WHAT HAPPENED

WHAT HAPPENED

*Inside the Bush White House and
Washington's Culture of Deception*

SCOTT McCLELLAN

PublicAffairs
New York

Published in the United States by PublicAffairs™,
a member of the Perseus Books Group.

Book design by Lisa Kreinbrink

Cataloging-in-Publication Data is available from the Library of Congress

ISBN-13: 978-1-58648-556-6

First Edition

10   9   8

To those who serve

CONTENTS

PREFACE

The UNIVERSITY OF TEXAS has always been special to my family and me. My grandfather, the late Page Keeton, was the legendary dean who led its law school to national prominence. I was born and reared in Austin, Texas, where it is located, and earned an undergraduate degree from the university.

I am very familiar with the UT Tower, the main building in the center of campus, with words from the Gospel of John carved in stone above its south entrance: "Ye shall know the truth and the truth shall set you free."

Those powerful words have always piqued my curiosity, as a person of faith and as an ordinary human being keenly interested in the larger meaning of life. But not until the past few years have I come to truly appreciate their message.

Perhaps God's greatest gift to us in life is the ability to learn from our experiences, especially our mistakes, and grow into better people. That uniquely human quality is rooted in free will and blossoms in our capacity for knowledge, based on understanding the truth—not as we might imagine or wish it to be, but as it is. And that includes recognizing our faults and accepting responsibility for them. Through contrition we find the truth and the freedom that comes with it, even as we improve ourselves and grow closer to the image that God our Creator has in mind for us to become.

My mother, who began her career in public service as a high school civics and history teacher, likes to say, "It is people, not events, that shape history." She couldn't be more right. History is rooted in the choices made by people—flawed, fallible people.

This is a book about the slice of history I witnessed during my years in the White House and about the well-intentioned but flawed human beings—myself included—who shaped that history. I've written it not to settle scores or enhance my own role but simply to record what I know and what I learned in hopes that my account will deepen our understanding of contemporary history, particularly the events that followed the tragic attacks of September 11, 2001.

I began the process of writing this book by putting myself under the microscope. In my efforts on behalf of the presidential administration of George W. Bush I fell far short of living up to the kind of public servant I wanted to be. Having accepted the post of White House press secretary at age thirty-five and possessing scant experience of the Washington power game, I didn't fully understand what I was getting myself into. Today, I understand it much better. This book records the often painful process by which I gained that understanding.

I frequently stumbled along the way and failed in my duty to myself, to the president I served, and to the American people. I tried to play the Washington game according to the current rules and, at times, didn't play it very well. Because I didn't stay true to myself, I couldn't stay true to others. The mistakes were mine, and I've suffered the consequences.

My own story, however, is of small importance in the broad historical picture. More significant is the larger story in which I played a minor role—the story of how the presidency of George W. Bush veered terribly off course.

As press secretary, I spent countless hours defending the administration from the podium in the White House briefing room. Although the things I said then were sincere, I have since come to realize that some of them were badly misguided. In these pages, I've tried to come to grips with some of the truths that life inside the White House bubble obscured.

My friends and former colleagues who lived and worked or are still living and working inside that bubble may not be happy with the perspective I present here. Many of them, I'm sure, remain convinced that the Bush administration has been fundamentally correct in its most controversial policy judgments, and that the dis-esteem in which most Americans currently hold it is undeserved. Only time will tell. But I've become genuinely convinced otherwise.

The episode that became the jumping-off point for this book was the scandal over the leaking of classified national security information—the so-called Plame affair. It originated in a controversy over the intelligence the Bush administration used to make the case that Saddam Hussein's Iraq represented a "grave and gathering danger" that needed to be eliminated. When a covert CIA officer's identity was disclosed during the ensuing partisan warfare, turning the controversy into the latest Washington scandal, I was caught up in the deception that followed. It was the defining moment in my time working for the president, and one of the most painful experiences of my life.

When words I uttered, believing them to be true, were exposed as false, I was constrained by my duties and loyalty to the president and unable to comment. But I promised reporters and the public that I would someday tell the whole story of what I knew. After leaving the White House, I realized that the story was meaningless without an appreciation of the personal, political, and institutional context in which it took place. So the story grew into a book.

Writing it wasn't easy. Some of the best advice I received as I began came from a senior editor at a publishing house that expressed interest in my book. He said the hardest challenge for me would be to keep questioning my own beliefs and perceptions throughout the writing process. His advice was prescient. I've found myself constantly questioning my own thinking, my assumptions, my interpretations of events. Many of the conclusions I've reached are quite different from those I would have embraced at the start of the process. The quest for truth has been a struggle for me, but a rewarding one. I don't claim a monopoly on truth. But after wrestling with my experiences over the past several months, I've come much closer to *my* truth than ever before.

MANY READERS WILL HAVE COME TO this book out of curiosity about the man who is a leading character in my story, President George W. Bush. You'll learn about my relationship with him and my experiences as part of his team as you read these pages. For now, let me observe that much of what the general public knows about Bush is true. He is a man of personal charm, wit, and enormous political skill. Like many other people, I was inspired to follow him by his disarming personality and by his record as a popular, bipartisan governor who set a constructive tone and got things done for the people. We all hoped and believed he could do the same for the nation.

Certainly the seeds of greatness seemed to be present in the Bush administration. Although Bush attained the White House only after an extended legal battle over the outcome of the 2000 election, he began his presidency with considerable goodwill. He commanded a rare, extended period of national unity following the unimaginable national tragedy that struck our nation in September 2001.

On paper, the team Bush assembled was impressive. Vice President Dick Cheney was a serious, vastly experienced hand in the top levels of government. Secretary of Defense Donald Rumsfeld had already enjoyed one successful run at the Pentagon and boasted a résumé listing a string of business and government achievements. Secretary of State Colin Powell, an able and widely respected military leader, was easily the most popular public figure in the country and could well have been the first African American president of the United States had he been interested in the job. Even Bush's chief political adviser, Karl Rove, had a powerful reputation as a brilliant strategic thinker who was helping to make the Republican party the nation's greatest political force.

I believed in George W. Bush's leadership and agenda for America, and had confidence in his authenticity, integrity, and judgment. But today the high hopes that accompanied the early days of his presidency have fallen back to earth.

Rumsfeld and Powell are gone, their tenures controversial and disappointing. Vice President Cheney's role is widely viewed as sinister and destructive of the president's legacy. And Rove's reputation for political genius is now matched by his reputation as an operative who places political gain ahead of the national interest.

Through it all, President Bush remains very much the same. He is self-confident, quick-witted, down-to-earth, and stubborn, as leaders sometimes need to be. His manner is authentic, his beliefs sincere. I never knew Lyndon Johnson (another Texan with a stubborn streak whose domestic accomplishments were overshadowed by a controversial war) or Richard Nixon (a president whose historically low poll ratings following Watergate have been rivaled only by Bush's). But according to historians, both men were consumed with defensiveness, anger, and ultimately anguish as their presidencies unraveled under the pressure of war and scandal, respectively. George W. Bush is different. He is very much the man he always was—though not quite the leader I once imagined him to be.

It was the decision to go to war in Iraq that pushed Bush's presidency off course. It was a fateful misstep based on a confluence of events (the shock of 9/11 and our surprisingly—and deceptively—quick initial military success in Afghanistan), human nature (ambition, certitude, and self-deceit), and a divinely inspired passion (President Bush's deeply held belief that all people have a God-given right to live in freedom). For Bush, removing the "grave and gathering danger" that Iraq supposedly posed was primarily a means for achieving the far more grandiose objective of reshaping the Middle East as a region of peaceful democracies.

History appears poised to confirm what most Americans today have decided—that the decision to invade Iraq was a serious strategic blunder. No one, including me, can know with absolute certainty how the war will be viewed decades from now when we can more fully understand its impact. What I do know is that war should only be waged when necessary, and the Iraq war was not necessary.

Waging an unnecessary war is a grave mistake. But in reflecting on all that happened during the Bush administration, I've come to believe that an even more fundamental mistake was made—a decision to turn away from candor and honesty when those qualities were most needed.

Most of our elected leaders in Washington, Republicans and Democrats alike, are good and decent people. Yet too many of them today have made a practice of shunning truth and the high level of openness and forthrightness required to discover it. Most of it is not willful or conscious. Rather it is part of the modern Washington game that has become the accepted norm.

As I explain in this book, Washington has become the home of the permanent campaign, a game of endless politicking based on the manipulation of shades of truth, partial truths, twisting of the truth, and spin. Governing has become an appendage of politics rather than the other way around, with electoral victory and the control of power as the sole measures of success. That means shaping the narrative before it shapes you. Candor and honesty are pushed to the side in the battle to win the latest news cycle.

Of course, deception in politics is nothing new. What's new is the degree to which it now permeates our national political discourse.

Much of it is barely noticeable and seemingly harmless, accepted as par for the course. Most of it is done unconsciously or subconsciously with no malicious intent other than to prevail in the increasingly destructive game of power and influence.

Some of it is self-deceit. Those engaging in it convince themselves to believe what they are saying, though deep down they know candor and honesty are lacking. Instead of checking their political maneuvering at the door when the campaign ends, they retain it as part of the way Washington works. The deception it spawns becomes the cancer on our political discourse, greatly damaging the ability of our elected leaders to govern effectively and do what is best for America.

Too many politicians and their followers have become passionately committed to a preconceived, partisan view of reality that allows little room for compromise or cooperation with the other side. The gray nuances of truth are lost in the black-and-white ideologies both parties embrace. Permanent division, gridlock, and a general inability to constructively address the big challenges we all face inevitably follow.

President Bush, I believe, did not consciously set out to engage in these destructive practices. But like others before him, he chose to play the Washington game the way he found it, rather than changing the culture as he vowed to do at the outset of his campaign for the presidency. And like others before him, he has engaged in a degree of self-deception that may be psychologically necessary to justify the tactics needed to win the political game.

The permanent campaign also ensnares the media, who become complicit enablers of its polarizing effects. They emphasize conflict, controversy, and negativity, focusing not on the real-world impact of policies and their larger, underlying truths but on the horse race aspects of politics—who's winning, who's losing, and why.

In exploring this syndrome and the way it helped damage at least one administration, I've tried to contribute to our understanding of Washington's culture of deception and how we, the American people, can change it.

Although my time in the Bush White House did not work out as I once hoped, my optimism regarding America has been strengthened. I've met many, many people who are eager for positive change and are ready to devote their lives and energies to the future of our country. I still believe, in the words of then-Governor Bush, that it's possible to show "that politics, after a time of tarnished ideals, can be higher and better." I'm convinced that, if we take a clear-eyed look at how our system has gone awry and think seriously about how to fix it, there's nothing we can't achieve.

This book, I hope, will contribute to that national conversation.

SCOTT MCCLELLAN
APRIL 2008

WHAT
HAPPENED

1

A MADE-FOR-
WASHINGTON SCANDAL

THROUGHOUT AMERICAN HISTORY, presidential administrations have undergone tumultuous periods of war and scandal. I happened to become White House press secretary at a time when the administration of George W. Bush was going through both, and they were intimately related to each other.

In late May 2003, when the president asked me to begin serving as his chief spokesman in July, I did not fully appreciate just how contentious and venomous the atmosphere in Washington was—and how controversial and polarizing the presidency of George W. Bush was about to become.

By October, less than three months after starting the new job, I was on the front lines defending a White House that was becoming engulfed in a growing scandal on the eve of a reelection campaign that had an increasingly hostile media clamoring and our partisan critics pouncing. For the American public, which had grown weary of the endless investigations and scandals connected with the Clinton presidency, the situation typified the worst of what they saw in Washington.

The emerging narrative in the Washington press was that the White House had deliberately blown the cover of Valerie Plame, a covert CIA official. Administration officials had anonymously leaked her identity to reporters in order to punish (at worst) or discredit (at best) her husband, former ambassador Joseph Wilson, who was publicly alleging that the administration had misled the country into war in Iraq. News stories suggested that White House aides had disclosed Plame's identity to at least five reporters. A concerted White House effort to disclose her identity would have meant that the officials involved, knowingly or not, had leaked classified national security information.

For nearly two weeks, following the September 29 disclosure of a criminal investigation by the Department of Justice, I vigorously pushed back at the notion that the White House was behind the leak. Even before then, I had batted down any suggestion that my colleague and fellow Texan Karl Rove, a frequent target of our critics as the president's closest adviser, was involved in the leak. Later I added the vice president's chief of staff, Lewis "Scooter" Libby, to the list of those I defended.

By the daily White House briefing on October 10, I was looking for a way to extricate myself from commenting any further about specifics of the Plame case, which were now part of the recently announced investigation.

The opening I sought came near the end of that Friday's briefing in the form of a question from Victoria Jones, a cordial yet skeptical liberal talk radio journalist and Bush administration critic.

"Scott," Jones said, "earlier this week you told us that neither Karl Rove, Elliott Abrams, nor Lewis Libby disclosed any classified information with regard to the leak. I wondered if you could tell us more specifically whether any of them told any reporter that Valerie Plame worked for the CIA?"

I was ready with a reply. "I spoke with those individuals, as I pointed out, and those individuals assured me they were not involved in this," I said. "And that's where it stands."

Another reporter, seeking clarification, jumped in: "They were not involved in what?"

"The leaking of classified information," I said.

It sounded final and definitive—just as I intended.

I'd chosen my words carefully. While I believed what I'd been told by Rove and Libby, I could never know with 100 percent certainty that it was true. So I purposely put the onus on them, noting that they had "assured me" about their lack of involvement. It was a firewall of sorts, designed to protect my own credibility if the truth turned out to be more complicated—or wholly different—from what I'd been told. Not that I expected it to be. After all, I was confident, at the time, that neither the president nor the vice president would knowingly send me out to mislead the public.

The public assurances I provided that October 10 would be my final comments from the podium denying that Rove and Libby had been involved in the outing of a covert CIA official, and my final comments on any other matters which might be part of the criminal investigation that the leaking of Plame's name had already spawned.

There was only one problem. What I'd said was not true.

I had unknowingly passed along false information. And five of the highest-ranking officials in the administration were involved in my doing so: Rove, Libby, Vice President Cheney, the president's chief of staff Andrew Card, and the president himself.

For my next two years as press secretary, the false words I uttered at that Friday's briefing would stand as the official White House position on the Plame case. Little did I know at the time that what I said, and the pervasive deception underlying it, would be my undoing as the president's chief spokesman.

I had allowed myself to be deceived into unknowingly passing along a falsehood. It would ultimately prove fatal to my ability to serve the president effectively.

I didn't learn that what I'd said was untrue until the media began to figure it out almost two years later. Neither, I believe, did President Bush. He too had been deceived, and therefore became unwittingly involved in deceiving me. But the top White House officials who knew the truth—including Rove, Libby, and possibly Vice President Cheney—allowed me, even encouraged me, to repeat a lie.

When the truth finally began to emerge, my credibility as White House spokesman was badly tarnished—a terribly painful experience for me.

I blame myself. I allowed myself to be deceived. But the behavior of the president and his key advisers was even more disappointing.

During 2003 and 2004, the White House chose not to be open and forthright on the Plame scandal but rather to buy time and sometimes even stonewall, using the ongoing investigation as an excuse for silence. The goal was to prevent political embarrassment that might hurt the president and weaken his bid for reelection in November 2004. The motive was under-standable, but the behavior was wrong—and ultimately self-defeating. And, in retrospect, it was all too characteristic of an administration that, too often, chose in defining moments to employ obfuscation and secrecy rather than honesty and candor.

As I reflected on this leak episode—one of the defining episodes of my tenure as press secretary—my view of Washington began to crystallize as never before. What I witnessed and have come to realize about my time in the spotlight—beyond just this episode—is a larger, very unpleasant truth. The deception was not isolated to one event or even to the Bush White House. It permeates our national political discourse. And while much of the deceit has been incidental and has not been embraced consciously by our elected lead-ers, it has become an accepted way of winning the partisan wars for public opinion and an increasingly destructive part of Washington's culture. Coming to Washington as a member of a Republican administration, I thought the mentality of political manipulation had been largely the creation of our pred-ecessors in the Clinton White House and that the leader I placed great hope in, George W. Bush, was dead set on changing it. He chose not to do so. In-stead, his own White House became embroiled in political maneuvering that was equally unsavory, if not worse, much of it related directly to his most con-sequential decision as president—the decision to invade Iraq.

SO MUCH HAS BEEN WRITTEN about the Plame leak episode in the past few years that even those of us who were part of its unfolding events have trouble piecing together the crucial details of how it all started. Let me lay them out for you.

The explosive controversy that eventually led to the leak scandal began with an assertion about Iraqi efforts to obtain fissile uranium concentrates— so-called yellowcake—from the west African country of Niger. Based on doc-uments that the CIA later acknowledged to be forgeries, this claim was one element of administration efforts in 2002 to demonstrate that the regime of Saddam Hussein was actively seeking to reconstitute its once-abandoned nu-clear weapons program and was maintaining a stockpile of biological and chemical weapons. Largely for these reasons, along with the regime's support for terrorism, the president said that Iraq posed "a grave and gathering danger" to peace in the Middle East and even to the security of the United States. This argument about WMD was, in turn, the centerpiece of his position that the United States was justified in leading its allies, as well as the United Nations, toward preemptive war against Iraq.

In the fall of 2002, as debate was swirling around Washington and the world over whether or not a war with Iraq was necessary, Congress requested a national intelligence estimate (NIE) about the status of Iraq's WMD program. An NIE represents the collective judgment of all the agencies that make up the U.S. intelligence community. And the NIE of October 2002, entitled "Iraq's Continuing Programs for Weapons of Mass Destruction," stated that Iraq had been "vigorously trying to procure uranium ore and yellowcake" (the "yellowcake" a reference to the Niger claim). Based partly on this NIE, Congress voted overwhelmingly and across party lines on October 11, 2002, to authorize military action against Iraq by the commander in chief.

The next step in the development of the Niger controversy was the president's 2003 State of the Union address, which largely focused on the threat posed by Iraq. He delivered the speech as rhetorical and military preparations for an invasion were intensifying and Saddam continued to defy demands from the United Nations Security Council.

After talking at some length about the Iraqi regime's continued pursuit of chemical and biological weapons as well as its ties to terrorism, the president briefly and ominously alluded to the greatest fear-provoking claim—that the regime was moving forward on an advanced nuclear weapons program. The president had already stated that Iraq could build a nuclear bomb "within a year" if it acquired necessary fissile material, such as uranium. Now he uttered what would become known as "the sixteen words"—his first personal reference to the Niger uranium claim: "The British government has learned that Saddam Hussein recently sought significant quantities of uranium from Africa."

Those sixteen words would become the nexus of the controversy that delivered a near-fatal blow to the credibility of the president and his administration.

As the push toward war continued, President Bush and others in his administration continued to make the case for action against Iraq. Because of Secretary of State Colin Powell's enormous bipartisan popularity, as well as his unquestioned honor and integrity, the White House recognized that he would be the most logical and persuasive person to help seal the case at home and abroad. So, on February 5, Powell made a special presentation before the

UN Security Council concerning the Iraqi effort to develop and stockpile weapons of mass destruction. This presentation did *not* include the Africa claim. After carefully scrutinizing the intelligence, Powell had chosen not to use it—a decision that, in retrospect, was both wise and highly revealing.

Still, that claim remained in the public mind one of the most potent bits of evidence in the administration's case for war. After all, the threat of nuclear attack by Iraq seemed far more frightening to most Americans than the more remote danger of a chemical or biological attack on U.S. soil. That is why the words of national security adviser Condoleezza Rice on September 8 had made headlines: "The problem here is that there will always be some uncertainty about how quickly [Saddam] can acquire nuclear weapons. But we don't want the smoking gun to be a mushroom cloud."

Then, just as America was on the verge of war, the Niger claim was seriously undermined.

On March 7, 2003, days before the president launched Operation Iraqi Freedom to disarm and topple Saddam's regime, Mohamed ElBaradei, the director general of the UN's nuclear inspection and verification arm, the International Atomic Energy Agency (IAEA), made a startling statement in remarks to the Security Council: the uranium intelligence was not credible and there was "no evidence or plausible indication" that Iraq had revived a nuclear weapons program. Furthermore, he implied that the documents on which the Niger claim had been based were forgeries: "Based on thorough analysis, the IAEA has concluded with the concurrence of outside experts that these documents which formed the basis for the report of recent uranium transaction between Iraq and Niger are in fact not authentic. We have therefore concluded that these specific allegations are unfounded."

Two days later, Secretary Powell was asked about ElBaradei's remarks by Tim Russert on NBC's *Meet the Press*. In response, Powell stated that the uranium information was provided in good faith and if it turned out to be wrong, then "fine." But he asserted to Russert that it was still an open issue to be investigated. Then he went on to restate another key administration talking point about how we had previously underestimated Iraq's nuclear capabilities. "We have to be a little careful about nuclear weapons programs," Powell warned. "We saw the IAEA almost give Iraq a clean bill of health in the early 1990s, only to discover that they had a robust nuclear weapons program that they had not discovered."

Powell was correct that intelligence reporting had previously underestimated the threat from Saddam Hussein's regime. His remark underscored many officials' lack of trust in the UN nuclear inspection agency, which some White House and administration officials used to convince themselves with an overabundance of certitude that the Iraqi regime was a real and growing threat in a post–9/11 world.

In any case, doubts about the accuracy of the Niger claim did little to slow the momentum toward military confrontation. On March 19, the war with Iraq began.

In a March 31 *New Yorker* article, Seymour Hersh discussed the Niger documents and flatly called them forgeries. Though Hersh was known for his liberal views (and therefore discounted by many on the conservative side of the political spectrum), he was also considered by the mainstream media to be a diligent reporter with good contacts in the policy arena, and his article shone a spotlight on doubts about the Niger documents.

The idea that the Bush administration might have based part of its argument for a controversial war on inaccurate intelligence was one thing. Most Americans would be inclined to forgive an honest mistake, especially if it stemmed from an excess of caution about a perceived threat in a dangerous, post–9/11 world. But if administration leaders deliberately chose to ignore the facts when assembling the case for war, and, even worse, if they knowingly dissembled in order to make the case appear stronger than it was, Americans might not be so forgiving. That was the new, far more potent charge leveled in a *New York Times* opinion piece written in May 2003 by Pulitzer Prize–winning journalist and Iraq war opponent Nicolas Kristof.

In his column, "Missing in Action: Truth," Kristof drew on information provided by an anonymous, albeit credible, source to suggest that the administration had deliberately misled the nation into war.

An unnamed "former U.S. ambassador to Africa" told Kristof that he had been sent to Niger to answer questions from the vice president's office about Iraq seeking uranium. Kristof wrote that the unnamed "envoy reported to the C.I.A. and State Department that the information was unequivocally wrong and that the documents had been forged. The envoy's debunking of the forgery was passed around the administration and seemed to be accepted—except that President Bush and the State Department kept citing it anyway."

They were tough words written by a prominent liberal columnist for what many consider the national newspaper of record. Doubts about the veracity of the Niger claim had been around for a long time. But Kristof was now suggesting something much more sinister—that the administration had cited the uranium claim *knowing* it was "unequivocally wrong."

The specific accusation being made by Kristof and his unnamed source fed into a broader, already burgeoning controversy over how the White House had used intelligence to make the case to Congress and the public for justifying going to war in Iraq. As U.S. forces swept through Iraq, the discovery almost everyone expected them to make—large WMD stockpiles—was failing to materialize. In response, administration critics, particularly the more partisan ones, were starting to charge that the president had deliberately misled the nation by exaggerating or hyping the intelligence to justify war. At best, critics of the Iraq war believed that the president had not been straight with the American people. They believed that he and his advisers had likely ignored or disregarded caveats and contradictory evidence about the intelligence to make the threat from Iraq seem more serious than it really was and thereby create a sense of urgency and gain necessary public backing.

While Kristof's column did not generate much immediate interest from the national media, it did get noticed by the White House, particularly the vice president and his office. And not unlike the Clinton White House, which quickly and aggressively countered criticisms, the Bush White House began taking steps to aggressively fight back. The vice president, whose credibility and integrity were specifically being questioned, and his office would take a leading role in these efforts, beginning in late May 2003.

Through inquiries at the State Department, the vice president's office quickly learned the identity of Kristof's unnamed source. It was former ambassador Joseph Wilson, who'd been sent to Niger to investigate the uranium allegation in January 2002. Under the cloak of anonymity, the vice president and trusted aide Scooter Libby soon began an effort to discredit Wilson with selected journalists. Unknown to anyone else in the compartmentalized, internally secretive White House—including the White House chief of staff, the national security adviser, and the CIA director—the president declassified key portions of information from the October 2002 NIE for the vice president and Libby to use in this effort.

At the same time, Libby and other high-ranking administration officials, including deputy secretary of state Richard Armitage, Karl Rove, and then-press secretary Ari Fleischer, would anonymously share another piece of classified national security information—the identity of Joe Wilson's wife, Valerie Plame, and her role as a CIA employee in helping to arrange Wilson's investigative trip to Niger. The purpose of these leaks was to discredit Wilson, by undermining his public assertions that he had been sent to Niger by the CIA at the vice president's request. But the circle of those who knew about these leaks was very small, and some of those who participated didn't even realize that Plame's identity was a state secret.

These decisions—to defend the president and to launch a stealth campaign to discredit Joe Wilson and expose his wife's CIA role as part of that campaign—would have profound long-term implications for the credibility of the Bush administration.

AS THE EFFORT TO DISCREDIT Wilson was getting under way, I was still deputy White House press secretary. I had just been tapped to replace Ari Fleischer, who'd announced his intent to leave in the middle of July. So my duties were still focused elsewhere and, therefore, I had no knowledge of the anonymous efforts to expose Plame and discredit Wilson. The sixteen words controversy was still taking shape and did not grow legs until early July 2002, about a week before I assumed my new position.

At the time, like others in the White House, I viewed Wilson's assertions as a malicious attack with partisan overtones. I knew of no real justification for questioning the case for war, and felt no reason to question it myself. I trusted the key members of the president's team, and I had no reason to doubt the president's integrity.

Of course, I realized that the administration was engaged in some back-and-forth jockeying with critics on Capitol Hill and in the press about the prewar intelligence and the case for war. But I felt it was all part of the modern-day Washington game—a permanent campaign between two sides, each trying to shape and manipulate public approval. As far as I knew, we were simply doing what we had to do—fighting back against unsubstantiated, malicious charges that the president had knowingly lied in order to take the nation to war. The partisan warfare of the 1990s was once again taking center stage, and the media were all too eager to cover who was winning and who was losing. Clouded in controversy once again were the larger underlying truths, including how the White House had made the case for war.

The resulting drama of secrecy and deception, of charges and counter-charges, was playing out in the theater of political power, Washington, D.C. And I found being part of the play exciting. While politics had been a focus of my life for as long as I could remember, I never imagined one day being cast as a prominent supporting actor in such a widely watched—and historically sig-nificant—drama.

2

A SMALL PART
OF SOMETHING GRAND

THERE IS AN IDEALISTIC STREAK in many of us who get involved in politics. We have a longing for a great leader—the one we imagine as the mythical president of strong character, free of debilitating personal flaws, and committed to striving for high ideals and bringing about something as close to Camelot as we can get, where truth, goodness, and beauty reign supreme.

Most of us are also grounded enough in reality to recognize that such a superhuman leader exists only in our imagination. Yet we still hope for the rare leader who possesses extraordinary talents, unique charisma, and a firm commitment both to striving for greatness and to achieving it the right way, honestly and nobly.

Our history immortalizes such rarities of leadership. Washington, Jefferson, and Lincoln watch over our nation's capital from their gigantic memorials of stone. Their granite heads (along with Teddy Roosevelt's) gaze out from Mount Rushmore, symbolizing the ideals of America: freedom, democracy, hope, and opportunity for people from all walks of life. Martin Luther King Jr. is revered in memory for challenging America to live up to its ideals of equality and justice for all.

While I did not view George W. Bush as the most charismatic or awe-inspiring leader in the world when I went to work for him, I believed he possessed enough of those qualities to be a very good, if not great, president. I also believed he had a rare understanding of what everyday citizens across America were looking for in a leader, and was committed to giving it to them. Consequently, in January 1999, when Governor Bush asked me to join his team, I was filled with excitement.

I was sitting and waiting, a little nervously, in the wood-framed communications office with its high ceiling inside the pink-domed Texas state capital building. Karen Hughes came back in and said, "The governor is ready to see you." As I entered the large, ornate reception area outside the governor's office, I put on my game face.

My mind went into tunnel-vision focus, as it used to do in my competitive tennis days, when in a moment of peak performance I could block out all the distractions around me—the people, the wind, the noise—and focus completely on the ball and the court. I could feel my adrenaline flowing. I was confident and anxious at the same time. It was a special moment.

I enjoyed my place in Texas politics and had never felt the pull of Washington. I found the partisan warfare that dominated national politics for much of the 1990s tiresome and off-putting. But I knew this offer from George W. Bush was a once-in-a-lifetime opportunity to be a small part of something grand. It was the equivalent in sports of joining a football team that has a real shot at winning the Super Bowl, and perhaps even at going down as one of the great teams in history.

Given Bush's performance as governor of Texas, I thought he had the potential to change Washington and accomplish some big things. And while I was only committing to working in the governor's office, I knew in the back of my mind that the opportunity to follow him to Washington would likely be an option should he run for president, as all expected he would, and prevail.

Karen Hughes was Bush's longtime communications director, and she and I had already talked about my joining Bush's team as a senior spokesman in his gubernatorial office. Now it was time for him to sign off on her recommendation. Bush and I had known each other since his first run for governor and my early days as a young Texas political strategist, though not on much of a personal level.

Officially he had not yet decided to enter the presidential race. But everyone knew, even if those inside team Bush did not say so out loud, that he would soon begin implementing a well-developed plan to do so. His chief political adviser Karl Rove was already deep into strategic planning for a national campaign. Soon Karen Hughes, his most trusted communicator, would move to join the presidential exploratory committee, leaving behind an experienced deputy and senior spokeswoman, Linda Edwards, who had solid journalistic credentials but lacked a background in politics. Linda would be elevated to communications director in the governor's office, while the position I was looked at to fill would be that of deputy communications director.

Karen had reached out to me to fill the void that would be created by her approaching departure. Since Bush was expected to enter the sweepstakes for the White House as the frontrunner, given his family name and his success as Texas governor, he and his gubernatorial record and policies would come under intense scrutiny by the national media. Karen wanted to make sure his government communications office, which would be on the receiving end, had the political experience and sensitivity needed to handle the expected onslaught of national media interest.

Only weeks earlier, Reggie Bashur, a savvy Texas political strategist who had mentored me through three winning statewide campaigns I'd managed, had said, "You've been noticed by the governor's people. They're looking for a senior spokesman with political experience. They want to talk with you, if you're interested."

It was only a few days after my job overseeing my mother's underdog campaign in the hotly contested 1998 race for the powerful Texas comptroller's office had ended in her surprising victory, and I had not really thought about what was next for me. Nepotism laws prevented me from following Mom into her new office. My immediate focus was on helping her transition into her new duties: managing one of the larger state office staffs; controlling the state's purse strings, including its more than $80 billion biennial budget; making revenue estimates on the cost of legislation; and certifying how much money lawmakers could spend, among other things. The goal was to help her assemble a trusted team of senior advisers.

Reggie Bashur was dangling a very tempting proposition. I was humbled by Reggie's words. I liked the governor. He always seemed approachable and down-to-earth, and came across as genuine when we visited. I thought highly of his style of bipartisan leadership and the outstanding team he had assembled to advance his agenda, but I had never imagined becoming a part of it. Members of Bush's team were understatedly bright, outwardly humble, and they seemed committed to serving something larger than their own interests—probably the reason they all seemed to work well with one another. Being one of them meant belonging to the top political talent in the state. Working for Bush was the pinnacle of Texas politics.

Now, walking into Bush's office at the dawn of a new legislative session following his landslide re-election as governor, I felt a deep sense of humility and gratitude. Why, I wondered, was I of all people being sought out by the popular Texas governor who might well be the next U.S. president?

The large, rectangular office was dimly lit, with the governor's desk at one end and his collection of autographed baseballs on the other. Near the baseballs were positioned a couch, a couple of chairs, and a coffee table. A portrait of the legendary Sam Houston, president of the Republic of Texas and governor of Texas after it joined the Union, showed him wearing a toga and a laurel crown in the style of an ancient Roman Caesar—not the way most Texans would ever picture their governor, particularly in the early years of statehood. Bush used to have fun at his legendary successor's expense by referring to the painting as a lesson for political leaders to be careful about what they agree to do.

The governor leaned back in his chair, one knee crossed. It was a typically relaxed posture I would see many a time in the years ahead.

"How ya doing, Scott?" Bush asked good-naturedly. "Have a seat."

"Good, Governor," I responded. "I'm honored to be here."

He said I was there because my talents had been noticed.

We chatted a little about my mother and her election race, and he complimented me for managing a well-run campaign.

"I just stayed out of her way," I said.

"That was smart," he chuckled, knowing what I meant.

My mother is a dynamic, type A personality with boundless energy, not unlike the woman who was seeking to bring me onto Bush's team. The biggest difference is that Karen is about a foot taller than my mother, who is barely five feet tall. I had already playfully told Karen that going to work for her would be no problem, since her personality was so similar to my mother's. Both are strong, charismatic women who are go-getters and talk rather fast.

Bush always had a fondness for strong women, my mother included. He liked her energy, enthusiasm, and straight talk. And he liked her feistiness and toughness. She was elected to a state office at the same time Bush was first elected governor, and they had been friends ever since.

As for me, I am about as reserved as Mom is animated, but I would not have been sitting where I was that day if she had not called on me to help her career in state politics.

"Why do you want to work for me?" the governor inquired right off the bat.

"Because I believe in you," I said.

"It's not about me," Bush jumped in. "It's about the agenda."

"Yes sir, you're right," I said. "That's what I mean. I believe in your agenda, and I believe in your leadership. I admire the way you have reached out across the aisle to get things done."

I went on to express how I thought people of my generation were tired of the political bickering at the national level and wanted leaders who could rise above partisanship, something Bush was doing in Texas even as Washington was moving in the opposite direction. We talked about his governing style, the positive tone he worked to set, his broader agenda, and how he had surrounded himself with some of the best and brightest in Texas to serve on his team.

Bush talked passionately about his agenda and his focus on achieving results. It was his strong belief, he said, that government programs which served a legitimate purpose should be made to achieve their intended results.

More broadly, underlying his belief that "it's about the agenda" was a lesson he had learned in politics (primarily from following his father's presidency)—results matter most. People judge leaders and history remembers them based on their success more than anything else. In time, I would come to learn that, in Bush's view of national politics, it mattered far less to the public how a leader achieved those results, whether with or without broad bipartisan support, and whether or not one was fully open and forthright in achieving them. As long as programs prove successful, the public tends to remember only the end results, not how leaders went about reaching them. As we began forging a long-term bond grounded in our working relationship and our shared affection for Texas, I didn't yet appreciate just how much that view would predominate, for better and worse, in Bush's approach to governing once he arrived in Washington.

Then he mentioned some of his expectations for his spokespeople—the importance of staying on message; the need to talk about what you're for, rather than what you are against; how he liked to make the big news on his own time frame and terms without his spokespeople getting out in front of him; and, finally, making sure that public statements were coordinated internally so that everyone is always on the same page and there are few surprises.

"I haven't made a decision about whether I will run for president," Bush added. "I'm still thinking about it. But you have good political instincts, and I'll need your help watching out for me in this office if I start to test the ground."

I told him I understood, and he wrapped up the conversation.

We had clicked. I'd made no fatal mistakes. I was hired.

Everything seemed pretty good to me at that moment. Here I was joining the team of an accomplished leader with a proven ability to calm the partisan waters, bring people together, and achieve positive results. I had no reason to anticipate serious disappointment over the horizon.

I WAS THIRTY YEARS OLD at the time. Having grown up around politics on the local level in the capital city of Texas and having worked on the state level for nearly a decade, I knew politics often turns into a contact sport.

Elections could be mean-spirited. But watching Washington during the 1990s was like watching the final weeks of a hotly contested political campaign that had turned wearily negative and was now being played out endlessly on television 24/7.

Deliberation and compromise, elements central to governing, particularly in a constitutional, representative democracy, all but disappeared. Who had the best ideas or policies mattered little compared to who was winning the battle for public opinion. Conflict, controversy, and negativity received growing emphasis in the media, and voices of partisanship and ideology grabbed increasingly more attention than voices of consensus and reasoned pragmatism. As a Republican, I tended to view Democrats as more shrill and unfair in their tactics, but it was abundantly clear that both parties shared the blame for the deteriorating climate in Washington, where elections might be held but the campaigning never stopped.

The Clinton presidency had taken the art of successful campaigning to new, unparalleled levels. It had begun during the 1992 election, when the

Clinton team, led by the colorful duo of George Stephanopoulos and James Carville, vowed not to allow their candidate to be mocked, belittled, and humiliated as Michael Dukakis had been in 1988. Campaigning with an effective aggressiveness shown by few Democrats in recent years, they captured the White House for their party for only the second time in seven elections. Unfortunately, once inside the White House, the Clinton administration maintained much the same partisan, chip-on-the-shoulder posture, cynically employing spin, "rapid response," obfuscation, dissembling, and bare-knuckle tactics to discredit those who challenged it openly.

Meanwhile, Republicans in Congress, led by Newt Gingrich, stung by their loss of the presidency, responded in kind. They sought to wrest political power out of the president's hands by pushing an ideologically driven agenda, tearing down Clinton and attacking congressional Democrats rather than reaching out to forge common ways forward in line with their political priorities. Some of what the Gingrich Republicans did was simply smart political positioning, as when they developed and trumpeted their Contract with America as a coherent agenda and set of shared talking points for congressional candidates to rally around. The gambit helped them wrest control of the House of Representatives from the Democrats in 1994. But some of what they did was based on exaggerated charges of dishonesty, immorality, and corruption, using Washington's scandal culture as a weapon to attack Clinton and his allies. The parade of scandals seemed endless: Travelgate, Whitewater, FBIgate, the Vince Foster case, the Rose Law Firm billing records affair, and, of course, the Monica Lewinsky episode.

In the eyes of history, some of these scandals will probably seem insignificant, others disturbing but less than earth-shattering. But their effect on politics in the 1990s is indisputable. Zero-sum politics became the rule. There could be only winners and losers. For the media, it was all about who was up and who was down. For elected leaders, the truth behind the story line mattered less than being on the offensive, shaping the narrative to your political advantage with the American people, or defensively responding to it. And as I think this book will show, there's a direct line between the attitude that truth is secondary to political victory and the obfuscation, dissembling, and lack of intellectual honesty that helped take our country into the war in Iraq.

But in Texas during the 1990s, something different was going on. A popular Republican governor was working closely with a Democratic lieutenant governor and a Democratic Speaker of the House to produce legislation and policies that met the needs and satisfied the desires of the majority of the state's people, whether conservative or liberal.

In large part because of Democratic Lieutenant Governor Bob Bullock's influence and Bush's keen grasp of Texas politics, there was little animosity between the leaders of the executive and legislative branches of government. It was not about who received credit for the results. Playing politics during the legislative session was viewed as unacceptable and was not tolerated. Governing was less about persuading or selling the public, and more about deliberating and compromising to serve the best interests of Texas. Most state leaders believed they had been elected to do that, and they worked to uphold their end of the bargain.

As soon as he was elected governor, Bush reached out to Democratic leaders, including the powerful Bullock, hoping to govern in a bipartisan manner. In Texas, the governor and lieutenant governor are elected separately. Bullock had deep roots in Texas government, having previously served four terms as the influential Texas comptroller. The Texas constitution placed great power in the lieutenant governor as head of the Texas senate, where he appointed committee chairpersons and determined the flow of legislation, directly influencing whether bills were passed or killed. Bullock's forceful personality, as large as Texas, made him even more effective than the average lieutenant governor.

For all these reasons, Bush knew that building trust and a close relationship with Bullock, as well as with the Democratic Speaker, Pete Laney, would be integral to getting his priorities passed. The three spoke frequently and met routinely at least once a week during session. By all accounts, Bush established far more collegial relations with Bullock and Laney than his Democratic predecessor, Ann Richards, had done.

Bush also reached out and built relationships with other Democratic leaders in the legislature, particularly but not exclusively key committee chairs. It was not unusual for Bush to stop by a member's office unannounced for a visit. And when election time came, Bush did not campaign against incumbent Democratic leaders who worked with him and helped advance his priorities.

This nonpartisan approach paid real dividends. During his first session, Bush managed to pass the largest revision of the state's education code in decades, strengthen juvenile justice laws, and implement reforms in regard to both welfare and lawsuits, core issues during his campaign for governor.

To me, leadership means uniting people around a common purpose, rather than dividing them along ideological lines, and I found Governor Bush's leadership inspiring. He adroitly joined forces with Bullock and Laney to build and sustain a strongly bipartisan, collegial approach to governing.

Could his leadership usher in a new political dynamic on the national level too, as it had in Texas? Many younger people were looking for just such a change. After all, shouldn't politics be about something higher and better than what our leaders in Washington were delivering? With the right presidential leadership, couldn't our elected leaders learn to set aside the excesses of perpetual campaigning and scorched-earth politics, and work together to serve our nation's best interests? Like many other Americans, I believed they could.

I always viewed politics as a way to make a positive difference for the common good—a belief that had been instilled in me early in life. It was for that reason, as much as any other, that I chose a career in the field. And George W. Bush, I genuinely believed, just might embody what I and so many others were seeking, a leader who could make us believe that it would be worthwhile to go to Washington after all—to see if we could change the destructive dynamic that dominated it during the 1990s.

As governor, Bush focused on big issues with broad appeal that affected all Texans. When it came to controversial issues like abortion, for example, he sought to find common ground by identifying practical ways to reduce the number of abortions, such as supporting parental notification and promoting adoption. He did not expend effort on divisive narrow issues, tailor his words to please a particular group of people, or strive to pit groups of people against one another for political gain.

His popularity in Texas spanned the spectrum of Democrats, independents, and Republicans. With an approval rating reaching well into the 70s, Bush attracted broad support for his leadership, policies, and governance.

It was a solid record of bipartisan accomplishment that he would highlight during his presidential campaign. Our campaign slogans captured what was unique about Bush. He was "a uniter, not a divider"; a "different kind of Republican" from the hard-edged, confrontational Gingrich and his group. He offered a "compassionate conservative" agenda and a commitment to change the bitter tone in Washington by bringing Republicans and Democrats together to solve the big problems.

Bush's principled leadership, bipartisan record, and compassionate conservative agenda inspired much hope in me and those whom I would soon call colleagues—fellow members of the Bush team.

And that's why I was there, seizing a once-in-a-lifetime opportunity to be part of something grand—because I believed that politics could be something far better than politics as usual. No wonder I was both thrilled and humbled at being hired to work for George W. Bush.

3

GROWING
UP IN POLITICS

MANY PEOPLE CHOOSE TO GET involved in politics as student activists in college, as young citizens involved in civic affairs, or as middle-aged people concerned with their community. A few, like me, are born with politics in their blood. I have been involved with politics in one way or another for as long as I can remember.

My mother was a trailblazer for women in politics. In 1972, when I was four years old, she was elected to the Austin school board. A few years later, she became the first woman president of the board. By the time I was nearing the end of third grade, she was elected the first woman mayor of Austin and would win election to an unprecedented three two-year terms.

I remember going to a U.S. mayors conference in Atlanta, Georgia, with my mother and older twin brothers during her first term in the late 1970s. The conference always featured chaperoned children's events while the elected officials participated in meetings.

Among other outings, we got to go to Six Flags Over Georgia. As a kid, I always loved the thrill of a roller coaster (little did I know what good preparation that was for someone who would enter politics). My older brothers were a little less adventurous (I'm not trying to imply any wimp factor here!) or perhaps less willing to wait in a long line for a two-minute adrenaline high. So I was left waiting by myself in line for the new, double-loop Mind Bender. As I stood there wearing my big name tag with the U.S. mayors conference logo, a college student the size of an offensive lineman looked down at it and asked, "So, your dad's mayor of Austin?"

All of ten years old and oblivious to how unusual my mother's accomplishment was in those years, I replied matter-of-factly, "No. My mother is."

The guy was stunned and yelled ahead to his buddies, "Hey, guys, get this. This kid's *mother* is mayor of Austin!"

I turned a bit red at receiving this unsought attention in the roller coaster line, though not enough to keep me from sharing a little more with them about one of my heroes—my mom. It was an early political lesson for a kid who thought little about the significance of my mayor's gender or how unusual it was in those days for a political leader to be a woman.

To me she was the high-energy supermom who packed school lunches, fixed dinner (when she could), drove me to my tennis matches, attended my little league games, helped me with school projects, paid for my hamburger and fries at the neighborhood Holiday House restaurant, disciplined my brothers and me when we misbehaved, let me play in her office or the back of council chambers, hauled me along to receptions (way too many, I would add), and happened to run a big city the rest of the time.

And during most of her time as mayor, Mom was a single parent. It all seemed normal to me in my preteen years. Only now do I fully appreciate what a remarkable woman my mother was and is.

My mother and father divorced when I was ten. Back then I did not understand why. My dad, an attorney, was a good father to me in those innocent years, but we grew apart as the years went by.

Like most kids, I've got warm memories of my dad: clinging to his chest hairs when he would playfully pretend to drop me, at age four or five, into the blue waters of a swimming pool's deep end, holding me up in his arms walking into the darkness of our front yard as he pointed out the Big Dipper or the stars of Orion, telling a story from Greek mythology, or helping coach my little league baseball team. But after the divorce, the times we talked and spent together grew shorter and farther apart. Nowadays we see or talk to each other very infrequently, but he is still the Dad I know, fondly recall, and will always unconditionally love.

My brothers and I were blessed to be close to all four of our grandparents, and they influenced us in a tremendously positive way as we were coming of age.

Grandmom McClellan, who volunteered at the church thrift store and taught Spanish to kindergartners in San Antonio, liked to spoil us and let us have fun. She raised four daughters and a son, my father, while Grandpop worked as a petroleum engineer, among the first to graduate from the University of Texas with a degree in the field. He was a good man of slender build and few words who grew up in small-town Texas. He enjoyed spending spare time with family, working in the yard of their modest house in San Antonio, and listening to Texas Longhorn football and baseball games on the radio he kept next to his recliner. His hearing wasn't great in his later years, but just being around him was nice.

While Granddad Keeton taught the law, as Mom likes to say, in our family Grandmom Keeton *was* the law. Grandmom Keeton came to the University of Texas in the early 1930s from the University of Georgia in her hometown of Atlanta, to attend the law school. She was enrolled in Granddad's class. He was a young professor who had recently graduated from the law school, and one thing led to another. Grandmom never quite finished law school. She looked after my brothers and me quite a bit, keeping us in line and making sure we knew our manners.

My granddad, Page Keeton, a legendary dean of the University of Texas law school, always had a great wit about him. He and Grandmom were married on March 4, or as Granddad used to quip, "two days after Texas gained its independence [celebrated every year on March 2], I lost mine." Instead of referring to how many years they had been married, he talked about how they had "gone sixty-three rounds" when celebrating their anniversary.

But the two were inseparable. To this day, I tear up when thinking about the time I took Granddad to visit my ailing grandmother in the hospital. She had been there for a few days, while he, aging and frail, unable to get around without the help of a wheelchair or walker, had been stuck at home worrying about his lifelong sparring partner.

I sat him down in the chair next to Grandmom's hospital bed. She was unable to sit up the day we visited. I noticed Granddad, using all his strength, starting to rock himself forward in the chair. He was trying to push himself up, and I grabbed under his arms to help him. He had one focus—my grandmother. Now standing and shaking a little, using every bit of his strength, he leaned down with some help from me to kiss her and said, "I love you, Madge. I hope you come home soon."

In that moment I thought, That's what it's all about. Here is this accomplished man of great intellect and strong character, and what matters most to him in these final years is not all he achieved in his profession, but all he shared with the family in which he instilled so much good.

Granddad grew up in northeast Texas on a small farm. After picking cotton in his early years in Red River County, he vowed to have a "sit-down job" when he was older. He found it, along with a lectern, at the University of Texas law school. Not long after he worked his way through school he worked his way into a professorship. He ended up teaching all the way to age eighty-six. He served twenty-five years as the dean of the law school and built it into one of the finest in the nation. He came to be known as one of the leading experts on tort law in the country.

A favorite story about my granddad was told to me by a family friend and UT law school graduate several years ago, not long after my grandfather passed away. This friend had been in a prelaw class that Granddad spoke to.

My granddad, standing at the podium in the theater-style classroom, looked over his glasses resting on his nose and asked students if they knew what made a good lawyer. One student toward the back of the room jumped up and said, "Dean Keeton, I believe right is right and wrong is wrong, and I believe in good over evil. Do you think I will make a good lawyer?"

Without missing a beat, my granddad peered up at the student and replied, "No, but you'll make a good Batman," to lots of laughter in the room.

I thought how much that sounded like the man I knew, who had a great, witty way of making a point. My granddad was teaching the students that the law is not always black and white, nor should a lawyer view it that way. The truth tends to involve plenty of nuance and shades of gray.

My granddad's class was often referred to by students as Keeton's comedy hour. But he was also renowned for his enormous knowledge of the law and his influence in shaping it for the better. To those in his profession who knew him and learned from him, Granddad was more than a good man; he was a great man, to be respected, admired, and emulated.

Some of my favorite times with Granddad and Grandmom were attending University of Texas football games. They had four tickets in the faculty section, and I usually brought a friend along.

I started attending UT football games at an early age in the 1970s, and warmly remember the days of Heisman Trophy winner Earl Campbell and our national title runs that fell short. UT football was part of our family life, and it became an inseparable part of my life, too.

Back in the 1950s and early 1960s, my granddad used to kick himself. For a brief period before becoming dean of the UT law school, he was hired as dean of the law school at the University of Oklahoma. He happened to serve on the athletic council that helped recruit Bud Wilkinson to OU. Wilkinson led the Sooners to many victories over UT in one of college football's great rivalries.

My future wife, Jill, knew our courtship was serious when I let her take possession of my season tickets. She was living in Austin and I was working in D.C. when we met.

In my youth, however, politics and current events, more than Longhorn sports, is what we spent time discussing and debating at our kitchen table. I learned that politics is a way to make a positive difference in people's lives. Granddad liked to say, "It's not the dollars you make, it's the difference you make," referring to what matters most in life.

Growing up in the local political spotlight of Austin had its ups and downs. Our mother the mayor tried to keep things pretty normal, and my three older brothers and I never let things go too much to our heads. Mom used to remind me, "What your friends do is one thing. What you do could end up on the front page of the paper."

We tried to avoid undue attention at all costs, while still taking life in a lighthearted way. Even if we were the mayor's kids, we were not about to let the pomp and ceremony of the political spotlight change who we were—just kids trying to grow up enjoying ourselves in a middle-class family.

Our mother did her best to keep us humble. I was none too happy the day she picked me up from junior high school and said we had to stop by a reception for the Texas A&M alumni downtown, and had no time to stop by home.

I wore my orange and white Texas #1 T-shirt to school that day because it was the week of the UT–A&M football rivalry. Now she was unconvincingly telling me how the alumni of the archrival Texas Aggies would have no problem with it.

"Oh, don't worry," Mom said. "They'll get a kick out of it. It'll be fun."

Yeah, right, I thought. All I remember from the downtown business attire reception upstairs in a balcony was the slightly inebriated, loud Aggie alum who came up behind me and tried to lift my shirt over my head. His fellow alums nearby enjoyed a laugh at my embarrassed adolescent expense.

Yeah, tons of fun, Mom.

Still, she did instill in my brothers and me the importance of public service as a way to make a positive difference and change things for the better.

My brothers and I grew up in a Democratic household, as had my mother and father. Mom was considered a moderate to conservative Democrat, a political centrist, when she served as mayor of Austin (although in Texas mayors and city council candidates do not run for office under any party label). Her coalition included the more affluent, conservative-leaning northwest part of the city and the heavily African American east, with the liberal urban areas near the university tending to oppose her. Generally speaking, she worked to keep taxes down, make sure city services were fully funded, and preserve Austin's wonderful quality of life while promoting economic growth. At the time, Austin was in the midst of a significant growth spurt—its population would go from 322,000 to 461,000 in just ten years—and becoming a technology hub in addition to being a government and university town.

Mom was plenty tough enough for the highly charged political environment, knowing how to form winning coalitions and finding common ground to get things done, at least until her third term when the council turned decidedly liberal. Spending a fair amount of time around city hall and in the back of council chambers tagging along with Mom, I learned about the political art of deliberation, thoughtful persuasion, and compromise for getting things done. Austin politics could be rough, though, and it was difficult to ignore the uglier things people said about Mom. But my brothers and I never let our distress show outwardly. It is hard not to take things personally when it's your Mom being attacked. But those tough boyhood lessons made it much easier for me to not take things personally later during my adult years in the rough-and-tumble world of politics.

Probably the most disturbing part of Mom's mayoral days was the death threats she received. I believe it only happened a couple of times, each during one of her three campaigns. I recall one of my brothers picking up the phone and hearing some guy say, "I am going to kill your mother."

The threats never materialized, but I remember Mom attending a little league baseball game of mine with some plainclothes Austin police officers who protected her around the clock when such a threat was made.

Politics, I learned, has an ugly side that most people never fully appreciate. This realization instilled in me a great respect for those willing to sacrifice much in order to serve. It also showed me that there are always going to be some people who are angry and hateful, and politics provides them a venue to vent their frustrations. You can't let that stop you from standing up for what you believe. As my granddad told my mother, "Carole, if you don't have somebody mad at you, you probably haven't done anything."

My brothers and I attended public schools, participated in extracurricular activities, and played a variety of sports from baseball to basketball to tennis, with some sandlot football thrown in. We would get into fights every once in a while, as young brothers tend to do. Being close in age made us competitive, but it also made us close when we needed one another.

Politics was something we each got involved with in school, too.

Following the landmark 1971 Supreme Court ruling in *Swann v. Charlotte-Mecklenburg Board of Education*, the Austin Independent School District was one of a number of cities nationwide under court order to use busing as a way to achieve school desegregation. "White flight" occurred in many parts of the nation after the ruling, including in Austin. From 1971 to 1972, a number of white families in Austin relocated to school districts neighboring the city.

In 1972, my mother was one of three candidates elected to the Austin school board who were opposed by a slate of antibusing (some said prosegregation) candidates. My mother won her seat on the board with 75 percent of the vote and still views with pride the way the school board peacefully and successfully integrated the schools during the five years she served.

During my mother's time as a member, the board developed a sixth grade center plan as an initial step to desegregate the schools. Under the plan, students who had attended predominantly white neighborhood elementary schools were bused along with students who attended heavily minority neighborhood schools to a school between the two areas of Austin for their sixth grade year. My brothers and I were bused from our west Austin neighborhood, where kids attended Casis Elementary School, to attend Baker Sixth Grade Center located in central Austin. Students from predominantly African American and Hispanic Ortega elementary in east Austin were also bused to Baker. The school board did not believe this plan placed an undue burden on any one area by having kids from just a single neighborhood bused cross-town. Instead, students from both areas would be bused to an in-between point.

I served as president of the student council at the Baker Sixth Grade Center. The school was diverse, quite a change from the neighborhood elementary school I had attended, which had only a small number of black and Hispanic students. I look back on my year at Baker with fondness. If there had been no busing, I might never have met Herman Hill, an African American student who served as vice president of the student body. Despite hotly contesting my claim to being the better basketball player, Herman, more than twenty years later, agreed to be a member of my wedding party.

At Baker, I also became friends with Hiep Pham, a recent immigrant from Vietnam. Hiep, a bright student who was still transitioning to English, used to refer to me affectionately as Chuck Norris ("Chuck Nor," as he would say in his accent) and in response I called Hiep, a young black belt, Bruce Lee. I did not study karate, but Hiep tried to teach me a few moves (the lessons did not stick). Before she lost interest in me, my smart, pretty sixth grade girlfriend was Camille Mojica, a Hispanic girl. Such a relationship was considered unusual in those days.

In favoring racial integration, I was carrying on a family legacy that extended back beyond my mom's school board service. During Granddad's tenure as dean of the University of Oklahoma law school, he testified in the case of Ada Lois Sipuel Fisher, a black woman who was challenging the state's new segregated law school for black students, which was held in a small curtained-off area inside the capitol building. The state had hastily opened the law school following the Supreme Court ruling in a previous case brought by Fisher that Oklahoma could not refuse to provide a legal education to all. "Not surprisingly, she did not feel that this was 'equal' protection to which the Fourteenth Amendment entitled her," recalled former Texas law school professor and nationally renowned constitutional law expert Charles Alan Wright at a memorial service for my grandfather in 1999. "She brought a new action in state court challenging the constitutionality of this instant law school."

Called to testify by the attorney representing Fisher, future Supreme Court justice Thurgood Marshall, my grandfather stated that there was "no way that the new law school could be considered equal to the long-established University of Oklahoma law school."

As Wright also noted in his eulogy, Granddad testified calmly and rationally, but a younger colleague on the faculty at OU law school who also sided with Fisher was more emotional and less restrained in his comments. The younger professor's testimony led vocal supporters of segregation in Oklahoma to demand that the university board fire him. As dean, my grandfather sent a letter to the chairman of the board of regents standing up for the professor's right to freely express his views, and pointing out "how the national reputation of the university would be hurt if it fired a professor for stating his honest view about segregation." Granddad's defense of the professor prevailed. The chairman of the board later told him that had it not been for his letter, the professor would have been dismissed. Granddad would become known over the years for hiring top professors with diverse viewpoints and loyally speaking up for their right to academic freedom when their comments created controversy.

Upon returning as dean, Granddad oversaw the peaceful integration of the University of Texas School of Law following the Supreme Court decision in *Sweatt v. Painter,* another landmark case that had been working its way through the legal system while Granddad was at OU. My whole family was proud of our patriarch's championing of equal rights and freedom of speech, and my own interest in public service owes a lot to his inspiration.

Eventually I served as president of my junior high student council and then as student council president of Austin High School, the same one my mother had been president of twenty-nine years before.

During my time as Austin High student body president, I came to befriend a colleague who was president at Johnston High School in Austin, John Barr. He, too, had grown up around politics. His father was a close friend and adviser to then-Congressman J.J. "Jake" Pickle, the longtime representative from Austin who succeeded Lyndon Baines Johnson in Congress. The year we came to know each other, my mother was running against Pickle (she lost). Over the years, John and I have talked about how, despite being in opposite political parties, our political views are pretty closely aligned. We have often discussed the dangers to democracy posed by each party's hard-line, uncompromising ideological purists.

In high school, I gave up all sports save for tennis and ended up becoming a top-ranked singles and doubles player. Our high school team ended up number two in the state my senior year.

I did well in high school, graduating with honors in the top 20 percent of my class, but not as well as my older brothers, who finished as valedictorian, valedictorian, and salutatorian (beaten out by his twin).

After briefly entertaining the idea of attending the U.S. Naval Academy and playing tennis there, I decided to stay home and attend the University of Texas. I joined the fraternity where two of my brothers were members and pursued a degree in government. The tennis coach, Dave Snyder, offered me a nonscholarship position on the top-ranked tennis team as well. Coming to the realization that my chances were slim for taking it to the next level, I ended up quitting the tennis team halfway through my sophomore year.

Midway through my junior year, I was elected president of the 120-plus member Sigma Phi Epsilon chapter for a one-year term. Fraternities at the time were undergoing closer scrutiny from the university and county attorney over concerns about continued hazing.

Hazing was part of the culture in the UT fraternity system, and the system had a long history of national notoriety. It wasn't an element of university culture that I felt comfortable with. During my freshman year, Mark Seeburger, a pledge in another fraternity, died of alcohol poisoning in a hazing incident. Later I lost a childhood friend and all-round nice guy, Scott Phillips, who joined a fraternal organization and got caught up in a hazing incident that resulted in his death. (While serving as a pledge trainer, he fell off a cliff while being chased through a park by a group of young pledges engaging in a bit of "reverse hazing.")

Incidents like these made me and others at UT feel that the hazing culture needed to change. Nationally, Sig Ep headquarters was working diligently to steer its chapters in a new, more positive direction. Such a change can be hard to bring about, but I would try—in part by necessity and in part by choice after a regrettable experience on my watch as the chapter's president.

I had taken over my presidential responsibilities just before Christmas break of my junior year. We had returned to school, and, as was the tradition, the fall pledge class was going through its unsanctioned hell week. This included sleep deprivation and mostly verbal hazing, but some physical hazing as well. Having experienced hazing as a pledge, I came to view it as a peculiar way to instill brotherly love.

During this particular hell week, however, things got out of hand. One pledge suffered eye injuries in a moment of near exhaustion from lack of sleep late one night. It was a freakish accident—hair dye from a crazy costume donned as part of the hazing ritual ran into his eyes, partially blinding him. One of my fraternity brothers brought him down to my room at the fraternity house. We immediately had him taken to the emergency room, where he was treated and returned home early the next morning.

At the time, doctors expressed concern that the eye injury could affect him for the rest of his life. Nevertheless, the pledge insisted he did not want to make an issue of what happened. I told him he needed to do what he felt was right, regardless of what it meant for others, but I also realized that the hazing problem was one our fraternity needed to deal with honestly and head-on, and that covering up an incident of this kind would not be constructive in the long run.

After the volunteer alumnus chapter counselor and I discussed the matter, we agreed it was best to inform the chapter alumni board, which included lawyers who were rightly concerned about potential liability. I told the alumni I would accept responsibility for whatever needed to be done. They ultimately decided to handle things internally, but we all agreed that we had to end the hazing culture inside the fraternity once and for all.

I stood up at chapter meetings and, in my role as president, strongly urged that hell week be eliminated in the future. This was a tough position for me to take. I was the one who had to bear the brunt of the criticism from fellow fraternity brothers who viewed hazing as something everyone does at UT and had done for a long time. They wondered why our chapter should change because of one incident involving a pledge who did not even hold the slightest grudge. The alumni board did little openly to back me. Perhaps understandably, they were squeamish about shouldering responsibility for this unpopular position. But despite being alone on this issue, I stuck to my guns. It cost me some friendships and created some vocal criticism. I held a firm line because I believed it needed to happen and it was the right thing to do. And some fraternity members joined with me. We effectively ended hazing within our fraternity—at least temporarily.

Unfortunately the change was short-lived. The following fall, a small group of members, after a drinking session, decided to take some pledges and show them what paddling felt like.

After my attempts to have those involved punished, I came to a moment of truth. If the fraternity wanted to continue down the path of self-destruction at a time when attitudes were swiftly changing about the acceptability of such behavior, then it was their choice as undergraduates. But I was not going to be a part of it. I ended up resigning as fraternity president a few months early. At the same time, I remained active as one of four student leaders who worked with university administrators to develop ways to move beyond hazing.

I eventually graduated wondering how much progress we had really made trying to bring about positive change in the UT fraternity system. Nonetheless, I was convinced that it was the right thing to do. Nationally, Sig Ep has taken a lead for many years to move beyond hazing, and I have heard reports that our Texas chapter has done the same in recent years as well.

Unfortunately, despite continuing efforts to end hazing, this social evil continues at UT and elsewhere. The state of Texas has passed antihazing legislation, and UT has adopted strict rules forbidding hazing and requiring victims to report incidents to the dean's office. Over the years, several student organizations have been suspended for violating these rules. Yet hazing still goes on. In December 2005, a young pledge in the Lambda Phi Epsilon fraternity died as a result of a hazing incident. Consequently the chapter was suspended until 2011, and three fraternity members received criminal indictments. It's terribly sad that tragedies like this continue to mar the fine record of an otherwise great institution like UT.

This college experience left a lasting impression on me. Most significantly, it showed me how difficult it can be to change a negative culture that has grown up in an institution over time. No matter how obvious it may be that change is needed, and no matter how hard people of goodwill fight to create that change, social inertia and the selfish motivations of a few individuals who benefit from the existing regime make systemic reform very challenging. It's a lesson that those who want to fix Washington's broken political culture will need to take very seriously.

RESIGNING AS PRESIDENT OF the fraternity in early fall 1989 opened the way for me to pursue another opportunity—one that turned out to be crucial for my career. I was about two semesters short of completing my coursework at UT and I hadn't yet decided what I was going to do after graduation. Since I was taking a somewhat lighter course load at the time and had some additional free time without my fraternity obligation, I reached out to Bill Tryon, an alumnus who had belonged to Sigma Phi Epsilon my freshman and sophomore years and was now working on a Republican gubernatorial campaign. I told Bill I had some time available and would be interested in volunteering to see what a statewide political campaign was like. This was a natural outgrowth of my family history, and I liked the idea because I thought it might give me an opportunity to work in Austin.

Why did I focus on an opportunity in the Republican party? The choice didn't reflect a particularly strong ideological bent. Overall, I did feel more at home in the conservative-leaning Texas Republican party, but my affiliation was more a matter of family history than rigid conservative belief. During the 1980s, I followed my mom and many other Texas Democrats in migrating to the Republicans.

Texas had been a one-party state for more than one hundred years, since the end of Reconstruction following the Civil War. Over the years, though, there had been a conservative wing and liberal wing in the Texas Democratic party. Since 1980, Texas has voted Republican in presidential elections. Many Texas Democrats over the course of the 1980s believed the national Democratic party had been moving too far left. My mother was one, as was I. She switched parties in 1985 during the period of the Reagan revolution. She ran for Congress as a Republican the following year (losing to the incumbent, Jake Pickle). It was also the year I turned eighteen; in fact, the first vote I ever cast was for my mother in the Republican primary. In 1988, I cast my first presidential ballot for George H. W. Bush, whom I also got to meet for the first time during a campaign event for my mother (little did I expect to get to know him personally more than fifteen years later).

Bill phoned me back that afternoon and asked if I would be willing to work part-time on Clayton Williams's gubernatorial campaign as a press assistant. Williams was a charismatic businessman who had built himself a fortune through successful investments in natural gas, real estate, banking, and telecommunications. He even appeared in a series of popular television commercials for his own long-distance phone company, ClayDesta, named after himself and his wife Modesta, wearing a business suit and a cowboy hat. Williams promised to bring his authentic Texas style, his businessman's intelligence, and a tough anticrime stance to the governor's mansion in Austin. But he was a novice politician, and his inexperience would prove fatal.

After meeting with the press secretary, Bill Kenyon, I was hired on the spot and started work immediately. Among other duties, the job entailed getting to the office at six o'clock every morning before anyone else had arrived, going through the major newspapers, and clipping and copying noteworthy stories relating to the campaign and prominent state issues so everyone, including the candidate, would have them to read right away. The twenty to twenty-five hours a week I committed to working quickly turned into thirty to thirty-five.

I'd signed on to the Williams for governor campaign early, which is always a good move for a young aspiring politico, and my dedication and hard work were noticed. Williams ended up winning the Republican primary overwhelmingly, defeating three notable rivals without a runoff—an impressive feat for a first-time candidate. The personal money he invested in the campaign helped, along with his down-home charm, and it looked as if he had great promise, capturing the electorate's perennial longing for something different from the typical politician.

Shortly after the primary, Kenyon asked if I would be interested in serving in a full-time press advance role, traveling ahead of Williams, the candidate, and making sure that public events, including news conferences, were properly staged with the right backdrops and visuals for the cameras and that Williams was fully briefed on the important aspects of the event. I jumped at the chance and put finishing school that summer on hold. It was exciting to move to the front lines of the campaign and have an opportunity to get to know the man who might be Texas's next governor.

Williams came out of the primary in strong position and with growing momentum, leading his Democratic rival, the charismatic and beloved Ann Richards, by a seemingly insurmountable margin. Williams had a populist conservative appeal. He was perceived as an outsider and successful businessman who could take on the state's bureaucracy in Austin, streamline government, fight crime effectively (he would teach felons "the joys of busting rock"), and best represent the values shared by the majority in conservative-leaning Texas. Richards, though well-liked personally, was perceived by many as too progressive or liberal for the state, and her 1988 speech at the Democratic National Convention attacking Texan George Herbert Walker Bush only reinforced that image.

Richards had served as a Travis County commissioner in Austin when my mother was mayor, so we'd crossed paths at political events when I was a kid. When Williams ran against her for governor, she was serving as the state treasurer. I knew she had lots of personal charm and would be difficult to beat, even when Williams was leading by twenty points after the primary. I viewed her as too left of center and knew she was vulnerable on the issues, but also knew she was adept at positioning herself publicly as more mainstream.

Right after the primary, however, Williams's lack of political experience began to hurt him, as he made a series of impolitic remarks and downright gaffes. For example, Williams refused to shake Richards's hand after an event, annoyed by an anonymous smear campaign against him that she had failed to denounce. But Texas men pride themselves on their gentlemanliness, and for Williams to publicly snub his opponent—and a lady, at that—was viewed as beyond the pale.

Much worse, however, was an ill-conceived joke Williams uttered during an informal press session at his ranch. The weather that day was lousy, and Williams quipped to a group of reporters that bad weather "is a little like rape. As long as it's inevitable, just relax and enjoy it." This wasn't just a case of political incorrectness, it was a horrendously insensitive remark, and the fact that Williams was running against a woman only made the circumstances worse. I was informed later that as soon as the words were out of his mouth, Williams's press secretary quickly spoke up and told the assembled writers, "This is all off the record." But at least one reporter pointed out, quite correctly, that no one had agreed to anything of the kind—and all the reporters were soon writing about the comment. It was inevitable that Williams's remark would make its way into the headlines of the papers and the TV coverage—and it did the following day.

Perhaps engaging in some wishful thinking, the candidate told his staffers that they were exaggerating the likely impact of his gaffe. Of course, he was way off base. The next day, the press secretary ordered me to collect all the news clips reporting and commenting on Williams's comment and get in early that weekend morning to answer phones, so that the candidate could see for himself the depth and breadth of the public outrage. The phones in our campaign offices were ringing off the hook, and I was the only one initially answering them as instructed. Texans took Williams's remark very personally. I remember one caller tearfully talking about her sister's tragic rape, a violent assault that left her permanently disfigured and emotionally scarred, and demanding to know how a candidate for governor could joke about such things. I had no answer or excuses to offer. All I could do was express my sincerest sympathy and let her know I would make sure to pass along the message. I did, to Williams himself over speakerphone when Kenyon, the press secretary, called in and told me to read out some of the calls.

One of my favorite classes at UT was a leadership course taught by Sara Weddington, a longtime friend of Ann Richards who was known for her involvement representing the anonymous "Jane Roe" in *Roe v. Wade*, the case that made abortion legal across the United States. The class was relatively small by UT standards, and quite a few bright, politically engaged students were taking it, and it was always interesting and informative. I was still a part-time staffer on the Williams campaign at the time. Our debates were intense but always cordial—except for the day after Williams's remark, when my more liberal-leaning classmates let me have it pretty hard. I eventually managed to get a word in and settle them down by letting them know that I agreed it was offensive and reminding them that I was not the one who said it.

Thanks to these and other missteps, Williams's substantial lead in the polls dwindled to virtually nothing by election day. Yet he still almost pulled it off because of his populist appeal. Richards came out on top with a very slim plurality.

It was a painful learning experience for those of us who'd worked long hours for a candidate we considered bright and promising. Vowing not to return to the up-and-down world of political campaigns, I briefly joined a small business started by some campaign colleagues before deciding that the next summer I would go back and finish my undergraduate degree.

But my vow to avoid political campaigns turned out to be temporary. After completing my degree that next summer, I spent six years bouncing back and forth among campaigns, grassroots political outreach, and Texas government.

In 1994, at Mom's request, I managed her first successful campaign to statewide elected office. Following her victory over the Democratic incumbent, I was asked by a new state senator, Tom Haywood, to serve as his chief of staff. I had managed his previous campaign in 1992, which he'd narrowly lost to an entrenched incumbent against heavy odds. I became a close friend of Tom's, as well as of his dedicated daughter Denise, who kept close watch over her father's interests, especially after he was diagnosed with Parkinson's disease.

Tom's illness didn't prevent him from serving in the senate, and I worked with him for eight months, including getting him through his first legislative session as we agreed. Mom came knocking again for her reelection campaign, which she easily won. Then it was off to a government affairs position in the Lower Colorado River Authority (LCRA), a quasi-state agency, before managing Mom's next race, this time for the powerful position of Texas comptroller. In each campaign, I also served as chief spokesman.

In January 1999, I was expecting to return to my position with the LCRA when Governor Bush's communications director, Karen Hughes, came calling, with an invitation that would change my life.

4

GOVERNOR BUSH
RUNS FOR PRESIDENT

Wʜɪʟᴇ ɢᴏᴠᴇʀɴᴏʀ ᴏғ Tᴇxᴀs, George W. Bush used to say he thought it was the best job in the world. For the most part, I believe he really meant it, and knowing Bush the way I do today, I have come to appreciate why.

Now, it is important to understand first that the Texas governorship is an inherently weak office constitutionally. The Constitution of 1876, written after the end of the Reconstruction period when most Texans still harbored great resentment toward the centralized, autocratic Republican administration that was imposed on them after the Civil War, substantially diminished the governor's powers and decentralized state government. The new constitution distributed power among an array of independently elected state officeholders, along with a part-time legislature. This so-called plural executive limits what the governor can do on his own, since the other officials with whom he shares power are elected on their own, are free to act independently, and may not entirely support his agenda.

Nonetheless, the Texas governorship does carry significant influence if the person occupying the office knows how to use the bully pulpit effectively. The Texas governor also has the power of the veto, as well as the ability to appoint a significant number of individuals to powerful and prominent positions within state government, including university boards and key regulatory commissions. And he or she can call special sessions of the legislature, which in Texas's unique (some might say odd) system otherwise meets for only four and a half months every other year. Relative to its power, the office also has a large staff and other perks and privileges, such as a mansion, a security detail, and the use of state government–owned planes. And it is considered the most prestigious state office, receiving far more media attention and public interest than any other.

The office suited Bush's personal style well. He is someone who enjoys living a full and balanced life, and—like most politicians—he finds being around people invigorating and uplifting. He also values discipline and routine in his schedule. The power of the office gave him the ability to do something meaningful and fulfilling—influence the state's direction in a positive way. Its largely predictable and normal hours coupled with its perks and privileges gave him great flexibility to balance work, exercise, and leisure time.

As we all should, Bush places great importance on daily exercise. I remember one day in 1997 when I was working at LCRA and had predictable, normal hours myself. Back then, before suffering a knee injury, I used to run three to four miles a day. I had taken my lunch hour to go running on the nearby Town Lake trail in Austin. As I was stretching and walking across the trail just before starting my run, a guy in hat and sunglasses flew right by me. I might not have noticed him but for the fact that he nearly plowed me over, which caused me to turn and see who it was. I saw a couple of guys follow on mountain bikes and another on foot. The guy in the hat was Governor Bush, who was sprinting as he finished his run for the day, and the guys trailing him were part of his protective detail.

Bush also used to like lifting weights at the nearby UT athletic facility, around lunch hour a few times a week, and had the flexibility to be able to do so. The prestige of his job provided him frequent access to a wide range of people, especially good, ordinary Texans, whom he could meet, greet, and address in speeches. I imagine there are few people, given the same opportunity, who would not enjoy such a prestigious, influential, and largely comfortable job.

I found working for Bush in the governor's office beginning in early 1999 to be rewarding and challenging. There were always a variety of issues or events to address, including his all but officially announced presidential campaign.

In my position as deputy communications director, I had frequent interaction with Governor Bush as I responded to press inquiries, attended public events with him in Austin and around the state, and wrote press releases and statements for him, among other duties. I started getting to know him as a person and a leader, and began to form a personal bond with him.

A governor's entourage, unlike that of a U.S. president, tends to be intimate and fairly small. And Bush always preferred it that way. He never much cared for a lot of people trying to handle him, follow him, or tell him where to go or what to say. On trips as governor, it was not uncommon for him to be accompanied only by a personal aide, his spokesman, and two or three members of his protective security detail, who were the best officers the Texas Department of Public Safety had to offer.

There are a few moments that I still remember well from those six months I spent in the governor's office before heading over to the presidential campaign.

It was in the governor's communications office that I first confronted a life-and-death policy issue—the death penalty. Governor Bush took a pretty tough line on stays and commutations. He believed that the death penalty helps save innocent lives through its deterrent effect. In his view, if the convicted felon had been afforded full access to the courts and there was no question about his or her guilt, then it was not the governor's place to overrule a jury. In any case, by state law, his options were limited to one thirty-day stay, and he could commute the sentence only if he received a recommendation to do so from the Texas pardons and parole board (whose members are appointed by the governor). As a spokesman, I had to respond to inquiries about specific cases as well as questions about how Governor Bush reviewed them before signing death warrants.

As the son of a former president and a possible future presidential contender, George W. Bush attracted more national scrutiny than other Texas governors had. Issues related to the death penalty were among the more contentious. Texas resorts to execution at a higher rate than any other state in the Union, and during Bush's tenure as governor the death penalty was implemented 152 times, a number that caused considerable controversy. Those executed included a handful of felons whose IQs were below what is often considered the threshold for mental retardation, as well as Karla Faye Tucker, a born-again Christian whose 1998 case attracted pleas for clemency from

Pope John Paul II and prominent conservatives including Newt Gingrich and Pat Robertson.

In any case, the death penalty was probably the first significant issue I had to deal with directly in the media where my view was not in line with Bush's. While I firmly believe in taking a tough stance on crime, I have always harbored some doubts about capital punishment. My thinking is grounded in a moral belief. I'm deeply troubled by the idea that even one innocent person could fall through the system and be put to death for a crime that he or she did not commit. I believe life without parole, which segregates convicted criminals from society, can serve the same purpose—keeping that individual from ever harming another innocent person—without forcing society to play a role that I believe is not ours to play. Such a convicted felon should be held in virtual solitude under maximum security and treated humanely but with few, if any, privileges of a free society. I also question, as have studies over the years, whether the death penalty has much of a deterrent effect.

To be clear, I'm not staunchly anti–death penalty. If ever there was a case in which it is deserved, it would be those responsible for planning the 9/11 attacks. For me, the issue is too complex and too nuanced for a black-and-white position. But I do feel significant doubts about it, much as I would later feel about the necessity of war in Iraq, another life-and-death policy matter where I was called on, as official spokesman, to defend a position despite inner qualms about it.

I didn't express my doubts about the death penalty publicly. After all, I was speaking for the governor, not myself. He was an unapologetic supporter of the death penalty, a position he had clearly articulated while running for the governorship and which the majority of Texans supported. Furthermore, the death penalty was Texas law. Even if the governor had not agreed with it, he had an obligation to uphold the laws of Texas and carry them out faithfully. For all these reasons, I told myself, my personal doubts didn't really matter. On Governor Bush's behalf, I issued statements defending his position and responded to the controversies the way he wanted me to. That's what a spokesman does.

Another notable moment occurred when a stricter Texas law against driving while intoxicated was passed. After determined lobbying by leaders of Mothers Against Drunk Driving (MADD), the Texas legislature passed a law in 1999 lowering the blood alcohol limit in Texas from 0.10 to 0.08. I remember suggesting to Karen Hughes that it might be good to hold a public signing ceremony for the bill, so that the governor could underscore the importance of the new law. Karen replied, "Oh, he won't want to do anything public on it. I'm not sure exactly what it is, but I think there is something in his past."

I found her response notable, but didn't think a lot more about it at the time. I'm not sure exactly why; probably the press of daily business simply pushed the issue to the side, until later events just before election day in 2000 made me recall the exchange with Karen and think about it in a new light.

Overall, my time in the governor's office was a good experience. I learned a lot about government, politics, and the art of communication. I helped support an administration that was producing good, bipartisan results for the state and the people of Texas. And I was playing a meaningful role in the career of a promising politician considered by many people to be a possible future president of the United States. All of this was heady, exciting stuff.

I enjoyed some delightful moments of personal bonding with Bush, flying on a small plane with just the two of us sitting up front or chatting with him in the governor's office. One of my favorite moments occurred on the day I was the first to arrive for a meeting to review bills from the just completed legislative session that the governor might veto. Since I had arrived early, the governor invited me back to the kitchen where he was fixing himself one of his favorite lunches, a peanut butter and jelly sandwich. Dressed down in a white T-shirt and blue jeans sans shoes, he asked if I wanted a sandwich. I said sure, and he fixed it for me. For the next twenty minutes or so we munched on the sandwiches and talked about a variety of topics, few of which had to do with politics.

Not long after I was beginning to settle in to the quieter times in the governor's communications office following the legislative session and the bill signing period that succeeded it, Karen Hughes, then-communications director for the Bush 2000 campaign, asked me to make another move. This time, in late July 1999, it was to join the now full-throttle presidential campaign as a deputy press secretary. Someone was needed to help fill the void left by departing national spokesman David Beckwith, a veteran Washington political communicator and former vice presidential spokesman. I had come to know Beckwith back in 1992 when he worked in Texas for then-U.S. Senate candidate Kay

Bailey Hutchison. I liked Beckwith, but Karen viewed him as a loose cannon who was less cautious and was not as on-message as she preferred. Karen had come to trust me to proceed cautiously and stay on message, and she felt I had a good sense of the tone Bush preferred to set in his comments.

I gained some valuable experience dealing with the national press during the lead-up to the primaries and early primary states. I spent most of my time responding to press inquiries from a variety of journalists and news organizations, both in person and on the phone, and participating in communications strategy meetings.

As Governor Bush seemed to be on his way to securing the nomination, Karen approached me about becoming the traveling press secretary when the campaign shifted to the general election. Karen would continue to travel regularly as the chief spokesman for the campaign, but with a full press entourage following the nominee's every move, another spokesman was needed on the road. I enthusiastically accepted the offer.

The primary victory was not secured as quickly or as easily as we thought it would be. Senator John McCain won a surprising victory in New Hampshire, followed by a Bush comeback in a hotly contested South Carolina race. Charges of smear tactics, dirty tricks, and other below-the-belt negative attacks flew back and forth beginning in the South Carolina contest and continued through the remainder of the primary battle, creating bitterness that I imagine endures in some quarters to this day.

You may be wondering whether such bare-knuckle campaign tactics are one of my targets when I decry the excessiveness of Washington's permanent campaign and its scorched-earth politics. I certainly don't advocate or condone distorting an opponent's record, disseminating lies about him, or spreading innuendo through whispering campaigns, and it's the media's job to help sort out the truth in such circumstances. But I am less concerned about tough election campaigns than I am about such tactics seeping into the conduct of governance. Harsh electoral tactics are as old as democracy itself. But once the election is over, elected officials of both parties—especially those in positions of leadership—owe it to the public to work together on solving the country's problems through deliberation and compromise. For most of American history, they have done just that, even after hard-fought, even brutally negative election campaigns. (We've had our share of those in Texas.) We need to find a way to return to that tradition.

McCain rebounded from the South Carolina loss with a win in Michigan, but it was his final hurrah for the 2000 season, as Bush went on to sew up the nomination.

Political campaigns are often described as "organized chaos." Presidential campaigns are organized chaos on a massive scale. There are many different areas of focus, from fund-raising to outreach to strategy to communications to advance work to policy to research to event planning, and each involves keeping multiple plates spinning at the same time. During the primary campaign, I spent most of my time serving as a press spokesman, responding to media inquiries, doing interviews, and participating in communications strategy meetings and discussions. After being named traveling press secretary for the general election, I spent the majority of my time on the road as part of Bush's traveling team. On nontravel days, I would return to doing phone, radio, and television interviews from campaign headquarters and sitting in on morning senior staff message meetings where we would discuss communications strategy, including talking points and the message of the day.

My memories of the campaign trail are a whirlwind of plane flights, motorcades, press buses, hotel rooms, large rallies, and traveling media relations. I coordinated messages and responses on the road with Karen Hughes, the chief spokesman, and from the road with the communications team back at our headquarters in Austin—including our national spokesman, Ari Fleischer, and rapid response director Dan Bartlett.

Part of my role was to function as an early warning detector and gather intelligence for the campaign. By establishing close relations with the reporters who covered Bush on the road, including consistently hanging out in their midst, I picked up useful bits of information—developing story lines that needed our input, incoming attacks from the opposition, or views of the internal Gore campaign from their colleagues covering the Democratic road show. As in any strategic battle, it's always good to know the opposition's mood and frame of mind.

The campaign was also a chance for me to get to know Bush better, since I spent much of my time in close proximity to him, including briefing him and filling him in on relevant communications information, often alongside Karen Hughes. The rigors of a presidential campaign demand discipline, energy, and focus from a candidate. The travel is grueling, often including multiple events in multiple cities on any given day with perhaps one or two days at home following several days on the trail. The candidate is constantly in the spotlight, giving speeches, being interviewed, attending fund-raisers, shaking hands on rope lines, and, yes, holding babies. He has to be on his game every minute of every day.

Bush dealt with the pressures remarkably well. He made time to clear his head, work out, and get a good night's rest (at least most of the time). He also understood the importance of pacing himself. A campaign is a marathon, which Bush recognized from watching and advising his father in 1988. He also had a great ability to stay focused on the big picture and not worry about the "process" stories—day-to-day analysis of the minutiae of the horse race that the press likes to report but which often has less interest among the general public.

Bush also understood the importance of keeping his sense of humor, particularly as the campaign heated up. He is famous for his locker room antics, and rather than add to the existing literature I will leave those stories in the locker room. But I will say that we had some great fun, particularly during our final campaign swing. The end was near, one way or the other (or so we thought), and after months of travel we would soon be heading home.

Keeping things lighthearted behind the scenes helps the candidate and everyone else survive the intense, pressure-filled campaign environment without losing their sanity. Bush liked to tease traveling staffers by asking toward the end of the day if they were tired from working so hard. He had a subtle way of hooking his prey. If they said they were, he would tell the other staffers present how tired that person was and what a hard day he had had. Then he would ask the staffer, "How many speeches did you give today? How many hands did you shake?" It was a humorous way of reminding us who had to do the heaviest lifting any given day on the road. It was a routine Bush tended to recycle during the 2004 campaign and on longer trips, too. And, yes, I recall falling for it—once.

One night near the end of the campaign, the governor turned around from his aisle seat at the front of the campaign plane and pointed at a staffer in the last row of the staff section, just a few seats behind him. The staffer, Eric Terrell, signed checks for minor traveling expenses. He was a soft-spoken, low-key individual who was easy to overlook. To Bush, he was "Check Dude," a nickname he'd been given early in the campaign. Eric had bet several of his road crew colleagues that he could go the whole campaign traveling with Bush without Bush knowing his actual name. But that night, Bush turned around, pointed to him, and said, "Eric Terrell. You're Eric Terrell. I gotcha. You're nailed."

As Governor Bush grinned triumphantly, Eric had to pay up on his losing bets.

In retrospect, one memorable moment I experienced while traveling with Governor Bush early in the campaign revealed more than just the repulsive tendency of contemporary Washington to spend an inordinate amount of time dredging into a candidate's personal past. It also showed a rather intriguing side of Bush's personality—one that proved significant at times in his presidential administration.

My recollection is that we were campaigning in the Midwest. It was not long after Bush had effectively secured the Republican nomination. Karen had been traveling during the hectic and fiercely fought Bush-McCain primary showdown, so she decided to stay home and focus on the bigger strategic picture for the general election, away from the demands of the road, while I stayed with the governor as the sole spokesman.

Following a campaign event, we arrived at a local hotel where the campaign had a few rooms reserved for some downtime. Governor Bush and I were visiting as we headed to his suite. His personal aide, Logan Walters, was in tow along with some Secret Service agents. On the way upstairs, Bush began asking questions and chatting about what was on the press corps' mind. As we approached his room, I mentioned that the cocaine issue was continuing to peek out from the shadows of the campaign.

Reporters earlier in the campaign had questioned Bush about whether he had used cocaine in his young adulthood. Rumors had circulated, but nothing had ever been substantiated. Bush had consistently brushed aside questions about his past with a deliberately ambiguous quip: "When I was young and irresponsible, I was young and irresponsible." Most reporters and commentators—and most voters too, I would bet—understood the message. Bush was, in effect, acknowledging that he had made some mistakes involving drinking and drugs, while at the same time refusing to be drawn into an endless line of questioning about exactly what he'd done and how it might affect his fitness for office so many years later. Bush would then segue into the broader point he wanted to emphasize: the most important message baby boomers such as himself could send to their children is that they have learned from experience and that their children should avoid repeating their mistakes.

In August 1999, a veteran Texas political reporter, Sam Attlesey of the *Dallas Morning News*, was able to elicit a new response and partial answer from Bush on the matter. The question centered on whether Bush could meet the standard in the FBI background check for security clearances of some federal appointees, which asked about drug use in the past seven years. Bush answered that he could and confirmed that he had not used cocaine in that time period. The next day he was asked if he could have met the standard during his father's administration, when he served as an informal adviser to the elder Bush. At that time, it was the past fifteen years. Bush said he could, laying down a marker that he had not used cocaine at least since 1974. After that, he returned to the "young and irresponsible" quip and made clear he was not going any further.

Nevertheless, news stories and columns periodically returned to the topic. Some critics asserted that it was a relevant issue. They suggested it was hypocritical for Bush to advocate tough mandatory sentences for users of relatively small amounts of cocaine if he had used it in his past, particularly when he hadn't faced any serious consequences for doing so.

All of this was in the background of the conversation that Bush and I were having on our way to his hotel suite somewhere in the Midwest. I mentioned to the governor that the local paper had run a tacky picture of him next to a story about the cocaine rumors. The photo was a head shot of Bush with his index finger touching the tip of his nose. The gesture, of course, was purely coincidental, but alongside the adjacent story it appeared at least suggestive. Bush shook his head incredulously and sighed, "Unbelievable. You gotta be kidding!"

As we arrived at the suite, the governor invited me to follow him into the back room. Logan stayed behind in the living room area, arranging for the governor to take a phone call from a supporter. Bush motioned for me to sit and relax in his room while he took the call. I didn't know who was on the other end of the line, but from the tone of the conversation, I could tell the supporter was probably a major contributor, though not necessarily a longtime friend. Bush had my comments about the picture in the local paper fresh on his mind. He brought up the issue behind it on the call.

"The media won't let go of these ridiculous cocaine rumors," I heard Bush say. "You know, the truth is I honestly don't remember whether I tried it or not. We had some pretty wild parties back in the day, and I just don't remember."

The overheard comment struck me and has stayed with me to this day—not for what it revealed or concealed about the young George W. Bush, but for what it said about Bush as an older man and political leader, especially as revealed through my later experiences working for him.

I remember thinking to myself, How can that be? How can someone simply not remember whether or not they used an illegal substance like cocaine? It didn't make a lot of sense.

I compared Bush's memory, or lack of it, to my own experience. When I was young, I had my moments of excessive drinking at parties or out on the town with friends. There was also a time or two when I was around others who smoked marijuana. But I always drew the line at illegal drugs. The closest I ever came was holding a smoldering joint in my hand at a friend's home, gazing at it for a second as if tempted—more to tease my friends than anything else—and then passing it along to the person next to me, saying something like, "Thanks but no thanks." After that happened a couple of times, my buddies knew better than to even tempt me.

Whether or not I smoked pot isn't that important. The point is, I *know* what happened. I remember. And I found it hard to understand how George Bush could say he simply had no idea about what happened in his own past.

I know Bush, and I know he genuinely believes what he says. He isn't the kind of person to flat-out lie, particularly when speaking in private to a supporter or friend. So I think he meant what he said in that conversation about cocaine. It's the first time when I felt I was witnessing Bush convincing himself to believe something that probably was not true and that, deep down, he *knew* was not true. And his reason for doing so is fairly obvious: political convenience. He is certainly not the only politician to embrace the hazy memory defense, especially in our ever-more transparent political culture where voters are exposed to more outlets for news than ever before and just about everything is considered fair game to some.

In the years to come, as I worked closely with President Bush, I would come to believe that sometimes he convinces himself to believe what suits his needs at the moment. It is not unlike a witness in court who does not want to implicate himself in wrongdoing, but is also concerned about perjuring himself. So he says, "I do not recall." The witness knows no one can get into his head and prove it is not true, so this seems like a much safer course than actually lying. Bush, similarly, has a way of falling back on the hazy memory defense to protect himself from potential political embarrassment. Bush rationalizes it as being acceptable because he is not stating unequivocally anything that could be proven false. If something later is uncovered to show what he knew, then he can deny lying in his own mind.

In other words, being evasive is not the same as lying in Bush's mind. The former is acceptable, but the latter is not. I've seen it happen during other private moments, around people he trusted, as well as at times during press availabilities and news conferences.

Self-deceit is a human quality, and we all engage in it at times. But for politicians it tends to be more discernable and probably more pronounced because of the intense spotlight they are under. Bush is certainly not the first or the last politician to deceive himself, but the extent to which he resorts to self-deception beyond personal matters, which one can argue should be off-limits anyway, and the sincerity with which he embraces self-deluding beliefs amount to a personality trait that goes directly to larger issues of character and leadership style and carry over into real issues of governance.

Another memorable moment was the time late in the presidential campaign when it was revealed that Bush had been convicted for driving under the influence of alcohol during a stay at the family home in Kennebunkport when he was in his mid-twenties. The momentum seemed to be with us in those final days, largely because Bush had essentially come out ahead during the three October debates. Bush had exceeded low expectations during the debates, whereas Gore had not met high expectations that he would decisively dominate Bush.

Gore's first debate performance, marked by sighs and exaggerations, played right into our hands. A key message we'd developed to undermine Gore's credibility was that he would say or do anything to get elected. Gore did not let us down, as comments he made and actions he took frequently underscored that perception in many voters' minds. It contrasted well with one of our key underlying messages: that Bush was honest and could be trusted to do what was right, not what was politically most convenient.

Now, four days before the election, Bush had just finished a rally in Chicago. I was heading toward the buses that would transport the traveling press corps back to our campaign plane when Karen told me that a local Fox News station in Maine would be reporting that evening that George W. Bush had been convicted of driving under the influence as a young man in his twenties.

I immediately thought back to my conversation with Karen a year earlier, when she'd said Governor Bush would prefer to avoid highlighting a law against drunken driving because of "something in his past." Suddenly Karen's words took on a specific meaning.

Minutes after my conversation with Karen in Chicago, Carl Cameron, the national Fox News political correspondent who covered the campaign as a member of the traveling press corps, approached me, indicating he had heard the news too, I believe via the local station through his network. He told me he was going to air with it at the top of the approaching evening news hour with Brit Hume back in Washington.

I contacted Dan Bartlett, who was our rapid response director back in Austin. One chief responsibility of the rapid response director is to keep close tabs on the opposition and find ways to put him or her on the defensive, such as pointing out when the opponent is saying one thing but has a history of doing the opposite. Another chief duty is to coordinate the campaign's efforts to quickly respond in the same news cycle to incoming attacks or damaging breaking news about its candidate. If it is an attack from an opponent, then the rapid response effort is usually aimed at counterpunching to avoid being put on the defensive. If it is damaging news, then the response usually tries to change the focus in the media, possibly by finding a way to frame it as nothing but a dirty trick from the opposition. I told him my efforts to hold off Cameron until we could get him some comment for the record were not proving successful. So Dan spoke with him and gave Cameron our initial response.

It's an old political truism: a candidate who has something controversial in his past needs to get it out early and on his own terms. Otherwise, his opponents may choose the time and manner of its release, usually calculated to maximize the political damage. This is why smart campaign teams perform opposition research ("oppo") not just on their opponents but on themselves, using public information sources as well as undercover investigations to find out the worst about their own candidate. After all, if we can discover embarrassing information about our candidate on the Internet, in old newspaper files, or in public documents, "the bad guys" can discover it too.

Everyone on the Bush team was aware of this principle, of course. I never had the impression that more than a few, if even that many, of Bush's top political advisers were aware of the DUI conviction. My conversation with Karen Hughes from a year before would lead me to believe that she had only a general sense of it but did not know any specifics. My conclusion was based on knowing Karen and the vagueness of her language ("something in his past").

By the time we finished the final event of the evening, Bush knew he had to address the media feeding frenzy about the DUI story. Breaking so late in the campaign, this story had the potential to alter the race. All the rumors about Bush's wild days of young adulthood were dramatically resurfacing with specific, documented evidence.

Bush told the assembled traveling press corps following his Wisconsin stop that the DUI story was, in essence, correct. "I've often times said that years ago I made some mistakes," Bush said. "I occasionally drank too much. I did on that night. I was pulled over. I admitted to the policeman that I had been drinking. I paid the fine. I regretted that it happened. I learned my lesson."

He had not disclosed the DUI conviction publicly before, he continued, because he did not want his daughters to know about it. He had told them as a dad not to drink and drive because he did not want them doing the things he had done.

Bush went on to talk about the suspicious timing of the news break, raising questions about whether it was politically motivated. It was an attempt to shift the topic of conversation from Bush's own misdeeds to the behavior of the opposition, in hopes that public revulsion against negative campaigning would produce a backlash against the Democrats. And indeed, a television reporter in Maine who first got the scoop later acknowledged that she'd been given the information by a local Democratic activist, a delegate to the Democratic National Convention.

What impact did the DUI story have on the extraordinarily close 2000 election? It's hard to say. Karl Rove, George Bush's chief campaign strategist, believed the revelation was responsible for the Republican loss of Maine, where the news had originated, as well as the loss of enough support nationally to cost Bush the popular vote and send the election into overtime. By undermining Bush's campaign refrain about restoring "honor and dignity" to the White House, the revelation likely led some social conservatives to sit out

the presidential race rather than cast a ballot for a candidate th now r -
ceived as flawed.

As for me, the DUI story didn't have much effect on my attitude toward
George Bush or his presidential campaign. I'd signed on as a Bush supporter
because I believed he could serve as a uniting force to help the nation overcome its bitter partisan divide, and I still felt that was true.

I didn't consider the mishandling of the DUI case a serious misdemeanor
on the part of George Bush but a minor peccadillo driven by understandable
motives: the desire to avoid political embarrassment over something personal
from his past and a father's reluctance to expose a seamy episode from his past
to his impressionable teenage daughters.

Most important, the story did *not* reveal anything detrimental about
Bush's ability to govern. The offense had occurred many years ago, and Bush
had given up alcohol altogether more than a decade earlier. In any case, the
crime had not involved violation of the public trust. Driving under the influence is serious and can lead to tragic consequences. But I don't think a single
episode of DUI automatically disqualifies a person from public office, unlike
crimes like bribery, embezzlement, or fraud, for example.

However, there is an important political lesson that could have been ap-
plied to more important matters of governance later in his presidency. While
Bush addressed the DUI story head-on and did so well, it was too little, too
late, and on someone else's terms. He allowed it to become a greater controversy than it needed to be by not dealing with it early and on his terms. The
result was that it added unnecessarily to the suspicions some had about his
strength of character and future ability to lead as president.

It would not be the last time Bush mishandled potential controversy. But
the cases to come *would* involve the public trust, and the failure to deal with
them early, directly, and head-on would lead to far greater suspicion and far
more destructive partisan warfare.

In any case, the election came down to the wire with the two candidates
neck and neck, and, as everyone knows, it led to one of the most contentious
and protracted electoral battles in American history.

My memories of the Florida recount, like my memories of the campaign,
are a whirlwind—this time a whirlwind of moving from county to county
across central and southeast Florida to oversee on-the-ground communications

efforts and make sure they were helping to inform and favorably shape public opinion.

On election night, Bush led Gore in Florida by about two thousand votes out of nearly 6 million cast. The extremely small margin triggered an automatic statewide recount under the state's election laws. Florida's twenty-five electoral votes would decide the contest, since neither Bush nor Gore had the necessary electoral votes without it. In addition to the automatic county-by-county machine recount, the Gore campaign decided to seek manual hand recounts of every ballot in a few select counties, and the legal battle that ensued over the constitutionality and fairness of the recount would drag on far longer than anyone expected.

On the morning of day two of the extended election period, I walked into a communications strategy meeting to discuss the rhetorical warfare that was beginning between the campaigns. Dan Bartlett said, "We need more spokespeople on the ground in Florida. Any volunteers?" (Whereas the Gore campaign had most of its paid communicators at the national headquarters or in Tallahassee, the state capital of Florida, one part of our communications strategy was aimed at spreading paid spokespeople out into select counties of interest.)

As a couple of hands went up, I thought to myself how worn-out I was from traveling and how eagerly I'd been looking forward to a well-deserved rest. "But a few more days on the road won't make much difference," I finally concluded. I raised my hand as well.

By midafternoon, a handful of us spokespeople were on a private jet to be dropped off in different strategic locales around Florida. I had almost no clean clothes left, since the end of campaign travel had been nonstop, but I managed to pull together what was wearable. "I just have to get through the weekend," I remember thinking. "Surely it will be over by then." Little did I know that I would not return home to Austin for three weeks, and that the recount marathon would last thirty-six days, causing confusion and uproar in newsrooms around the country and unprecedented angst for millions of voters.

Starting in Pinellas County near Tampa Bay, I traveled across the central part of the state, reaching Kissimmee, near Orlando, by the end of week one. Then things got particularly interesting when the Gore campaign targeted

Broward, Miami-Dade, and Palm Beach counties, each a Democratic strong-hold, for manual hand recounts.

I remember joining up in Broward with a volunteer organizational team made up of advisers to Ohio Governor Bob Taft. They were there to help make sure tables were staffed with Bush volunteers and that the volunteers understood when and when not to challenge ballots. We coordinated our efforts out of the office of the county GOP chairman, Eddie Pozzuoli, who was helping lead the Bush efforts. The machine recount had already been conducted as required by law because of the closeness of the election. Bush remained in the lead. A campaign could request hand recounts, but Broward, like other counties, could order a hand recount only after a vote by the county canvassing board, typically made up of the county judge and two county commissioners. Technically the canvassing board was supposed to vote for a hand recount only after an initial sampling of precincts had been conducted and there was reason to believe there were errors serious enough to warrant one.

Initially, the Broward County canvassing board voted against ordering a full hand recount. The Taft volunteers, Pozzuoli, and I had a brief celebration that day, thinking the result was final and believing nothing would change. I was dispatched to Miami-Dade County, and by the time I got there, Team Taft from Ohio had arrived as well. The canvassing board there likewise voted against a full hand recount. Another victory, we thought. But then we learned that the Broward canvassing board had reversed course under pressure from Democratic trial lawyers enlisted by the Gore campaign. Suddenly we were headed back to Ft. Lauderdale in Broward County.

The recount process was moved to a larger venue, the Broward County hurricane center. Around fifteen or twenty long tables were brought into a large room so both GOP and Democratic volunteers could sit at the tables and jointly review ballots, one by one. The county people knew they were under a time limit to get the ballots reviewed, so they wanted as many tables going as reasonable. If the opposing party volunteers at a table could not agree on the voter intention revealed by the ballot, it would be set aside for the three-member commissioner's court to determine by majority vote. The canvassing board was made up of two Democrats and one Republican (you may remember pictures of the Republican commissioner with his glasses perched on top of his head and eyes wide open, glaring at the ballot as he holds it up to the light).

I believe it was around midnight of the first full day of recounting that we discovered a potential issue of concern—and a great angle for a news story. Ed McNally, a lawyer who had worked in the first Bush administration (and later the second), had come to Broward to help with legal issues. A Bush volunteer approached us just after the hand recount was halted for the day. "There's something over here that you should see," he said. He walked us over to the table he had helped man and pointed to the floor. On the floor were sprinkled a significant number of chad.

As the world came to learn that month, for voting purposes, a chad is a tiny, confetti-like rectangular piece of paper that is made when someone makes a hole in a punch card. A chad can take several different forms. A hanging chad is connected to the ballot by one of its four corners, a swinging chad is attached by two corners, and a tri-chad, by three corners. Then there is a pregnant or dimpled chad that has an indention in it, supposedly from a voter who may have been trying to cast a vote, but the chad remains attached at all four corners. I never thought I would be a chad expert, but the 2000 election made chad-ology an essential topic.

As we stood looking at the tiny bits of paper scattered all over the floor, Ed came up with a clever idea. "These chad could be considered evidence of a crime," he said. If people had been handling the ballots too much or too carelessly, or, worse yet, if they'd been deliberately poking pieces of chad out of the ballots to alter the election results, that could explain why so much confetti was littering the floor.

The local Democratic leaders had already dispersed for the night. We sought out the local election official still present as the ballot boxes were being secured in the back room, which bore a large glass window on the entrance side. A sheriff's deputy was present to guard the room. At our request, the election official ordered the fallen chad on the floor to be collected and placed in a large envelope marked "CRIME SCENE EVIDENCE."

Our campaign and supporters had already questioned the integrity of the hand recounts, given that the ballots were now being handled yet again after being put through a machine twice. The wear and tear of multiple handlings, we contended, could be altering the votes or knocking chad loose. Now we had evidence to back up our claim.

After consulting with Ed, I quietly went around to reporters individually the next morning to alert them of the previous night's development. "Did you hear about what happened last night?" I asked. When they replied they had not, I explained. "They [election officials] seized a bunch of fallen chad late last night," I said. "You ought to ask to see the envelope they put them in." I knew that, in the heated atmosphere of Florida 2000, an envelope marked "CRIME SCENE EVIDENCE" would make for great pictures.

I also coordinated a news conference with Eddie Pozzuoli. Eddie did a great job, standing outside the building, with the words "hurricane center" plainly visible, talking about how "Hurricane Chad hit Broward County last night" and raising questions about the integrity of the whole hand recount process. Just as we hoped, the news coverage added to the nation's doubts about the legitimacy of the recount.

A couple of days later, I was sent to nearby Palm Beach County, where a hand count was also under way. I took a clear plastic bag filled with more fallen chad from the second night. The election officials turned down our request to seize another batch of fallen chad. So we did it ourselves, and marked the bag with the words "Fallen Chad, Broward County" and the number of paper fragments, well over a hundred, that we'd picked up off the carpet and tables. I held up the bag when I arrived in Palm Beach County for assembled reporters and again raised questions about the process.

Marc Racicot, the Montana governor and Bush adviser, went out on the Sunday political shows that week. At his request, I sent him the bag of fallen chad. He referred to it as "clear and compelling evidence" of the "completely untrustworthy" hand recounting process.

Personally, I viewed the recount process as selective, unfair, and sometimes wacky. Allowing canvassing boards that were majority Democratic to decide the fate of disputed ballots based on what they believed voter intent to be did not strike me as particularly objective. In Palm Beach County when the canvassing board was running up against the deadline to finish its hand recount, our lead lawyer on the ground there, John Bolton (named American ambassador to the UN in Bush's second term) and his team, including Florida attorney Mark Wallace, reportedly caught the Democratic commissioner on the board directing sheriff's deputies which specific precinct boxes to bring out for recounting. The problem? The boxes were supposed to be selected randomly, and this commissioner was allegedly telling the deputies to get ones that were considered heavily Democratic—and therefore most likely to help pick up votes for Gore.

Frankly, I believe the Gore campaign made a strategic mistake by not calling for a manual hand recount in every county. That would have been hard to dispute as anything but fair.

At any rate, the fallen chad provided us some great fodder for questioning the selectivity and subjectivity of the hand recounts. But the Florida recount continued for a couple more weeks. No one had ever witnessed anything like it. Certainly nothing in my political background had prepared me for it. I remember, as a third grader, staying up until 3:30 A.M. to follow the results as my mother won the closest mayoral election in Austin history. That seemed like a rare anomaly to me. (Mom later won her reelection by the largest margin ever.)

On day twenty-one of the recount ordeal, I was granted a reprieve and allowed to travel home for the weekend. As I was waiting word on whether I needed to return to Florida, Ari Fleischer, who had already been named the transition press secretary, called from Washington to offer me the deputy press secretary position for the transition. He also asked me to be his principal deputy should the Florida results hold. I accepted fairly quickly.

Rather than returning to Florida, I headed to Washington to begin work on the transition team. We had a temporary space already set up for our use until Bush was recognized as the official winner and given taxpayer space and funds from the General Services Administration in Washington.

My focus shifted quickly to helping Ari with press management and dealing with the multitude of transition issues. When Florida secretary of state Katherine Harris certified Bush the winner in Florida, Dick Cheney was already overseeing the transition out of temporary space near his home in McLean, Virginia, just outside of Washington. He formally requested that the GSA provide us the keys to the government transition office near the White House. The GSA, under White House direction, refused. This did not make Cheney happy.

On December 12, when the Supreme Court made its controversial ruling ending the Florida recount and dispelling questions about the result, the GSA invited the vice president-elect to a press event at the transition office. Still stewing about the initial snub, Cheney had Ari send a lower-level official— me—to receive the keys. The idea was to send the GSA a message.

I had no idea what I was supposed to do. When I got to the transition office, I was given a brief tour, then handed the keys in front of a battery of television and still cameras. Although the assembled reporters seemed to expect some sort of speech, I said little other than "thank-you." I think the GSA got the message from Cheney, and they worked to make up for the displeasure they'd caused him from that day forward.

Within days, I was standing in my new office behind the briefing room—a barren space with a couple of chairs and a computer. It all happened so quickly that I barely had a chance to absorb the amazing fact that I was now working for the nation's forty-third president in the West Wing of the White House.

BY AND LARGE, BUSH AND his campaign did a successful job of defining him and starting the process of changing the image of the Republican party nationally. Bush was elected with a clear agenda—tax cuts, education reform, strengthening Social Security, strong defense, and military transformation. He was also elected with a clear public image as a different kind of Republican—a "compassionate conservative" who understood and cared about the needs and interests of the middle class, the working class, and the poor, and was willing to use the government when necessary to help meet those needs.

As Bush took office—buoyed by the nation's relief over the ending of the prolonged election process, as well as by Al Gore's gracious concession speech—Bush was promising to bring the country a fresh start after a season of cynicism. His intention, it appeared, was to reach across the aisle as he'd done in Texas to forge cooperative links with Democrats in Congress and elsewhere in pursuit of goals that would benefit all Americans. The days of endless scandal and partisan warfare in Washington were coming to an end—or so I believed.

Events of the months and years to come would test the sincerity of Bush's intention to end the excesses of the permanent campaign era, as well as the depth of his promised commitment to ensuring that every member of his administration adhered to high ethical standards.

5

THE PERMANENT
CAMPAIGN

PLANNING FOR THE BUSH transition quietly began more than a year and a half in advance of Election Day. The process was led by the president's trusted lifelong friend Clay Johnson, whose background in business management (he had held executive positions at firms ranging from Neiman Marcus to Frito Lay) served him well in this role. He had become the governor's executive director (equivalent to chief of staff) once Joe Allbaugh had moved over to manage the presidential effort; before that, he'd been the appointments director during most of Bush's governorship, overseeing the nearly three thousand appointments to boards and commissions that a Texas governor makes. Johnson was able to do the transition planning discreetly, unbeknownst to the media and the public and on a separate track from the campaign.

The decision to start the transition planning early with Clay in charge proved highly beneficial, particularly given the extended election period. In large part because of Clay's detailed planning, the president and his team hit the ground running and got off to a successful early presidency. (Clay later served as the White House personnel director and currently is deputy director for management at the Office of Management and Budget.)

One feature of contemporary politics had a profound impact on the transition, probably without Clay Johnson's intention or awareness, since he was neither a creature of politics nor had a background in it. I'm referring to the "permanent campaign," a shorthand term for the way political leaders today work 365 days a year, year in and year out, to shape and manipulate sources of public approval as the primary means for governing. Because of the power and ubiquity of the permanent campaign, the jockeying for power during the 2000 presidential race did not end with the inauguration but simply morphed into a different phase—governance.

I don't believe that any of Bush's senior advisers took time during the transition period to read and absorb the lessons offered in the book *The Permanent Campaign and Its Future*. I know I didn't. If they had, they might have taken steps to minimize the impact of the permanent campaign and prevent some of the problems that plagued Bush at defining moments of his presidency. Instead, the permanent campaign was firmly ensconced in the Bush White House from the beginning, virtually guaranteeing that it would play a major role in the administration.

Edited by a pair of respected scholars at two influential Washington think tanks—Norman J. Ornstein of the conservative-oriented American Enterprise Institute and Thomas E. Mann of the liberal-leaning Brookings Institution—*The Permanent Campaign* was published in June 2000, partly in the hope it would help guide future presidents-elect and their teams as they planned their transition into office. For me, it elucidates one of the core phenomena of today's Washington.

As the preface to the book explains, when the phrase was first coined (perhaps in 1976 by Pat Caddell, an assistant to Jimmy Carter), the permanent campaign referred to the process of governing in a way that builds and sustains public support for an administration and its policies. In this sense, continual political campaigning is the means by which any administration exerts a lasting impact on the nation, since policies that the public doesn't understand or support are likely to be short-lived and ineffective.

However, the meaning of the term and the excessive way the permanent campaign is practiced have evolved in a disturbing direction. As government professor Hugh Heclo explains in the first chapter of Ornstein and Mann's book, today's permanent campaign is "a nonstop process seeking to manipulate sources of public approval to engage in the act of governing itself." In other words, campaigning and governing have now become indistinguishable. The aim of Ornstein and Mann's book, as Heclo notes, is "to make sense of this new meaning of the permanent campaign, to understand how and why it has evolved, to weigh its consequences for our ability to govern ourselves effectively, and to consider whether steps might be taken to ameliorate its more damaging effects."

Understanding the permanent campaign's impact on governing, both in the White House and Congress, is integral to grasping how Washington has gone astray, becoming ensnared in constant partisan bickering and warfare, and, in particular, how the presidency of George W. Bush wandered and remained so far off course by excessively embracing the permanent campaign and its tactics.

The permanent campaign is a concept that would have baffled our nation's founders. When they created our system of representative democracy as enshrined in the Constitution, Heclo notes, they envisioned an ideal system of governance in which disinterested legislators and high-minded executives would determine policy free from interest group pressures and partisan loyalties. They assumed that members of Congress would be citizen-statesmen, serving their country a few months each year and tending their farms, businesses, or professions the rest of the time. They considered parties pernicious and hoped they would never become a feature of the American system (the word "party" doesn't even appear in the Constitution). They deliberately provided that senators and presidents would *not* be chosen by popular vote but rather by elites in the state legislatures and the electoral college. If that insulated them from public opinion, so much the better. In much of eighteenth-century discourse, the people were the "mob," a collection of ill-informed, emotional, self-interested individuals who could not be trusted with high affairs of state. The idea of running the government to cater to this mob would have horrified men like Washington, Jefferson, Madison, Monroe, and Adams.

Today, of course, the game of politics has been dramatically redefined. The people are more deeply and directly involved in government than ever before. In many ways, this is a very good thing. Certainly government is more responsive to the needs of the citizens than it was in the eighteenth century. But some of the ways in which the desires of "the people" (however defined) are reflected in governance are dubious at best. We all know many of the problems. Narrowly tailored partisan and other special interest groups influence Congress to shape policies for the benefit of their members, not necessarily the citizenry as a whole. Opinion polling is used not only to read the mood of the electorate and guide political leaders in the ways they communicate their messages but also, at times, to determine the policies they will advocate. Continuous fund-raising, a necessity in an era when expensive television advertising and other costly forms of communication are essential for political success, binds powerful interest groups and wealthy donors to parties and politicians in a way that often shuts out the needs of the average American.

In this new system, governing is *primarily* focused, in Heclo's phrase, on "manipulating sources of public approval," using such tools as the news media, political blogs, popular web sites, paid advertising, talk radio, local organizations, and propaganda disseminated by interest groups to shape narratives to one's advantage. In the age of the permanent campaign, governing becomes an offshoot of campaigning rather than the other way around. Bills at times are written as much to create talking points for boosting one's own party and embarrassing the opposition as they are to improve the operations of government or to promote justice. Presidential initiatives from health care programs to foreign invasions are regularly devised, named, timed, and launched with one eye (or both eyes) on the electoral calendar. Budgets are drawn up not solely with the pressing needs of the public at the forefront but rather to reward political loyalists, punish enemies, and win votes in contested districts and states when November rolls around.

The infiltration of politics into governance has been a feature of democracy from the beginning. But during the second half of the twentieth century, it became increasingly prominent and pervasive. The administration of Richard Nixon—the first president to begin institutionalizing a permanent political operation inside the White House—exemplified many of the pitfalls of the permanent campaign, with its enemies list, its abuse of the IRS and the Justice Department for political ends, and the dirty tricks associated with the Watergate affair, which ultimately destroyed the administration.

Too much of the permanent campaign mentality can cripple an administration. It brought down the Nixon presidency and nearly ended Clinton's, despite—or because of—what *Washington Post* media reporter Howard Kurtz called its "spin doctors and well-oiled propaganda machine." And as I'll show in this book, it severely damaged the Bush White House, which arguably embraced and institutionalized the permanent campaign even more deeply than its predecessors.

A second force shaping today's political environment is the perpetual scandal culture, which was born as the permanent campaign was growing deep roots in Washington. This is a lasting legacy of the Nixon presidency, as described by Bob Woodward, one of the dogged young journalists who exposed the cover-ups orchestrated by the Nixon White House. Woodward gave an authoritative account of the scandal culture's effect on succeeding presidents from Ford to Clinton in his book *Shadow*.

As Woodward explains, Watergate created a deep distrust of the White House and a more cynical view of politics. Obvious questions arose. Could another president engage in criminal conduct? Did every president secretly plot behind closed doors as Nixon had done? A scandal-based cottage industry was born, including emboldened congressional inquisitors, investigative reporters, and determined prosecutors and ethics investigators. "The habit of deception and hedging practiced by presidents would no longer be acceptable," writes Woodward. However, the endless investigations haven't ended deception in Washington, but rather turned it into just another part of an elaborate warlike game with operatives on both sides of the aisle and both inside and outside of government.

Surprisingly, Woodward notes, none of Nixon's successors has managed to fully "comprehend the depth of distrust" he left behind. Controversies significant and not so significant were allowed to grow legs in this less trusting environment of inquisition, some turning into notorious and enduring scandals. There was Ford's withholding all details of the deal he believed he had rejected to pardon Nixon; Carter's Bert Lance controversy; Reagan's Iran-Contra scandal and the defeat of Robert Bork's nomination; and the elder Bush's involvement in Iran-Contra (in the loop or out of the loop) and a series of lesser controversies, from passportgate and the John Tower nomination to the alleged involvement of Bush's own son, Neil, in the savings and loan scandal. Finally, there was the seemingly endless string of controversies and scandals that ensnared Clinton, from Whitewater to Lewinsky.

Each of these presidents, Woodward concludes, had failed to heed the two fundamental lessons of Watergate:

First, if there is questionable activity, release the facts, whatever they are, as
early and completely as possible. Second, do not allow outside inquiries,
whether conducted by prosecutors, congressmen or reporters, to harden into
a permanent state of suspicion and warfare.

Inevitably, as these lessons went unheeded and the controversies and
scandals took on lives of their own, lasting suspicion and partisan combat resulted, undermining each presidency to some degree. The presidents fueled
the controversies by not addressing them openly and directly, fueling a cycle
of payback and retribution as congressional leaders of both parties sought to
shape public opinion to their own advantage. The result was the creation of a
destructive culture of endless scandal.

My experience and involvement in politics leads me to conclude that
presidents and their inner circles have in fact learned some of the *wrong* lessons. They've taken a cynical approach to dealing with the scandal culture.
Fear of short-term political embarrassment leads them to reflexively manipulate, hide, and distort the truth. Top presidential advisers come to view their
job as protecting the president above all else. They create a wall of protection
around the Oval Office, making sure the president is sufficiently detached
from, and preferably unaware of, the more unsavory side of politics. When
controversy arises, they convince the president to embrace defensive tactics.
This invariably cedes control of a president's reputation to outside investigations and allows the scandal machine to set the terms of a controversy's duration. "What did the president know and when did he know it?" becomes the
central question. But, ironically, by seeking to protect themselves, presidents
damage their honor and integrity, and often put their presidency in jeopardy.

The answer is not to get rid of the advisers and lawyers who seek to protect the president from the taint of scandal. The answer, as I'll explain in detail
later in this book, is more principled presidential leadership.

A third core element of the bitterly partisan Washington environment,
one that is part and parcel of the current excessive embrace of the permanent
campaign and the deep-seated scandal culture, is the increasingly ruthless,
win-at-all-costs attitude that guides many politicians and their advisers in
governing to manipulate public approval to their advantage—the philosophy
of politics as war.

The emergence of the permanent campaign and the scandal culture was bound to lead to growing animosity between the parties. What caused it to spill over into the all-out ideological wars of the 1990s were a series of historic turning points. Even before Watergate, as Lanny Davis, the former special counsel to President Clinton, persuasively argues, the culture wars of the 1960s helped launch the trend.

In his book *Scandal*, Davis talks of the true believers of the "New Right" who began to dominate the national Republican party in 1964. They viewed liberals as "cultural enemies who were traitors to American values and who needed to be destroyed." The same period saw the emergence of the ideological purists of the "New Left." They embraced radical politics and frightened Middle America with the rhetoric of revolution, which they used to express their anger over Vietnam, race, and mainstream culture in general. Both the New Right and New Left took their hard-line ideologies far beyond what traditional conservative and liberal standard-bearers had advocated. As Davis writes:

> The result was that, by the end of the 1960s and the 1972 presidential election, both parties were in danger of domination by ideological purists who had personalized their political differences into hatred and vitriol. A dangerous new symmetry had set into the American political culture. For both the New Left and New Right, it was not enough to defeat the political opposition and criticize their policies. It was necessary to destroy the opposition and describe their policies as evil.

The cycle of attack and payback rooted in the high-profile controversies and scandals that followed Watergate were further defining moments, Davis suggests. The tearing down of Bert Lance, Jimmy Carter's budget director, was in part Republicans' revenge for Watergate. The defeat of Supreme Court nominee Robert Bork through negative attacks and leaks was a big win for Democrats. Republicans came back with a fury during the Clinton years. The cycle showed no signs of stopping.

Davis, a Democrat, focuses on the Bork episode, calling it "the keystone event that triggered the most vicious subsequent manifestations of the scandal culture and gotcha politics." The issue is not whether there were legitimate reasons for opposing Bork's taking a seat on our nation's highest court. Liberals and experts in constitutional law raised legitimate philosophical concerns and questions about whether Bork had a suitable temperament for the Supreme Court, all of which warranted rational debate. But as Davis notes, the tactics used for defeating Bork crossed a line. Misinformation, distorted accusations, and self-serving leaks for political gain—all part of the unsavory side of today's politics—played a huge role in derailing the Bork nomination. Liberals leading the effort probably justified their tactics as necessary, simply the rules of Washington—the politics-as-war mentality. But conservatives were left fuming and would not forget the underhanded way liberals brought Bork down, even coining a new verb for the vicious attack strategy, "borking."

In looking back, I think another significant turning point was the 1988 presidential campaign. No campaign was more single-mindedly centered on bringing down an opponent than that of George Herbert Walker Bush. With their candidate trailing badly in the polls, his political strategists believed he could not win through an honest debate on the real issues. Instead, they developed a calculated strategy to go negative that had little to do with building their candidate up and everything to do with tearing their opponent, Michael Dukakis, down. The campaign was by most objective accounts full of distortions, misrepresentations, and zero-sum politics, accusing Dukakis of everything from embracing furloughs for dangerous criminals to disliking the pledge of allegiance (the innuendo being that he was unpatriotic). It was, as recorded in *The Quest for the Presidency* by Peter and Tom Matthews Goldman, "the systematic dismemberment of Michael Dukakis" based on a "scorched-earth strategy."

The elder Bush certainly believed in civility and decency. Everything about his record and his personal behavior indicates that. And he is one of the most decent and honorable men I have ever met. But during the 1988 campaign, he acquiesced to certain advisers, including Roger Ailes and the late Lee Atwater, who were intent on winning at all costs (within the bounds of legality). I am sure that many conservatives viewed it as part of the game, and necessary for achieving the right end. But the blood left on the pavement at the end of the one-sided and mean-spirited political street brawl between Bush and Dukakis spilled into the corridors of Congress. The controversies and scandals that engulfed the forty-first president's White House were motivated, at least in part, by the desire to exact retribution for what he'd wrought in his campaign. These were the new rules by which politics-as-war would now be practiced, by Democrats and Republicans alike.

By 1992, Clinton and his political advisers felt they had learned the lessons of the 1988 campaign: answer every attack; counter misrepresentations and distortions of one's record by using the same tactics against the opponent; play by the same rules the opposition plays by, but do it better. Beginning with the 1992 election campaign, the Clinton political machine became famous for its aggressive pushback tactics, its subtle and not so subtle intimidation of reporters, its mastery of spin, and its rapid response to charges. An admiring documentary film, *The War Room,* made Clinton operatives George Stephanopoulos and James Carville media stars as it showed the world how a canny, tough-minded campaign team could control the news cycle and help shape the attitudes of millions of people, for good or ill.

Which party shares more blame for the ascendancy of the politics-as-war philosophy? That is an interesting question that would likely require a lengthy book to dissect. One thing is certain: the philosophy of politics as war has been developing for decades and elected leaders of both parties bear responsibility for it.

Some put the primary responsibility at the media's doorstep. I don't. The media has its problems, and the most notable for me is its complicity in encouraging ideological combat to flourish because of its insatiable appetite for something or someone to pick on. But our elected leaders have the greatest power and highest responsibility to do something about it, and I think that is what most Americans want and expect them to do. Instead, most have chosen the more destructive route of practicing politics as war in order to achieve their short-term political goals.

During the era of the Clinton presidency and Gingrich Republicanism, the permanent campaign, the perpetual scandal culture, and politics-as-war coalesced as never before. The result was all-out partisan warfare. I only have to mention some of the "lowlights" of that era to remind you of how it demoralized and repulsed the citizenry, halted progress on addressing our national problems, and dragged the reputation of Washington in the mud: Vince Foster, Whitewater, Travelgate, Filegate, the Gingrich government shutdown, Paula Jones, Monica Lewinsky, "wag the dog," the Marc Rich pardon. What a roster of national embarrassments—some substantive, some not—all fueled by two factors: the White House's lack of candor and honesty and the partisan determination to destroy political enemies, no matter what the cost!

By the time of the 2000 election, the permanent campaign and its attendant ills had become status quo for the Clinton team, Congress, and Washington. The Clinton White House came to epitomize this style of governing via
endless campaign, institutionalizing it as never before. It was the accepted way
of doing things. Most people involved in governing and campaigns understood that political manipulation was a necessary part of how things are
done—particularly in a climate of partisan war. They gave little thought to its
overall effect on national politics, beyond occasional hand-wringing complaints and ineffectual sighs about the good old days.

The national media became complicit enablers, as the twenty-four-hour
news networks jumped on every scandal and conflict, no matter how trivial,
to fill airtime, stir the pot of controversy, and attract viewers. Political news
came to resemble sports coverage, with its entertaining "plays of the week," instant analysis, constant anointing of winners, losers, heroes, and goats. Many
"pundits" did not dedicate themselves to dispassionate analysis but cheered
on one side and shouted down the other.

And when partisan warfare breaks out on such a large scale, the results are
terribly destructive and do lasting damage to our national political discourse.
Vicious, negative attacks, distortions, spin, unsubstantiated innuendo, and
misinformation become the norm. The headlines and sound bites that receive
the greatest emphasis in the media too often are grounded in such unsavori-
ness. Caveats are deemphasized. Contradictory information is downplayed,
dismissed, or simply disregarded. Complex issues are too often oversimplified
in the context of winners and losers, and portrayed in stark black-and-white
terms. The side that most effectively manipulates the narrative often prevails,
and is lifted up as being on the offensive—at times regardless of any nuances
and the larger underlying truth. Deception nudges truth to the side.

I believe most of those engaging in the deceptive ways on both sides of the
partisan aisle, including our elected leaders, are good people who have fallen
prey to the destructive nature of the Washington game. But as manipulation is
embraced more widely and becomes more accepted, a new culture starts to
develop as a result of the all-out partisan warfare—a culture of deception.

Sun Tzu, an ancient Chinese general, is known for his military treatise *The
Art of War,* written centuries before the birth of Christ. It is one of the oldest
and most widely read books in existence on military strategy. It has also made

a lasting imprint on business leadership and political campaigns for its strategic insights.

I can't remember which political strategist first recommended the book to me years ago, but one relevant passage in the book notes that "all warfare is based on deception." *The Art of War* goes on to discuss the many ways of employing deception when preparing for battle, ways not unlike those that might be useful for winning a campaign for elected office or exercising power when in office. Sun Tzu even points out that effective military strategy includes deceiving not just the enemy but one's own troops as well, making them follow orders without full knowledge of their leader's true intentions.

In warfare, the goal is to literally destroy the enemy. Using deception in this context is probably reasonable, since damaging relationships is a small price to pay when a life-and-death struggle for survival is involved. In politics, there may be a few limited, minor instances where deception is acceptable; for example, when a campaign pretends to be more active early in the process than it really is, in order to trick the other campaign into spending money and resources too early. But applying the strategy of deception broadly to politics and governance is a step too far.

Unfortunately, the Sun Tzu approach has become the norm in politics, as deception is considered vital today for defeating campaign opponents and for governing. This "all's fair" attitude now permeates political campaigns and has crossed excessively into governing, especially when the stakes are high. Washington, as a result, has become a breeding ground for deception and a killing field for truth.

Make no mistake, governing inevitably has an adversarial element. People and groups will always differ about the proper use of limited government resources. But should government be a process of constant campaigning to manipulate public opinion rather than one centered as much as possible on rational debate, deliberation, and compromise? Should it be based on all-out war and deception, or grounded in a high level of openness, forthrightness, honesty, and a search for truth? All too often, in today's politics, the spirit of warfare rules.

Clinton and his team played the game extremely well. They showed an uncanny resilience and an ability to persevere and prevail in the high-stakes political combat of attack and counterattack. In the end, Bill Clinton's undeniable personal flaws proved to be debilitating but not fatal to his presidency. Why?

Because Clinton had a magnetic personality, extraordinary charisma, and a rare ability to charm many Americans, as well as a deep appreciation—whether based on principle or political pragmatism–for governing toward the center. He succeeded on the policy front, enlisting Republican support and enacting policies that Middle America cared about, from welfare reform to deficit reduction. He understood that a successful agenda can overcome personal shortcomings and partisan ill will. His team knew that their greatest persuader was Clinton himself, and they knew how to play the Washington game of the permanent campaign better than any previous White House. But their excessive embrace of the modern day rules—shared by the Gingrich Republicans—came at a heavy price to the nation.

Unfortunately, the incoming Bush administration learned some of the wrong lessons from watching the Clinton White House. As they planned for the new regime in Washington, they did nothing to change the status quo. Rather than thinking outside of the box of the permanent campaign, they accepted the new rules of the game and focused on how to play it better, not how to change the game to one that would better serve the American people.

Ironically, much of Bush's campaign rhetoric had been aimed at distancing himself from the excesses of Clinton's permanent campaign style of governing. The implicit meaning of Bush's words was that he would bring an end to the perpetual politicking and the deep partisan divisions it created. Although Washington could not get enough of the permanent campaign, voters were seemingly eager to move beyond it.

Bush emphasized this sentiment during the campaign. He would "change the tone in Washington." He would be "a uniter, not a divider." He would "restore honor and dignity to the White House." He would govern based on what was right, not what the polls said. He would, in short, replace the cynicism of the 1990s with a new era of civility, decency, and hope. There would be no more permanent campaign, or at least its excesses would be wiped away for good.

But the reality proved to be something quite different. Instead, the Bush team imitated some of the worst qualities of the Clinton White House and even took them to new depths.

Bush did not emulate Clinton on the policy front. Just the opposite—the mantra of the new administration was "anything but Clinton" when it came to policies. The Bush administration prided itself in focusing on big ideas, not playing small ball with worthy but essentially trivial policy ideas for a White House, like introducing school uniforms or going after deadbeat dads.

But a significant aspect of the Clinton presidency that George W. Bush and his advisers did embrace was the unprecedented pervasiveness of the permanent campaign and all its tactics. In hindsight, it is clear that the Bush White House was actually structured to emulate and extend this method of governing, albeit in its own way.

The most obvious evidence that the Bush White House embraced the permanent campaign is the expansive political operation that was put in place from day one. Chief political strategist Karl Rove was given an enormous center of influence within the White House from the outset. This was only strengthened by Rove's force of personality and closeness to the president. He would be one of the three key players—along with Karen Hughes and Andy Card—beyond the president himself who most defined the way the Bush White House operated.

I first started getting to know Karl in 1992, when I was managing a Texas state senate campaign that hired his political consulting firm to do direct mail. My conversations with him during that period were not extensive; he had plenty of other clients to tend to, and his work for us was primarily limited to the mailings. But Rove already was establishing himself as the guru of Republican politics in Texas.

A couple of years earlier, in 1990, while the Republican gubernatorial nominee I worked for narrowly went down in defeat, two Rove clients on the statewide ballot, Kay Bailey Hutchison and Rick Perry, had won races for treasurer and agriculture commissioner respectively, winning Rove some of his early renown as a rising political star in the state.

After the state senate campaign in northwest Texas, which we lost ever so narrowly against an entrenched incumbent, I moved back to Austin to figure out my next move. I had some time on my hands and volunteered to help on Hutchison's nascent campaign for the U.S. Senate. It was a special election to replace Lloyd Bentsen, who had become Treasury secretary. Hutchison would challenge the incumbent Bob Krueger, previously Texas railroad commissioner, who had been appointed by the governor to serve until a replacement could be elected. The fledgling campaign was operating out of Rove's office space at the outset. I was helping make calls to get people to show up for Hutchison's upcoming four-day, twenty-city announcement tour.

Just as Hutchison was to begin the tour, her campaign manager asked if I would travel with her for the first day. At the time, Rove had already given my name to some communications strategists from a D.C. firm who were seeking talent to help one of their clients, the American Tort Reform Association, with its lawsuit reform efforts in Texas. But the thought of traveling with someone who could be the next U.S. senator from Texas sounded like a good experience, so I quickly agreed.

The day of travel turned into four full days on a small plane with Hutchison and her husband, Ray. It was great fun, and at the end of the tour I was offered a paid position on the campaign. But at the same time, I was offered a job working on the lawsuit reform effort. In part since I had just finished a campaign, I was not sure jumping into another competitive race was something I was ready to do, so I accepted the lawsuit reform position. I would not have gotten the job had Rove not suggested my name.

Rove was becoming the dominant force in Texas politics. He was viewed by many political observers in the state as a fierce competitor who at times could be ruthless and vicious, operating with a take-no-prisoners mentality.

I stayed in contact with Karl sporadically over the next few years. In 1994 his company did some work for my mother's election to the Railroad Commission (which regulated the Texas oil and gas industry), the first statewide campaign I managed. But that year he was mainly focused on Bush's gubernatorial campaign. Texas had already been trending Republican, and Rove engineered a Republican sweep of all statewide executive offices in 1998.

I remember election night well. My mother had been in one of the more closely contested races, and many pundits rated her chances against the incumbent as poor. But we pulled off the upset and helped ensure the Republican sweep. All the Republican candidates were holding their individual victory parties at the same hotel in downtown Austin, the Capitol Marriott. Our room was a few steps from the main ballroom where the Bush campaign was celebrating.

Later in the evening, as it was starting to become apparent that my mother would also win, Rove appeared at her party. I was sitting in a cordoned-off area just to the right of the door where we had tables and computers set up to monitor the votes as they came in. In a loud and energized voice, Rove said, "I want to congratulate the person responsible for this victory—

and there he is!" he added as he turned to his right and pointed to me. "She could not have won without you, buddy. You did a fabulous job."

This was heady praise for a twenty-six-year-old. Here was the top Republican political strategist in the state—and the new kingmaker of Texas politics—going out of his way to offer words of validation. We shook hands and embraced. "I don't know that it was me, but thanks," I said. "Your words mean a lot, and I appreciate them very much."

Rove was the go-to guy in Texas for young politicos such as myself. If you wanted to get a political job in Republican politics, Rove was at the top of the list of people to visit. And despite his busy schedule, he was always generous with advice and help.

Many younger operatives in Texas considered themselves dedicated followers of Rove and his school of politics. I never really felt that way. I always viewed myself as a more independent political operative, one who was not necessarily tied to any one strategist or camp within the Texas Republican party. But I knew that Rove was the kingmaker in Texas Republican politics, and I appreciated and welcomed his support.

After I joined Bush's team in 1999, I would see Karl occasionally at a senior staff meeting in the governor's office. By the time I moved over to the campaign months later, I would see him frequently in the hallways of our campaign headquarters in downtown Austin, especially after I became traveling press secretary. When not on the road, I would attend the daily message meeting of senior aides which Karl also attended, and frequently he would join us on the campaign trail. I came to know Karl even better when I joined him on the senior White House staff.

I will always recall fondly how Karl inserted his brand of levity into the demanding, draining life inside the White House bubble. He has an endearing goofy side that he used to boost morale, especially during the rigors of an election campaign, when every day in another hotel felt like yet another Groundhog Day.

Toward the end of the 2004 election campaign, for instance, Karl used to rev up his fellow Bush team passengers in the staff vans by loudly leading us in some of the famous chants from the Republican Convention in New York that August. He would just start yelling, "U-S-A, U-S-A; Four more years, four more years," or one of our favorites, "Flip-flop, flip-flop!" (You may recall the large "flip-flop" beach sandals that conventioneers waved to symbolize John Kerry's tendency to change his position on issues.) I would usually follow right along, and others would join in at times. I think sometimes our volunteer driver, usually a local supporter, would wonder whether Karl had been on the road too long or needed to get out of the sun. I'm sure many an onlooker must have wondered, "Is *this* the famous political genius?"

In the 2000 campaign, I remember hanging out late on election night in Karl's campaign office. Several other aides were in his office or nearby. Karl was working the phones, checking emails, and crunching numbers from the Florida counties. He had been energized by the way the networks had earlier called Florida for Gore, only to reverse themselves. Karl had been going around headquarters saying that conservative precincts in the Florida panhandle were still voting and that the closeness elsewhere made the network projections premature. Now, after their reversal, Karl seemed emboldened and determined, almost as if his sheer willpower was magically turning things in our direction.

Shortly after 1:00 A.M., Fox News became the first network to project a Bush win in Florida, and with it a victory in the national election. This was a thrilling development, but like others I stayed silent, not sure whether to believe it and watching to see whether Karl and his usually spot-on number crunching agreed. But a few nail-biting minutes later, the other networks followed suit, reversing their earlier projections. The euphoria could not be contained. The other staffers and I let out enthusiastic yells, raised our arms, and high-fived one another. Rove led staffers who had remained behind at campaign headquarters to follow results in a march down Congress Avenue in Austin to the front of the state capitol. Bush was supposed to appear there, but later results caused the networks to reverse course again and say it was too close to call, and Gore withdrew his congratulatory call.

Karl is without a doubt one of the brightest political talents of our time, thanks to his boundless energy and enthusiasm, his deep historical knowledge, and his keen insights into the electorate. He is a sharp strategic thinker and a savvy, shrewd, and devious strategist. Karl lives, eats, and breathes politics, and he loves everything that comes with it, particularly the competition and verbal combat. To him, politics is a contact sport, and he relishes the partisan warfare. Karl also has a reputation as a ruthless, perhaps unscrupulous operator and has always struck me as the kind of person who would be willing, in the heat of battle, to push the envelope to the limit of what is permissible ethically or legally.

Rove likes to have his hands in just about everything, relishing policy shaping as much as political strategizing. He views governing and politics as completely interconnected, and he occupied a key seat at the center of both in Bush's White House.

Named senior adviser to the president just weeks before the inauguration, Rove was charged with overseeing politics and political strategy, and he headed four key offices aimed at one overarching objective: shaping and manipulating sources of public opinion, much as in a political campaign, to help advance the Bush agenda and policies. Each office was influential in its own right, and combined under Rove they formed a massive, powerful operation that would drive a campaign-like effort to strengthen the president's standing with the public, as measured by his all-important approval ratings. And they often did so very effectively.

The Office of Strategic Initiatives served primarily as a long-range strategic planning outfit. This office hadn't existed in previous administrations. My sense is that it built on and consolidated into one operation a number of equivalent functions carried out by previous White House staffs. But in its current form, it was Rove's grand creation. This office looked weeks and months down the road, planning the president's public focus in terms of his policies and agenda. But it also stayed integrally involved in day-to-day White House operations, sending a staffer to attend most key meetings. It also routinely engaged in research, monitored polling data, coordinated key strategy meetings, and daily played an integral role in helping the president set his agenda.

The Office of Political Affairs coordinated a broad range of politically oriented events and activities, keeping in close contact with the Republican National Committee and with Republican leaders and activists in states and communities around the nation. It was also responsible for preparing detailed political briefing papers for Bush's trips to various states and localities, including an overview of each state's political climate, demographic characteristics, noteworthy issues, recent election results, media markets, congressional delegation, state leaders, and GOP party leaders, and a summary of previous visits to the state by Bush and his cabinet members. In effect, it prepared an information kit that provided the president an instant overview of the political context for anything he would say or do during a visit, making it easier for him to couch his message appropriately for a particular setting.

The Office of Public Liaison worked closely with key constituencies and public interest groups, from trade associations like the chamber of commerce to groups like national Right to Life to African American leaders and organizations. Staffers were assigned various constituencies—business groups, social conservative organizations, Hispanic outreach, and many others. Public Liaison helped mobilize such constituencies as needed to advance important priorities and managed their meetings with the president. Sometimes its job was to neutralize a group, attempting to dissuade an influential organization from openly opposing an initiative that might cause consternation for its members. An example might be keeping a group that represents the elderly from openly opposing personal or private retirement accounts for younger workers during the Social Security debate of 2005, using the argument that future reforms would not impact any currently retired people.

The Office of Intergovernmental Affairs focused on state and local officials. It coordinated closely with mayors, county commissioners, governors, and other state officials on policy, presidential meetings in Washington, and visits to localities.

Individuals of enormous political savvy and intellect headed each of the four offices throughout President Bush's time in office. Each also had an energetic staff of up-and-comers to help develop and execute various strategies, duties, and initiatives. The director of each office reported directly to Rove and worked under his direction and guidance.

The existence of these four powerful political offices inside the White House—most established prior to Bush's presidency—helped solidify the place of the permanent campaign in the national political landscape. The concept of politics as war was reinforced by the sharply partisan approach to both campaigning and governing that Karl Rove practiced and taught.

Rove tended to look at everything from the political viewpoint, particularly the impact on core constituencies. He saw the electorate as divided more sharply along partisan lines than ever before in recent history. And he felt it was absolutely essential to keep the party base of social, economic, and foreign policy conservatives happy and solidly in support of the president. Having a solid conservative base of support and not alienating the party faithful, in Karl's view, would allow the president then to reach out to independents and swing Democratic voters to maintain a majority in the country of at least 50 percent plus one.

As distinguished from the broad majority political strategy of consistently governing from the center and not catering too heavily to single-issue or narrowly focused partisan constituencies, the 50-percent-plus-one strategy emphasizes catering to ideological purists. For example, Bush appeased social conservatives by forcefully advocating passage of a constitutional amendment banning same-sex marriage as we headed to Election Day in 2004; on another occasion he dramatically returned to Washington in the middle of the night from his home in Crawford to sign a federal law transferring the fate of Terri Schiavo to the federal courts, thereby involving the national government in a controversial issue typically handled by the states. Bush's decision in 2001 to narrowly limit the federal government's role in embryonic stem cell research and his later vetoing of legislation expanding it kept social conservatives appeased too, as did his support for legislation to ban partial birth abortion.

Each move to the right garnered enormous coverage in the media and did much to shape public perceptions of the Bush administration. Regardless of the merits of these issues, Bush's emphasis on them created a perception of a president who was focusing on ideologically rigid issues tailored to a single-issue constituency, pro-lifers, rather than addressing pressing priorities that the broad majority in the center (center, center-right, and center-left) cared most about, such as the economy, health care, energy, and the environment.

Rove had enormous influence in putting these issues front and center on the president's public agenda. It was a far cry from Bush's days as governor of Texas, when he consistently governed from the center and avoided overemphasizing controversial issues embraced by single-issue, socially conservative constituencies and that tend to pit groups of people against one another.

Washington is a much different political environment than Texas was when Bush led it. More is expected from the ideological purists who represent partisan base organizations and the opinion leaders who influence the same constituencies. Rove and Bush both recognized this. By keeping the social conservatives happy (with initiatives like the ones mentioned above), passing substantial tax cuts (which kept the economic base happy), and taking a hardline, confrontational approach on national security (which pleased the hawks), Bush could have greater liberty to push centrist policies on immigration, public education, and Medicare prescription drug coverage.

It was a strategy that worked well in the first term and helped Bush get re-elected. But its shortcomings and flaws were exposed in the second term as Bush's Iraq policy began to cripple his presidency. When things started deteriorating in Iraq, Bush and Rove knew that it was politically impossible for him to appear as if he was backing away from his vision for a free and democratic Iraq even by a single iota. If he did, they knew, his base would see him as weak and begin to fracture. Under this base strategy, compromising on an acceptable outcome that Democratic and Republican congressional leaders could support was essentially out of the question and never seriously contemplated. Add the excessive public catering to social conservatives, and Bush's problems and his poor standing with the public are exacerbated even more.

Having a brilliant political strategist and grand manipulator of sources of public approval like Rove working in the White House isn't necessarily a problem in itself. It's a problem, however, when political strategy takes over excessively, and governance becomes merely a subset of campaigning. And when the strategist is someone with the skills, personality, and reach of Karl Rove, it's all too easy for that to happen. He liked to have his hands involved in, if not controlling, anything and everything that could affect Bush's approval ratings. Sometimes he worked quietly, behind the scenes. Other times he asserted himself in meetings. Generally speaking, on most policy and strategic decisions, and particularly on campaigns to sell policy to the public, his views were given great weight and deference.

Rove was specifically excluded from National Security Council war meetings. Obviously, the presence of the controversial Rove in those meetings would have given critics a field day. But his exclusion in itself seems to raise the question of why there was not equal concern about whether politics unduly affected policy considerations in the otherwise almost all-encompassing role in governing Rove played.

Within the Bush administration, Rove's controlling personality and substantial influence over policy, strategy, political communications, and message expanded unchecked, particularly after the departure of Karen Hughes, another strong personality and a key member of the Bush troika of advisers.

Karen represented a second sphere of influence created at the beginning of the administration. She too was a longtime trusted Bush aide from Texas. The president sought her advice and input, and usually agreed with it. I recall a conversation in the early days when I was traveling with him *sans* Karen. He was asking how I liked working for her. During the conversation he said, "Karen gets it right most of the time. Not all the time, but most of the time she is right." Bush's trust in Karen and her closeness to him, her dynamic personality, her savvy strategic thinking, and her ability to grasp the views of Middle America made her, like Rove, an instrumental player in all aspects of the White House, including policy. Of course, her designated role overseeing the large White House communications apparatus, which in today's politics plays an ever more prominent role in the permanent campaign, was very important in itself.

My first experience with Karen was back in the early 1990s when she was executive director of the Texas Republican party. She was looking for a finance director to oversee the organization's fund-raising. Although I was not really interested in working for the state party and my experience was not in fund-raising, I was encouraged to explore the possibility, and my name had been suggested to her as an up-and-coming political operative. For a twenty-three-year-old it could be another way to establish myself on my career path.

I was not offered the job, which was fine because working for the state party or any explicitly partisan organization was not where my main interest was. Soon thereafter, I headed off to Wichita Falls, Texas, to manage my first campaign—the Texas state senate race for a man who would later become my friend, Tom Haywood.

It was not until I met with Karen in late 1998 for the position she was looking to fill in Governor Bush's communications office that I really got to know her. I thought highly of her abilities as a communicator, and I liked her take-charge style and dynamic personality.

Karen mentored me in political communication. I had a good base of knowledge to begin with, having grown up with a mother who occupied the local political spotlight and then later serving as a campaign manager and spokesman in her successful statewide campaigns. The latter role caught Karen's attention. Once I was on the job, I found that she followed what Bush's spokespeople said very closely. If she felt it could be stated more strongly, more cautiously, or more reflectively of Bush's tone and style, she would let the spokesperson know. She viewed her job as making sure spokespeople adhered to her and Bush's style and tone of communication. They were one and the same. I honed my communication skills under her direction.

But Karen's communication strength was in some ways her weakness. Though well-liked, she was viewed by many in the media as overzealous at times in her devotion to Bush. She was at times too disciplined a communicator for him—always on message, always emphasizing the positive, always downplaying the negative, always protective of Bush, and rarely if ever giving an inch. But that's exactly how Karen and Bush wanted it. Having come from the media, Karen knew the media always tended to seek the limelight and controversy, especially in the high-stakes, competitive national environment. She was not going to hand them anything to exploit. Message control required great discipline in Karen's and Bush's minds. And spokespersons who could not be pulled off message, like Karen, were highly valued.

In her capacity as counselor to the president, Karen initially had purview over four offices and later added a fifth (Global Communications). The Communications Office was responsible for strategic communications planning, looking a week to two weeks down the road, and for execution of the overall strategy. It was the central office for coordinating Bush's message throughout the White House and the administration. And it was the office responsible for making sure that the picture of the day reinforced the message and image of Bush that we sought to portray. I'm referring here to a literal picture, which was carefully planned in the hopes that it would end up above the fold in the next day's newspapers or prominently featured on the evening news—from a simple picture of Bush greeting soldiers if the day's theme was military preparedness, to the elaborately choreographed scene of Bush speaking in front of the Statue of Liberty on the anniversary of 9/11. Reagan's team had perfected this art of stagecraft, and the man in charge for Bush, deputy communications director Scott Sforza, took it to new heights.

The Office of the Press Secretary was a round-the-clock operation that focused on the national and White House press corps and handled daily media relations with them, conducting daily briefings and being the chief spokesman for the White House. There was close coordination with other communicators, but the press secretary had plenty of autonomy to run the office as he saw fit. When I became press secretary, the role was to faithfully articulate the president's views, decisions, and policies, and publicly advocate for and defend them with the national media.

The Office of Media Affairs focused on local media across the United States and daily media relations. The media affairs team responded to inquiries from local media outlets, helped coordinate with those outlets when the president traveled to their respective areas, and was responsible for coordinating presidential interviews with local reporters.

The Office of Speechwriting was responsible for churning out countless presidential speeches and remarks. The speechwriting process played a vital role in driving policy. Drafts of speeches would be circulated to all relevant White House offices, including the president's senior advisers and specific policy advisers. The president had the final say, but if an adviser wanted to influence policy, the speechwriting process was one way to do so.

In addition to her abilities as a communicator, Karen had a strong force of personality and a keen understanding of the more traditional political views of Middle America, as well as where the broad majority in the center usually comes down on an issue. Both attributes benefited Bush greatly. Karen had her own assertive and imposing presence within the White House. She was not afraid to assert her views in meetings or go directly to the president privately. She also had a good grasp of how to connect with everyday Americans and helped the president better communicate his policies and decisions and set the right tone with them.

Just as important, Karen provided a good counterbalance to Karl Rove. He had strong beliefs about the way things should be done. So did Karen. While Karl's views were oriented largely around the conservative base, Karen's focused on everyday Americans toward the center of the political spectrum. The differences were less over policy than over tone, message, policy framing, and public emphasis. The two worked well together but were not shy about disagreeing openly in front of the president. It was what one would expect from two strong-willed, opinionated, and knowledgeable individuals who both had the full and extraordinary confidence of the president.

The third member of the White House troika was Andy Card, a tireless public servant who brought years of experience to his position as chief of staff. His sphere of influence was built on both his position and his closeness to the president, though he was more of a facilitator for the president, noticeably less domineering and softer spoken than either Karl or Karen. His role was to serve as an honest broker among the staff inside the White House and help make sure all views were heard, while privately offering his views to the president as needed and appropriate, usually once the policy process had time to work its course.

Andy understood how Washington and the White House operate, since he had served both Reagan and the president's father. He also understood the unparalleled trust Bush placed in Rove and Hughes, and how much he valued their viewpoints. Andy worked to make sure the policy processes ran their full course and that staffers felt included in them. He managed the president's most valued commodity—his time—in part by making sure that people saw the president only when they really needed to. Most notably, Andy managed and oversaw the White House exactly the way Bush preferred—firmly, with discipline, focus, and thoughtful, deliberate planning. When Bush required it, Andy kept the administration compartmentalized in a way that restricted information to a select few.

I first met Andy on the campaign trail back in 2000. My recollection is that it was ahead of the Republican convention, which he had been tapped to oversee. He came across as a very likable person, courteous and dignified, but I did not really get to know him until we worked together in the White House.

Toward the end of the transition, just ahead of the inaugural, Andy assembled all the staffers who would be working in the West Wing. Most, like me, had never worked in the White House before. We listened intently as he talked about what we should expect and what he expected of us. He talked about the honor of working there. He stressed the importance of working together as a team. We were all there to serve the president. He talked about the importance of humility, not letting our jobs go to our head. He talked about the intensity of work there. And he let us know that the average tenure of someone who works in the West Wing is about two years. He told us to remember to "know when it is time to leave." He cited the example of John Sununu, chief of staff to the first President Bush, who had failed to recognize when it was time to go until it was forced upon him.

It was hard to appreciate what he was saying then, but after serving in the White House I understood his remarks much better. One can become too comfortable inside the bubble. When that happens, one's perspective becomes stale and one's energy is drained. Burnout can set in. A president needs change, fresh perspectives, and new energy from his staff. That's why turnover is important and, when correctly timed, a very beneficial process.

Of course, Rove, Hughes, and Card weren't the only powerful figures in the Bush White House. Two other prominent advisers at the beginning were the national security adviser, Condoleezza Rice, and the vice president, Dick Cheney.

Rice, who mentored Bush on foreign policy, was the person whose advice the president relied on most when it came to national security issues starting during the presidential campaign. Lacking a deep background in foreign policy, Bush counted on a team of foreign policy heavyweights with diverse expertise to help him formulate policy based on his guiding principles, such as freedom, a strong military, and free trade. Rice headed the group, referred to as the Vulcans. It included Richard Armitage (Colin Powell's alter ego), Paul Wolfowitz and Steve Hadley (two protégés of Dick Cheney), Richard Perle, Bob Blackwill, Bob Zoellick (a James Baker protégé), and Dov Zakheim. George Shultz was often called on for advice, and once Dick Cheney became the vice presidential nominee, he too was directly involved. The name of the group was based on the imposing statue of Vulcan, the Roman god of fire and metalworking, that is a landmark in Rice's hometown of Birmingham, Alabama. Bush developed a strong personal bond with Rice and came to trust her judgment, instincts, and insights. As Hughes' and Bush's style and tone of communicating were one and the same, so too were Rice's and Bush's views on foreign policy.

From the beginning, the president wanted the vice president and his staff included in his White House processes and operations. Dick Cheney and his key advisers were considered integral members of the team. Bush valued Cheney's experience and knowledge, particularly on national security matters, and sought his counsel. At the same time, Cheney and his advisers essentially ran their own operation, as I will discuss later in this book.

Bush and Cheney's relationship was close—and substantially private. Cheney tended to offer his counsel in private to the president. He or his top advisers were included in all presidential policy briefings, world leader meetings, congressional meetings, and the like. Of course, Cheney heavily influenced foreign policy. He also took particular interest in economic policy, especially tax and energy issues. Bush showed Cheney great deference, especially when he designated him to take on a specific task, such as heading the energy task force early in the administration or bird-dogging buy-in from congressional leaders on the controversial warrantless wiretapping program instituted after 9/11. Bush also relied on Cheney's ability to shape what Bush considered vital national security policies on matters such as al Qaeda detainees.

But it was the troika of Rove, Hughes, and Card—especially Rove—who drove the permanent campaign inside the Bush White House, embracing and emulating the manipulative political and communication tactics used by

Bush's predecessor that had put off many Americans. It was all done through carefully orchestrated campaigns to shape sources of public approval to Bush's advantage, such as the ones developed to advance tax cuts, education reform, and the selling of the war in Iraq.

At least in the early days of the presidency, the troika and the structure of the White House served Bush well. While Cheney declared in early 2001 that "the days of the war room and the permanent campaign are over," the reality was far from it. The permanent campaign was simply being re-structured, re-defined, and expanded to how it best suited the Bush White House. Permanent campaign–style methods proved highly successful as the early Bush White House sold two high-priority agenda items to the public and got them passed in Congress. These early successes may have contributed to the air of invincibility that set in, leaving the administration vulnerable to the mistakes that later damaged the Bush presidency.

6

THE EARLY DAYS

———

THE FIRST SIX MONTHS AFTER Bush took office on January 20, 2001, would be a crucial time for defining the president and his administration. Bush and his top advisers recognized the importance of achieving some early victories on signature policy items, especially tax cuts and education reform. They also wanted to portray the new president as a strong leader who could unite the American people and who had the necessary heft in foreign policy (one notable area of concern about Bush's leadership ability).

At the same time, the tone set by the new administration would also be of great importance. Most Americans were more than ready for a return to civility in the national political discourse. They were weary of the excessive partisanship of the previous decade, ready to move beyond Bill Clinton's personal scandals, and exhausted by the extended 2000 election period. But whether Washington was prepared to respond by working together in a spirit of bipartisan cooperation remained uncertain.

During the campaign, Bush had tapped into the mood of the broad majority of Americans who were in or who leaned toward the vital political center. He had urged an end to "the politics of anger" and the beginning of a "fresh start after a period of cynicism." Washington, Bush said, did not have to be "a place of zero-sum politics, with one winner and one loser."

Now, at the outset of his presidency, it seemed to me that Bush was committed to making it happen. In his inaugural address, Bush returned to this campaign theme:

> America, at its best, matches a commitment to principle with a concern for civility. A civil society demands from each of us goodwill and respect, fair dealing and forgiveness. Some seem to believe that our politics can afford to be petty because, in a time of peace, the stakes of our debates appear small. But the stakes for America are never small . . . We must live up to the calling we share. Civility is not a tactic or a sentiment. It is the determined choice of trust over cynicism, of community over chaos. And this commitment, if we keep it, is a way to shared accomplishment.

No one in the White House, including me, was naive about the difficulty of ending Washington's deep-seated partisan warfare in those early days. But I believed Bush was willing to make a concerted, sustained effort to rise above the destructive partisan squabbling and the distractions created by the Washington noise machine. Unfortunately, it would turn out otherwise. And looking back on the inner workings behind the White House's public performance during these early months, I've come to better understand some of the factors that would later contribute to the Bush presidency's veering off course.

Those first few weeks were a flurry of chaotic activity. Everything was happening at once. I moved into my small downtown apartment halfway between the Capitol and the White House over inaugural weekend. The demands of transitioning into the White House as the principal deputy press secretary gave me little time to enjoy all the festivities. Like many others, I'd just packed up my belongings at the transition office the day before. In order to allow time for a quick cleaning and makeover, Joe Hagin, the new deputy chief of staff for operations, had suggested we wait until late Sunday before entering our West Wing offices. When I first stepped foot inside the building, a box of my personal belongings in my hands, it was definitely a moment when I was wowed. There would be many others during those first weeks of the Bush administration, including when I drove home late at night after a long day of work in the West Wing, taking E Street along the south lawn side of the White House. I glanced to my left, and there was the White House—the people's mansion—

glowing in the soft yellow radiance of the floodlights against the blackness of a Washington night. The sight never got old.

On Monday, our first full work day, we hit the ground running. I was up at 5:00 A.M., reading the *New York Times* and *Washington Post*, the two newspapers that more than any others dictated the direction of the national media and shaped the national story lines. Then it was off to the White House, where I arrived before 7:00 A.M. There were a few early meetings to discuss press issues of the day and message strategy, followed by the press secretary's morning press gaggle and the afternoon briefing, the two public sessions that would become focal points of the day in my new role. The cycle quickly became routine but never less than demanding—and never dull.

Even at the outset, Iraq was looming in the background. That very first Monday, the *New York Times*, citing a new internal U.S. government intelligence estimate, ran a front-page story about Iraq rebuilding factories "that the United States has long suspected of producing chemical and biological weapons, according to senior government officials." The *Times* called it an early test of Bush's pledge to "take a tougher stance against" Saddam Hussein than his immediate predecessor had.

Iraq would continue to be a top issue of administration focus and media interest in months to come. The National Security Council made Iraq an early priority of the policy formulation process. As for that first day, with no new policy yet firmly in place, we simply told the press that the president expected Saddam Hussein to live up to his agreement with the United Nations that his regime not produce weapons of mass destruction.

That same day, Bush issued a presidential memorandum addressed to the administrator of the U.S. Agency for International Development (USAID), instructing that the so-called Mexico City Policy be reinstated. This policy, originally put in place by Ronald Reagan, stated that any nongovernmental organization (NGO) receiving USAID funding could not perform or actively promote abortion as a method of family planning, with exceptions for rape, incest, and the life of the mother. It was an early signal to the president's social conservative base that his administration was strongly committed to supporting their causes.

As planned, the president focused publicly on education reform in week one. We began the formal rollout on Tuesday, hitting the main elements of the initiative, including the requirement that states develop their own systems of annual testing to measure student progress, the increased flexibility provided in spending federal money, the provision of additional assistance for low-income schools, and the principle of offering school choice for students in schools deemed to be failing.

Plenty of attention was paid to showing that the president was reaching out to Republican and Democratic members of Congress. The Congress was closely divided, but both houses were controlled by Republicans. The Senate was split 50–50, but Vice President Cheney had the tie-breaking vote, giving Republicans control, though they agreed to a power-sharing arrangement with Democrats. In the House, the breakdown was 221 Republicans to 211 Democrats with 2 independents. (Due to a handful of deaths and resignations, the numbers would fluctuate ever so slightly in the coming months.)

In the early weeks, Bush held a series of meetings with leaders in both parties to discuss top domestic priorities, including education, tax relief, his faith-based initiative, and a patients' bill of rights—what Bush termed "front-burner issues." We made a point of drawing attention to the bipartisan outreach.

My first White House trip with President Bush was to the retreat for Democratic House members, held at a resort just outside Pittsburgh the first weekend in February. Bush had already attended the Senate's Democratic retreat. Clinton had never attended Republican retreats, so the move was given due notice in the media and credit for its bipartisanship by Democratic leaders. The event was not open to the press.

The president began his remarks at the retreat by saying, "I'll do my best to change the tone of the dialogue in Washington. It is my hope that people can disagree in an agreeable way. One of the things I resolve to do is say, here's my position and I want to hear you out. Bipartisanship is going to require more than words to put forth good public policy—and I believe we're all here to do that."

Then he added, "I ran on an agenda. That's what I'm here to talk to you about. I believe the right thing to do is to do what you said you were going to do" during the campaign. "The expectation is that nothing will get done because of the closeness of the election," he added, making it clear that he intended to prove that expectation wrong. "Part of coming here today is to tell you who I am and about my agenda and listen to what you have to say."

He then took several questions. The respected elder congressman Charlie Rangel of New York said in his unique voice, raspy yet oddly captivating, "Mr. President, you're good!" He then remarked that it took "a lot of political courage" for Bush to come to the retreat and reach out to Democrats, and asked whether Bush would urge his party leaders to work across the aisle, too. Bush replied that he was "committed to taking the same message of civility to the Republican leadership."

A few years later, I would hear Rangel, then minority ranking member on the powerful Ways and Means committee, more than once express his appreciation to the president for bringing leaders of both parties to the White House—followed by complaints that Bill Thomas, the Republican chairman of the committee, had failed to follow suit, giving Democrats little voice in the committee's deliberations.

As for the retreat, it was a cordial meeting, but it was difficult to tell whether Democrats were genuinely open to a bipartisan effort and believed in Bush's sincerity. Some were still upset about the Florida recount process, including one speaking for the Congressional Black Caucus. They pressed Bush to act on electoral reform in tones that reflected an underlying tension. But among the leadership and most of the attendees, there appeared to be a willingness, though tempered by skepticism, to see whether the president was going to govern to the center and take into account the concerns of Democrats.

Much of the first six months had been planned in advance by the president's senior advisers, almost the way a smart head coach will script the first dozen plays of a football game. Controlling the agenda in Washington meant keeping the focus on the big picture, even while reacting to the daily news and responding to the unexpected. Karl Rove understood this well, and he drove the strategic planning efforts with input from a number of top White House aides, particularly Karen Hughes, Andy Card, and Condi Rice.

One of the ways we tried to set the agenda was by having a "theme of the week," around which most of the president's public schedule would center. One week, he would do education events, appearing at schools and speaking with groups of teachers and parents. Another week, he would focus on tax cuts, meeting with "tax families" and small business owners to highlight how much they would benefit from his tax cut plan, much as he'd done during the election campaign. Another week, he focused on defense and made his first trip to a military base, Fort Stewart in Georgia, to talk about his initiative for better pay and housing for troops, followed by an event promoting military transformation to address new threats in the post–cold war era, a key foreign policy priority during the campaign.

It was all part of our well-choreographed plan to get the president off to a quick start and define him as a strong leader focused on redeeming his campaign promises and getting things done.

I was spending my early days becoming a part of the White House policy, legislative, and communication operations. I got my fill of meetings: legislative strategy meetings to discuss important initiatives; daily communications meetings held by Karen Hughes; prebriefings with my immediate boss, Ari Fleischer, ahead of senior staff, the morning gaggle, and the afternoon briefing; twice-a-week message meetings to coordinate the president's upcoming public events; and policy meetings on specific domestic issues, including the patients' bill of rights, campaign finance reform, racial profiling, the environment, Medicare, stem cell research, and education.

My fellow deputy Claire Buchan and I split responsibilities by issues. Claire took most of the economic issues and I took most of the other domestic issues, while the National Security Council press office handled foreign policy. We made sure all issues were covered for the press secretary, preparing talking points for him and helping him stay on top of the issues to avoid surprises in the briefing room. When I filled in for Ari, I would of course have to focus more broadly. At times, I would also attend presidential meetings in Ari's place, including congressional meetings and policy briefings.

In addition to reaching out to members of Congress from both parties, the president also reached out to key world leaders. It was an effort to show the president engaging in "personal diplomacy" aimed at strengthening our alliances abroad. Bush's ability to establish strong personal relations with allies was important to highlight, given his very limited experience in foreign policy.

As deputy press secretary, my duties also included traveling on selected presidential trips. Whenever a president travels, he is accompanied by a virtual traveling White House, including advisers, support staff, Secret Service agents, and military staff. The White House Communications Agency (WHCA), an arm of the White House Military Office, sets up secure and nonsecure communication lines for presidential holding rooms and staff holds at event sites, as well as staff offices and presidential suites at hotels, press filing centers with a podium for any briefings, and a press office stocked with notebook computers and phone lines. The press secretary typically traveled aboard Air Force One, while one of the deputies, Claire or I, would travel aboard the press charter plane. On foreign trips, the NSC spokesperson would also travel with the White House press corps.

Our first foreign trip was a day trip to San Cristóbal, Mexico, in February, where the president participated in events and meetings with President Vicente Fox. In an odd bit of foreshadowing, Bush's first joint news conference with a world leader, at President Fox's ranch, was dominated by questions on Iraq. British and American military aircraft had just struck a number of radar and air defense command centers, including around Baghdad. The action required approval from the president since it was outside the no-fly zone in Iraq that we and the British enforced. It was a response to intensified Iraqi efforts to shoot at our aircraft in the no-fly zone, including the launch of surface-to-air missiles. It was the first notable military action approved by the new president. Bush called the response part of a "routine mission" to enforce the no-fly zones and to make clear to Saddam Hussein that he was expected to abide by the agreements he'd made following the Gulf War.

Following the visit, Ari headed back with some of the staff to Washington for the weekend. I took his place and headed to Bush's ranch in Crawford with the president for the weekend. It marked my first of many rides aboard Air Force One, and included a tour from the chief flight attendant—another early moment when I was wowed by life inside the White House bubble.

The president and Mrs. Bush attended the dedication of the Oklahoma City National Memorial that next Monday before heading back to Washington. I still vividly remember walking through the interactive museum honoring those who'd been killed in the terrible 1995 bombing of the Murragh Federal Building by Timothy McVeigh. The Gallery of Honor, one of the stops on the tour, is a dark room in which visitors hear a recording of a hearing under way in a meeting room, suddenly interrupted by loud explosions. As the lights come on, you glimpse a wall filled with pictures of the 168 people who lost their lives in the bombing.

Later in February, the president hosted Prime Minister Blair of Great Britain at Camp David. Iraq was on the agenda, and of interest to reporters who covered the press conference during the visit. Bush and Blair talked about restructuring the sanctions on Iraq through the United Nations. The idea was to impose what we labeled smart sanctions aimed at restraining the regime without hurting the Iraqi people by tightening controls on goods that could be used for military purposes and preventing the regime from getting illicit funds from oil smuggling.

Echoing Blair, Bush said, "A change in sanctions should not in any way, shape, or form, embolden Saddam Hussein. He has got to understand that we are going to watch him carefully and, if we catch him developing weapons of mass destruction, we'll take the appropriate action. And if we catch him threatening his neighbors, we will take the appropriate action." Saddam was viewed more as a "problem" to deal with than a "grave and gathering danger" in the early days. Talk centered on if he was developing WMD, not that he was developing them.

Another responsibility of mine in the early months was occasionally sitting in on senior staff press interviews. In early February, I attended some interviews we arranged for the new chief of staff, Andy Card. During an interview with the Associated Press, Andy succinctly summarized his view of the three core responsibilities of the White House staff: to manage the "care and feeding" of the president, to run a disciplined policy formulation process, and to effectively manage the marketing and selling of the president's policies. Andy had a keen grasp of the big picture. Like Karl Rove, Karen Hughes, and President Bush himself, he knew that the marketing and selling of policy—another way of describing the permanent campaign—were instrumental to getting things done and key measurements of presidential power and success.

Karl Rove oversaw the strategic planning process within the White House for the marketing and selling of policy. Rove instituted regular "strategery" meetings, using a term derived not, as some might have believed, from a real Bush remark but from a *Saturday Night Live* skit in which Will Ferrell played off Bush's penchant for "mangling the English language" (as Bush himself would say).

Strategery meetings were focused on long-range planning and strategy weeks and months down the road. Rove's Office of Strategic Initiatives helped coordinate the efforts, including preparing materials and doing research to see how previous White Houses might have handled similar challenges. Electoral success was the ultimate objective—winning more Republican seats in Congress in 2002 and getting George Bush reelected to the presidency in 2004.

Those attending strategery meetings included Rove, Karen Hughes, Andy Card, Deputy Chief of Staff for Policy Josh Bolten, Staff Secretary Harriet Miers, Domestic Policy Adviser Margaret LaMontagne, National Security Adviser Condoleezza Rice, National Economic Adviser Larry Lindsey, Vice Presidential Counselor Mary Matalin, and Legislative Liaison Nick Calio. The deputies of all these key advisers attended their own regular strategy meetings. Priority issues from the strategy meetings would filter down through the White House policy, communications, and legislative divisions so that ideas could be discussed and developed for discussion at future sessions. That's how I first became familiar with the formulation of strategy, as Karen Hughes would regularly seek ideas and input from all of us on the communications team at her meetings.

As counselor to the president, Karen Hughes was responsible for managing the president's message and overseeing all his communications efforts. Her chief role was to help instill and enforce message discipline throughout the White House and the administration as a whole. She also served as an adviser on most important decisions made at the senior staff level and by the president.

Thus politics and policy were deeply interwoven within the fabric of the Bush White House. Most of us who had been around politics for any length of time found this completely natural and far from sinister. We considered the president more open, forthright, and honest than his predecessor, and we viewed him as right on the issues as well as closely in synch with the views of most Americans. As far as we could see, there was no contradiction between these assumptions and the existence of a large political operation within the White House dedicated to setting the public agenda. It was just part of the political process, a job that needed to be done and that we were happy and honored to perform.

But stepping outside the White House bubble and looking back from today's perspective, it's easier to see that much of what we were doing was no different from the things our immediate predecessor had done. Like the Clinton administration, we had an elaborate campaign structure within the White House that drove much of what we did. We were always focused on how to control the agenda, shape the media narrative, and build public support for our policies—the same things Democratic leaders in Washington sought to do. Bush had promised to change the way things were done in Washington. But how could he change the game if his administration continued to play by the very same rules? At the time, I didn't recognize the contradiction, and neither, I think, did most of my colleagues.

However, the system worked—at least in those early months. It helped us pass the president's tax cuts by late May. We had argued that a large portion of the projected $5.6 trillion budget surplus (which included $2.6 trillion designated for Social Security) ought to be returned to taxpayers. This would help stimulate growth and job creation, and bring the economy out of its downturn (determined by later economic reports to be a recession). Bush visited twenty-six states during his first one hundred days in office, and many of these trips were focused on getting the public to pressure Congress to act. There was plenty of skepticism in the media coverage and, at first, not a lot of support in the polls. But the campaign effort proved remarkably successful. The package as passed was not everything Bush had wanted, but he largely got what he sought: a $1.35 trillion tax cut over ten years, just below the $1.6 trillion he'd advocated. Bush received some bipartisan support, including garnering yes votes from twelve Democrats in the Senate.

The president's No Child Left Behind (NCLB) education bill was another beneficiary of the administration's campaign posture. Aimed at closing the achievement gap between high-performing and low-ranked school districts, NCLB also made it through both the House and Senate on the heels of a carefully orchestrated public outreach effort. After differences in numerous details, including some extended partisan wrangling over funding levels (particularly in the soon to be Democratic-controlled Senate), were worked out and agreed to by conference committee members, the bill would be signed into law in January 2002.

There were plenty of bumps in the road in those early months.

Senator Jim Jeffords of Vermont, a lifelong moderate Republican, decided to bolt the party just as the tax cut legislation was set to pass in late May. He became an independent and caucused with the Democrats, giving them effective control of the Senate and making Tom Daschle of South Dakota the majority leader.

Our sixty-day regulatory review of Clinton era regulations, which had yet to go into effect, caused some public perception problems; when certain rules were rolled back or weakened, some critics used the decisions to paint Bush as being antienvironment or more concerned about corporate interests than with protecting individual Americans.

The president's energy task force, chaired by Vice President Cheney, held a series of meetings with outside interests whose identities were withheld from the public. This created an early impression of an administration prone to secrecy and reinforced the image of the Bush White House as in thrall to corporate interests.

As with any new administration, there were some glitches that caused us to change our procedures. For example, there were a few leaks to the media concerning White House message strategy discussions—something that Bush intensely disliked, as did Card, Rove, and Hughes. To prevent future leaks, some strategy planning meetings were reconfigured. The twice-weekly message meeting turned into more of a general run-through of the public schedule and what the topics would be than an open discussion and deliberation about ideas. Those strategic decisions were left to much smaller meetings of top advisers.

As summer arrived, we seemed to be having some trouble defining a clear, big-picture message to cut through the news clutter. We were struggling to get high-priority legislation like the patients' bill of rights and the faith-based initiative passed. Criticism of the White House communications and legislative operations began to surface. There was plenty of discussion internally about how to come up with new ways to highlight our top priorities so that the media would follow our lead and we would not fall into the trap of engaging in "small-ball" issues and reacting to the agendas of others.

As for me, I was settling into my new life, getting fully acclimated to the internal White House operations, traveling with the president, and dealing with the national media. In April, I had to face a lively press corps covering the first foreign policy crisis for the Bush White House—the heroic emergency landing on Chinese territory of a U.S. surveillance plane, an EP–3 Aries, after a midair collision with a Chinese fighter jet sent to intercept it (the Chinese fighter pilot crashed to his death). Our American service members were in Chinese custody at the time. Over the course of several days, the president and his national security team managed to bring the crisis to a successful conclusion without escalating the situation, including the safe return of our military men and women. I also had to handle the live briefing on the morning of the president's controversial decision on stem cell research, which was announced in his first prime-time address as president from Crawford in early August. Moments like these constituted my baptism by fire as a presidential spokesman, and gave me some early confidence that I could handle future challenges if necessary.

Bush's early presidency was mainly focused on the domestic agenda, but the president did start to define himself on the foreign policy front. He was pushing ahead on missile defense, which would ultimately lead to the U.S. withdrawal from the ABM Treaty with Russia. Military transformation was a top priority for Bush, and his Secretary of Defense Donald Rumsfeld began pushing ahead on it. The president gave his first major foreign policy address in Europe during a stop in Warsaw when he urged the spread of freedom across the world. He also focused heavily on personal diplomacy, establishing close personal relationships with world leaders to strengthen our alliances.

And Bush and his national security team made clear that we were determined to pursue a tougher approach for dealing with Saddam Hussein and his rogue Iraqi regime, though no one, at the time, was predicting an imminent crisis in the region. Still, Bush and his advisers were sending clear signals that more robust military action, rather than a tit-for-tat response, was likely if the regime stepped out of line. As concern grew within the administration that the sanctions of the previous decade were continuing to weaken, Russia prevented the new smart sanctions approach toward Iraq proposed by the United States from getting through the Security Council in the summer of 2001.

The first seven months of the Bush administration were not devoid of political push and pull. I could certainly tell that Washington was not Texas. Trust was lacking between leaders of the two parties in Congress. Memories of past affronts were long and distrust ran deep. Bitterness over the contested 2000 election result still lingered among some Democrats. Suspicion over whether the president was sincere about wanting to be "a uniter, not a divider" was commonplace, and some liberals doubted the phrase "compassionate conservative" could ever be more than a meaningless paradox. But we in the Bush administration had enjoyed enough bipartisan success with our tax cuts and No Child Left Behind that we were still optimistic about the possibility of unifying the nation behind an agenda that most Americans, if not all, could be proud to embrace.

And then came the day that changed everything.

7

SEPTEMBER 11 AND
THE PARTISAN CEASEFIRE

LIKE MOST AMERICANS, I will never forget where I was the morning of
September 11, 2001. It is etched in my memory forever. I was traveling with
the president as he was preparing to talk about education reforms, and his
reading initiative in particular, at an elementary school in Sarasota, Florida. It
was part of a two-day swing aimed at urging Congress to finally get Bush's education package passed. I was the deputy press secretary at the time. Press Secretary Ari Fleischer was traveling with the president aboard Air Force One,
while I was traveling with the larger press corps accompanying the president
in their chartered plane.

The president had participated in an education event at an elementary
school in Jacksonville, Florida, the day before, and we all had spent the night
at the Colony Beach Resort in Sarasota (which was planning to close for the
season after we left that day).

The press buses with the larger traveling White House press corps left the
resort about a half hour ahead of the president's motorcade so they could
preposition at Emma E. Booker elementary school. Typically the networks
set up a transmission room that has all their broadcast needs, including a
pool feed of the president's remarks on television screens. A filing center

where reporters can write and send their news stories and receive briefings is
set up for the entire press corps, usually including a podium for briefings by
the press secretary or other administration officials. A White House press office is always located nearby.

After arriving at the school and checking out the transmission room/filing
center and press office (in this instance they were all located together in a classroom), I went into the school library where the president was scheduled to
speak following a classroom visit. The network camera and sound crews and
the local media stations were already in place on the press platform behind the
seats for the audience members, which would include school administrators,
teachers, and parents. Seats in the back were reserved for White House reporters. I sat down between Judy Keen of *USA Today* and David Sanger of the
New York Times.

We were chatting casually when my pager went off. I pulled up the incoming
message. Brian Bravo, a young aide in the press office, was on top of the breaking
news as it was being reported right around 8:50 A.M. that morning: a plane had
hit the World Trade Center in New York. I wondered how such a weird accident
could happen. Was it a small plane whose pilot had suffered a heart attack and
lost control of his craft? Had there been some massive failure by the traffic control system? It seemed very mysterious.

"That's terrible," I said aloud.

Judy asked, "What?"

I said, "The AP is reporting that a plane has hit the World Trade Center."
She and David were both as shocked as I.

We quickly moved into the filing center to see it on television. Most of the
traveling press corps joined us, if they were not already there. We were all listening and watching intently, trying to find out what had happened, when
suddenly a reporter shouted out, "Another plane just hit the other tower!"

I think I'd noticed another explosion out of the corner of my eye as I was
talking to someone, but I'd thought it might have been a secondary explosion.

"Are you sure?" I inquired. Others were questioning whether it was a new
one as well.

Moments later it was replayed, and we all saw the second plane crashing
into the second tower. Chills went up my arms and back. The idea that someone had attacked America in a dramatic and deadly way began to penetrate
my consciousness. Instantly, most of the reporters turned and looked at me,

standing at the back of the small filing center. It was a natural reaction on their part. This was big news, and they were looking for answers. What is the White House hearing and doing? But they knew I would need to go find out.

"I'll be back," I said. I needed to track down the senior staff traveling with us that day and see what they knew. As I walked out of the filing center, one of our advance staffers saw me and said without my asking, "Follow me. I'll get you to the hold."

This was a private room set up as a quiet work space with secure and non-secure phones for us to use during a presidential visit. On this occasion the presidential hold was the same as the senior staff hold. It was next to the classroom where the president was observing a class of second graders participate in a reading lesson and reading along with them. The only way to get to the hold was to walk through the small classroom.

As the advance staffer and I approached the classroom, the press pool was leaving. They had just filmed the president reading to the class and now were being escorted out, as would usually be the case in a photo-op of this kind. Just a moment earlier, the pool had filmed Andy Card walking up to the president and whispering into his ear, "A second plane hit the second tower. America is under attack." It's a moment that has since been replayed countless times.

As we entered the classroom, some in the press pool asked if I knew anything more about the plane crash in New York. They hadn't heard about the second plane yet.

"We just saw a second plane hit the second tower on television," I informed them. Ann Compton of ABC News couldn't hear me very well. She asked me, "Did you say there was a second plane?"

"Yes," I replied. "A second plane hit the second tower. That's all I know."

The advance staffer then pointed me to the staff hold on my left. As I entered the classroom and walked across the back toward the hold, I looked at the president, who was sitting in a teacher's chair in front of the students. A student was reading, but the president's mind was clearly on the attacks. I had never seen that kind of distant expression on his face before. I could see in his eyes that he knew we were at war.

I joined the other traveling staff in the hold. Moments later, the president entered and saw the burning towers on the television set. Then he sat down and took some phone calls, seeking more information. I remember him instructing someone to turn off the television. (Bush usually likes a distraction-free environment.) Ari Fleischer was there, as were Dan Bartlett, Andy Card, Karl Rove, and Deborah Loewer, an NSC staff member and director of the White House Situation Room.

Bush spoke individually by secure phone with the vice president, FBI director Robert Mueller (who'd been on the job just one week), and Governor Pataki of New York. Cheney and Mueller told the president what they knew, which as far as I could sense was not much more than we already knew. The president told Pataki to let New Yorkers know that the federal government would do all it could to help with the response.

After the calls, the president got a yellow pad to scribble some notes about what he would say before departing the school. The senior staff present huddled with the president. The visit had been scheduled as a two-tiered event: a stop in the classroom and then some remarks on education to the thirty or so audience members assembled in the library. The plan now was to have the president say a few words about what had happened and let those present and the media know that he had to return to Washington immediately to tend to the unfolding tragedy. I stood just to one side near the president, Dan stood next to him, and Ari was seated with him at the table.

The president had indicated he didn't need a formal prepared statement. Now he spoke out loud, writing parts of what he would say as Dan and Ari offered input. "Today we've had a national tragedy," the president said. "Two airplanes have crashed into the World Trade Center in a terrorist attack on our country."

"We don't know for sure it was a terrorist attack," Dan interjected.

"Sure it is," said Bush. "What else do you think it is?" Ari and I agreed that it was clearly a terrorist attack.

"I'm just saying we have not confirmed anything yet," Dan replied. "We don't know who is responsible."

"Then just say 'apparent' terrorist attack," I said, offering my two cents. The president added the additional word.

Then the president headed to the library to make his brief remarks, staff in tow. At one point he talked off the cuff about hunting down "those folks" before stating that "terrorism against our nation will not stand," echoing similar words his father had once said about the Iraqi invasion of Kuwait. The president's initial comments were viewed by some as casual and not as strong and reassuring as they should have been. But he would quickly gain his footing and come across as firm, resolved, and reassuring in his words and actions in the days to come.

As the president was wrapping up his comments, Ari looked at me. We were standing behind the curtains that were always used to cordon off a closed, protective area for the president.

"Should you come with us to Washington?" Ari asked.

"I don't think so," I said. "I'm the press corps' only link to the White House. I think I need to stay with them and get them what information I can."

Moments later the president departed.

I returned to the filing center and was informed by press assistant Harry Wolff that the broadcast correspondents were getting ready to go live in the school yard. I walked outside and provided them color about who the president had spoken with and what he had said. In a time of crisis, I believe it's best to provide information and facts as quickly as possible to the press, and that's what I was trying to do.

As I headed back to the filing center, Fox News producer Nancy Harmeyer came running up to me. I knew Nancy well. She had covered us on the campaign.

"Scott, our guys in Washington are saying that the Executive Office Building has been hit," Nancy said.

"The Executive Office Building?" I asked incredulously.

"Yeah, they're saying there is a cloud of smoke coming out from it," Nancy said. "Are you hearing anything?"

Now it was hitting even closer to home for me. My oldest brother Mark, a member of the President's Council of Economic Advisers and his senior health policy adviser, worked in the Executive Office Building. Many colleagues I knew worked there, too, including some close friends. Once again I felt chills.

"I haven't heard any such thing," I said.

I immediately proceeded to the filing center to see what I could on television. Reports were coming in that the Pentagon had been hit. Nancy soon confirmed that apparently some of their people had been looking at the smoke from the Pentagon, but thought it was coming from the Executive Office Building, which blocked the Pentagon in their line of sight. It was hard to believe that the home of the Department of Defense could be hit by terrorists. I felt great pain, even as I felt some relief that the Executive Office Building had not been hit.

Knowing she might be worried, I thought about my mother at that moment (I was still single at the time). She was in Austin, working as the state comptroller. I stepped outside and phoned her office from my cell. With the un-folding crisis on my mind, I didn't even pause to ask if she was there. I just told her assistants, Nora Alvorado and Lisa Wright, "Tell my mother I am in Florida with the president. I am fine. Let her know I love her and I will call her tonight."

Then I went back to work. I had some trouble connecting with Claire Buchan, my fellow deputy press secretary back at the White House. I remem-ber it took some time to get through because of the communications network in Washington being overloaded. But once we connected, Claire kept feeding me whatever information she knew, so I could provide what the White House knew to the press corps. Ari also passed along what he knew and what the president was doing as they flew by a circuitous route back to the White House, including stops at two Air Force bases. The Secret Service was con-cerned that the president had been targeted. I later learned that Andy Card and the vice president had agreed with the Secret Service that the president should hold off on returning to Washington until more could be learned about the extent of the threat.

I did not know it at the time, but most of the nonessential staff was being evacuated from the White House. As the senior press spokesman at the White House, Claire would stay put in the Situation Room, fulfilling our office's communications duties.

As the afternoon wound down, I headed back to the Colony resort with a few other staff members who would be remaining in Florida, including press advance director Kelley Gannon, travel office aide Bo Bailey, and Harry Wolff, as well as the members of the White House press corps who had been left be-hind. The White House travel office was responsible for coordinating logisti-cal needs like buses, planes, and lodging for the traveling press corps. It had been relatively unknown to the public until Travelgate, the first of a series of ethics controversies to embroil the Clinton White House.

Bo was the first to inform me that there would be no way to get the press corps—and therefore me—home that evening. It was already known that transportation secretary Norm Mineta had grounded all civilian aircraft and prohibited any unauthorized flights. A number of military aircraft were being put on alert for air defense and response support. I stayed in contact with Claire into the early evening. That night, back at my room at the Colony, I watched the president's brief remarks to the nation from the Oval Office. He came across as considerably more sure-footed and strong that night than he had seemed earlier in the day.

The next morning, I headed to the press filing center at the Colony and set up shop in the White House press office. It was in the same room, cordoned off by large blue curtains. Bo and his fellow travel office colleagues back at the White House continued to pursue avenues for getting the press home. While we eventually got permission for the press charter to take off from Sarasota and land at Andrews Air Force Base, the airline refused to allow their plane to fly under such circumstances.

We'd told the press we would try our best, but now we had to inform them that we could not get them back home on the press charter.

By this time, one of the network correspondents had grown particularly anxious about returning to D.C. to cover the biggest story of the Bush presidency, and he was not timid or shy about expressing his frustration. A solid reporter, he wanted to be in the thick of the reporting. He was upset at seeing his colleague at the same network, who'd remained in D.C., reporting from outside the White House, standing on the familiar reporter's staging area then known as "Pebble Beach," with the stately North Portico in the background, while he was stuck in Sarasota.

"Scott, c'mon," the correspondent belted out in front of all the other reporters. Pointing his finger at me, he added, "You're a deputy assistant to the president. You have the ability to get us a military plane. This is absurd!"

I was a little annoyed at the reporter's presumptuousness. "I think there are more important priorities for the military than you right now," I shot back. My retort silenced him, as a hush fell across the rest of the room.

I felt a little bad about putting the reporter down in front of his colleagues, but later a network producer came over to me and said, "I just want you to know you did the right thing. What he said was off base, and you were right to put him in his place."

I expressed my appreciation. I hadn't been pleased at the reporter's outspoken complaint in front of the entire group. We all shared his frustration about being away from the action; he didn't need to take it out on me in front of everyone we worked with.

By that afternoon, the travel office had arranged for three buses to transport the press corps back to D.C. It would be a sixteen-hour trip. Kelley Gannon invited me to ride back with her in the advance head's Ford Expedition, which would get us home faster. I told her that would be great, "but if I am going, my man Harry has to go." Harry Wolff had been working hard, providing great support help for two days in the middle of the unfolding tragedy.

Kelley and I then remembered the Secret Service press agent. Ever since John Hinckley attempted to assassinate President Ronald Reagan after making his way into the press area outside the Washington Hilton, the Secret Service has positioned an agent with the press corps. Kelley said, "We should ask him if he wants to come back with us."

"Yeah, and if we want to get home quickly, it won't hurt to have him along," I said lightheartedly. I was thinking that his badge was sure to impress the highway patrol if we got pulled over. As for Bo, we couldn't help him. He had to stay with the press corps.

Once the press buses arrived and things looked under control, the five of us loaded into the Expedition and hit the road. It was around 3:00 P.M. We decided to take turns driving in four-hour shifts and get back as fast as possible. The agent had the heaviest foot—maybe it was the weight of his badge!

Somewhere just south of the North Carolina border, I awoke from a brief nap in the backseat and looked to my right out the window. We were passing a big truck with a crane, and draped across the crane was a large American flag. I was only half awake, but a sense of pride came over me. It was just one flag among many that were appearing on cars and trucks, in homes and classrooms, and in offices and store windows across the United States. Whatever divided us as Americans mattered not at that moment in time. We were standing together, one nation indivisible.

The Bush White House I returned to later that morning would never be the same. Others before us who had served in the White House had been called to action in the face of adversity. Now it was our turn to rise to the challenge. It was a responsibility none of us could have imagined when we assumed our duties eight months earlier.

All the elaborate planning of the "strategery" meetings for the fall was set aside. Our focus shifted from being domestic-centered to foreign policy or national security–centered. This was now a wartime presidency. We would still push forward on important domestic priorities, especially much needed economic stimulus measures and the No Child Left Behind Act, but protecting the homeland and prevailing in the war on terrorism was now the highest priority.

Those initial days after the attacks were notable. I remember sitting in the National Cathedral in Washington during the prayer and remembrance service that first Friday, just three days after the attacks. The president's remarks were moving and reassuring. He noted the generosity and kindness and bravery of rescue workers "past exhaustion," blood donors and thousands of others offering to work and serve in whatever way they could help. He highlighted the character of America found in specific "eloquent acts of sacrifice." And then Bush spoke about our sense of national unity:

> In these acts, and in many others, Americans showed a deep commitment to one another, and an abiding love for our country. Today, we feel what Franklin Roosevelt called the warm courage of national unity. This is a unity of every faith, and every background.
>
> It has joined together political parties in both houses of Congress. It is evident in services of prayer and candlelight vigils, and American flags, which are displayed in pride, and wave in defiance.
>
> Our unity is a kinship of grief, and a steadfast resolve to prevail against our enemies. And this unity against terror is now extending across the world.

That afternoon in New York, the president would grab the bullhorn standing at the side of New York firefighter Bob Beckwith and speak to the multitude of tireless rescue workers at ground zero. When someone yelled out that they could not hear him, Bush responded in one of the most memorable and defining moments of his presidency, "I can hear you. The rest of the world hears you. And the people who knocked these buildings down will hear all of us soon."

On September 20, I well remember witnessing history, not too many feet from the platform where the president was addressing a joint session of Congress. He put the repressive Taliban regime in Afghanistan on notice, made clear that we would relentlessly pursue the al Qaeda terrorist network until it was dismantled and defeated, and announced the creation of an Office of Homeland Security within the White House to be headed by Governor Tom Ridge of Pennsylvania. The war against the terrorists, Bush said, would be a lengthy campaign fought on many fronts—intelligence, diplomatic, military, law enforcement, and financial. Some actions would involve dramatic, visible military moves, while others would be unseen covert operations. Bush declared, "Every nation, in every region, now has a decision to make. Either you are with us, or you are with the terrorists. From this day forward, any nation that continues to harbor or support terrorism will be regarded by the United States as a hostile regime."

And he told the military to "be ready." Just over two weeks later, those called to battle in Afghanistan began to show us they were. Our military took the offensive in Afghanistan with help from Great Britain and the support of a broad international coalition that would grow to more than ninety countries.

The administration also took action at home. In the immediate aftermath, there was no higher priority than the response and recovery efforts, and helping New York rebuild. Airline safety was of paramount importance, and a number of steps were taken, starting with improving passenger screening, including an eventual agreement on federalizing screeners under the new Transportation Security Administration. Congress also acted within weeks to pass the Patriot Act, giving law enforcement a number of new tools to fight terrorism, some of which would become controversial in later years as questions were raised about possible violations of civil liberties. Bureaucratic walls that had prevented the FBI and CIA from sharing intelligence were brought down, and other steps were taken to strengthen the gathering and sharing of intelligence. Perhaps most significant was the effort to clamp down on those permitted to come into the country.

The attacks of 9/11 had dealt a serious blow to an economy that had been in a downturn and that we would soon learn had entered into a recession in March (according to the National Bureau of Economic Research, the official arbiter of business cycles). Assistance was needed to help stabilize the airline industry financially. We also pushed forward in Congress a new economic stimulus package to help displaced workers, sped up the tax cuts passed early in the year, and provided additional relief to moderate and low-income Americans. However, while the House passed the package quickly, the Democratic-led Senate refused to act. Final passage of a scaled-down stimulus package would not happen until the following year.

Looking back on the post–9/11 period, however, I think that one event with an enormous impact on President Bush's mind-set has been almost forgotten by many people—the anthrax attacks.

One of the biggest concerns within the White House and intelligence community in the days and weeks after 9/11 was the possibility of a second wave of attacks. When word reached the White House on the morning of October 4 that a man in Florida had contracted a lethal dose of inhalation anthrax, those concerns were heightened.

There were indications later that day that the case might be isolated and not an act of terrorism. But the Centers for Disease Control and FBI quickly began investigating the matter. The following day the Florida victim, Bob Stevens, died. Traces of anthrax were found at his office building in Boca Raton on Sunday, October 7, leading officials to evacuate it and begin testing those who worked in the building. (Earlier that same day, the president had addressed the nation to announce the beginning of Operation Enduring Freedom, the military campaign aimed at removing the Taliban regime from power and bringing to justice the al Qaeda terrorists in Afghanistan.) The source of the anthrax that killed Bob Stevens remained uncertain.

One of my new duties in the post–9/11 White House was helping Ari Fleischer to stay on top of this potential bioterrorist threat. I stayed in contact with my counterparts at the Department of Health and Human Services, and began working closely with Lisa Gordon-Haggerty, an exceptionally bright and tireless public servant who worked in the counterterrorism unit of the National Security Council under Richard Clarke. Lisa was running point for the NSC on the anthrax attacks.

Several days after Stevens's death, letters containing anthrax began turning up in New York and Washington, including ones sent to the offices of NBC News and Senate Majority Leader Tom Daschle. The letter to Daschle contained a particularly lethal strain of the bacterium, heightening fears in Washington and beyond.

Reports of white powder that people feared was anthrax started to pop up all over. Most turned out to be false alarms. But the fear permeating the country was real. And it wasn't long before the press began asking whether the source of the anthrax could be a foreign government. The early indications we had been getting privately didn't appear to point overseas, but as Ari and the new Homeland Security Adviser Tom Ridge held their early briefings, nothing could be definitively ruled out.

The anthrax situation continued to become more troubling. We were starting to wonder when it would stop. Two postal workers from a northeast D.C. postal facility, Thomas L. Morris Jr. and Joseph P. Curseen, died later in October from inhalation anthrax. The White House remote mail facility tested positive for small traces of anthrax. For months to come, as I remember well, delivery of all White House mail was delayed for inspection and irradiation.

Amid all the reports, mostly false, of possible anthrax cases, around 9:00 P.M. on the night of October 23, I received a call from Bill Pierce, a Department of Health and Human Services public affairs official, warning of a possible case of smallpox in the Orlando, Florida, area. A man had showed up at a local hospital and was quarantined out of caution for exhibiting what medical personnel thought could be signs of the deadly disease. We could only imagine the panic it would cause if it turned out to be true.

I alerted Ari to the story and waited anxiously for further word from Bill Pierce. I got it a short time later that evening. It was a false alarm. The man did not have smallpox but syphilis. "Syphilis?" I asked Bill. "How could they confuse that with smallpox?" Bill didn't know, but we were both relieved.

I went up to Ari's office right after that call. "Well, I've got good news for us. The man in Florida does not have smallpox. But there's bad news for him—he has syphilis."

As Ari later recounted in his memoir, *Taking Heat,* he replied with a joyful shout, "Yes! It's syphilis! He's got syphilis." We all went home a little more relaxed that evening.

But the source of the anthrax attacks remained uncertain. We received a private briefing a couple of days later about the anthrax in the letter to Daschle. Analysis revealed that it was from the same strain as the others, but more sophisticated. Thousands of FBI agents were now involved in the investigation into the 9/11 hijackings and the anthrax attacks—pursuing any lead, interviewing friends and neighbors of those who'd come into contact with the anthrax and seeking to determine its origin.

I also remember Ari's frustration with an inaccurate ABC News report the evening of October 26, another story he recounted in *Taking Heat.* Since no source could be officially ruled out, the media were pursuing all angles. Brian Ross, a highly respected investigative reporter for ABC News, led the newscast that night stating that he had learned from "three well-placed but separate sources" that initial tests had found the chemical additive bentonite in the anthrax, and that the only country known to have used this substance to produce biological weapons was Iraq. Bentonite, Ross reported, was "a trademark of Saddam Hussein's biological weapons program." Peter Jennings indicated that some would conclude this was "a smoking gun" linking the anthrax attacks to Iraq.

ABC did mention that Ari had denied "in the strongest terms" that it was bentonite. But Jennings also talked about the "raging argument in the administration about going after Saddam Hussein."

Ari relentlessly pursued the story and "continued to badger a variety of people at ABC to see if they were going to correct the story" in the days after it aired. On October 31, ABC backtracked from its previous report, saying only that "a further chemical analysis" had ruled out bentonite in the anthrax, although it did contain silica, which is "not a trademark of any country's weapons program." They refused to offer a full retraction, however, which frustrated not only Ari but all of us who were concerned with getting accurate information out to the public. Perhaps it was an early vivid signal of the national media focusing on a potential conflict with Iraq at the expense of important truths about the actual necessity for war.

By early November, there had been sixteen confirmed cases of anthrax exposure. A New York woman, Kathy Nguyen, had died in late October. The FBI had determined that the NBC, Florida, and Daschle letters had all been sent from the same mailbox in Trenton, New Jersey, and agents were trying to track down who might have placed them there. Still, it could not be determined definitively whether the source was domestic or foreign.

To this day, no one has been charged with the anthrax killings, though many law enforcement personnel believed that the source was domestic. One person of interest was mentioned publicly though never indicted.

The influence of the anthrax attacks on policymaking within the Bush White House shouldn't be underestimated. Soon afterward, Vice President Cheney, along with Health and Human Services Secretary Tommy Thompson, led efforts to push ahead on a smallpox vaccine program for all Americans, in hopes of minimizing the impact of a bioattack using smallpox. While many potential first responders and hospital personnel—those who might first come into contact with a smallpox outbreak—were eventually vaccinated, the more ambitious plan never materialized. We also pressed ahead with funding for Project Bioshield, aimed at developing vaccines and stockpiling them to protect Americans in the event of a bioterror attack.

I know President Bush's thinking was deeply affected by the anthrax attacks. He was determined not to let another terrorist attack happen on his

watch and to challenge regimes believed to be seeking weapons of mass destruction. While his strategies for pursuing those objectives would later be
questioned, his concern was sincere.

That Christmas, shortly after the anthrax stories had finally faded from
the headlines, I flew home to Austin to spend time with my family. Upon
boarding the airplane, I looked down at my seat and noticed what appeared to
be a trail of white powder on the edge of the seat. I paused ever so briefly,
shook my head, and thought to myself, "You've got to be kidding! Of all the
seats, I pick the one with the white powder on it." I took a deep breath,
brushed it aside, and sat down, glad to be going home to my family.

Later I wondered what would have happened if someone else had found
the powder. Maybe the flight would have been delayed or canceled as the powder was tested and the plane swept for residue. Personally, I have a theory as to
the source of this particular contamination. I think someone on the previous
flight had been eating a donut—the kind with powdered sugar on top.

THE UNITY IN WASHINGTON during those first few months following the 9/11
attacks was a welcome change. The outpouring of unified sentiment was unlike any Washington had seen in decades. Would the politics-as-war mentality
and the excesses of the permanent campaign era end as a positive side effect of
an unprecedented national tragedy?

It was not to be. The forces that had transformed Washington over three
decades into a nexus of partisan warfare were far too powerful. And those
forces were at work on both sides of the political divide.

In January 2002, the first cracks appeared in the facade of bipartisan
comity. During an open press Republican National Committee meeting in
Austin, Texas, Karl Rove stated that the GOP would make the president's leadership in the war on terror the top issue for retaining control of the House and
winning back the Senate in the midterms.

Rove was the first administration official to publicly make the case for using the war as a partisan issue, a marked shift in tone from Bush's repeated
emphasis on unity and bipartisanship in confronting and defeating radical
Islamic terrorism. "We can go to the American people on this issue of winning

the war," Rove said. "We can go to the country on this issue because they trust the Republican party to do a better job of protecting and strengthening America's military might and thereby protecting America."

At the time, polls showed the Republican party with a sizable lead (38 points in a Gallup survey) as the party Americans trusted most to deal with terrorism, and an even larger advantage on military and defense issues. While both parties would see the benefit of using such a sizable advantage on a major issue to their advantage in an election, Rove's candor about this strategy infuriated suspicious Democrats, who condemned Rove for trying to politicize the war.

Soon the president began campaigning openly again for Republican congressional candidates, including against incumbent Democratic members of Congress, touting his and GOP leaders' management of the war. As governor, he'd maintained good relations with friendly legislators by refusing to campaign against them, even if they were members of the opposing party. Bush's actions prompted concern and anxiety among Democrats.

The brief period of bipartisan peace initiated by 9/11 ended for good in May.

The new round of warfare was set off by what seemed to be a startling revelation from CBS News. On its evening newscast of May 15, 2002, based on information it had received anonymously, CBS reported in dramatic fashion that the president had received an intelligence briefing in early August 2001 that "specifically alerted him of a possible airliner attack in the United States."

Correspondent David Martin went on to report, "The president's daily intelligence brief is delivered to the president each morning, often by the director of Central Intelligence himself. In the weeks before 9/11 it warned that an attack by Osama bin Laden could involve the hijacking of a U.S. aircraft."

The report left much open to question. Was it suggesting that the president had received information that *should* have led him to act? Was it just a possible warning sign, like many others that may have gone unheeded? Or was it something else, possibly a nonspecific bit of intelligence from years earlier?

These questions were unanswered at the time, but that mattered little to Democratic leaders in Congress. They saw an opportunity to attack the president's strong suit—his leadership in the war on terrorism—and cut into his enormous popularity ahead of the midterm elections that coming November.

The morning after the CBS News report, Senate majority leader Tom Daschle stated how "gravely concerned" he was to learn "that the president received a warning in August about the threat of hijackers" by al Qaeda. He called for the president's intelligence briefing to be provided without delay to congressional investigators.

House minority leader Richard Gephardt, a Missouri Democrat, invoked Watergate, saying, "I think what we have to do now is to find out what the president, what the White House, knew about the events leading up to 9/11, when they knew it and, most importantly, what was done about it at that time."

But the Democrat who most aroused the ire of the White House and Republicans was New York's Democratic senator, Hillary Clinton.

While saying she was not trying to engage in finger pointing but simply seeking answers, Clinton rose on the floor of the Senate to declare, "We learn today something we might have learned at least eight months ago: that President Bush had been informed last year, before September 11, of a possible al Qaeda plot to hijack a U.S. airliner." She followed her declaration by holding up the cover of the tabloid *New York Post* with the glaring headline "BUSH KNEW" just below a slightly less glaring "9/11 BOMBSHELL."

"The president knew what?" Clinton asked.

The implication was clear: the president might have had information that could have been used to prevent the 9/11 attacks, yet he did nothing.

My White House colleagues and I were incensed. To us, such grandstanding appeared to be a return to the ugly partisan warfare that had come to define Washington and its culture during the 1990s. Politics as war, the innuendo of scandal, and the egregious implication that the president had deliberately neglected the country's safety—it was all in service of the November election results.

All the familiar elements were there. The story and the partisan accusations that followed provided great controversy for the media to cover. The story line would play out for days and even return two years later when the president's highly classified daily intelligence brief referenced in the report would be made available to the public and to the 9/11 Commission charged with investigating what had happened.

The next day, a front-page story in the *New York Times* began:

After months of unstinting support for President Bush's handling of the war on terror, leading Congressional Democrats changed course today and demanded full disclosure of what Mr. Bush was told last summer about the danger of terrorist hijackings. They also called for a broad public inquiry into what the government knew before Sept. 11. . . . For the first time since Sept. 11, the bipartisan unity over how Mr. Bush has conducted the war on terror appeared to be dissolving in sharp questions, accusations and partisan finger-pointing. . . . Democrats, who until now have been reluctant to speak out against Mr. Bush on foreign policy, said it was their duty to seek information.

To the White House and its supporters, Clinton's remarks seemed calculated to manipulate the narrative concerning who should be blamed for 9/11, placing blame at the doorstep of the current occupant of the Oval Office. Was she trying to shield the legacy of her husband's presidency by shifting blame for overlooking available intelligence on bin Laden away from him and onto his successor? The White House pointed out that Senator Clinton had not even bothered to call anyone there to find out more about the facts behind the headlines before delivering her speech.

To us, the disingenuous way Democratic leaders rushed to create a damning story line about the president and his administration crossed a line. Republicans objected vehemently and aggressively in a counteroffensive led by the White House. Soon the same Democratic leaders started stepping back from their initial insinuations and blame casting, particularly as they realized that their haste to create a narrative involving a terrible tragedy before the facts were known might backfire with the public. But prior to their retreat, the story dominated the news coverage from Washington for several days, and Democrats like Clinton initially fanned the flames of the media feeding frenzy, in part to gain support for the creation of an independent commission to investigate the 9/11 attacks. The White House initially resisted the idea and argued that House and Senate intelligence committees should handle any needed probes.

The administration fired back. Vice President Cheney referred to the Democrats' suggestions as "incendiary," and President Bush declared, "Had we had any inkling, whatsoever, that terrorists were about to attack our country, we would have moved heaven and earth to protect America." And in a gesture toward the rapidly vanishing spirit of bipartisanship, he added, "And I'm confident President Clinton would have done the same thing. Any president would have."

Is there blame to be doled out here? Maybe so. It would be naive to think Democrats were not seeking political gain just months before the midterm elections. But it would also be wrong to suggest that their over-the-top accusations and partisan finger pointing were unprovoked and that Democrats alone were responsible for the breakdown in the post–9/11 spirit of bipartisan cooperation. Democrats were responding in part to perceived efforts by Republicans seeking political advantage from the president's aggressive efforts to wage war against Islamic terrorists.

And if the shoe had been on the other foot—if a Democrat had been president at the time of the 9/11 attacks—would Republicans in Congress have challenged him in an equally inflammatory fashion? Probably. Republican accusations that President Clinton had "wagged the dog" in 1998 by launching military strikes against Iraq in order to distract attention from the Monica Lewinsky scandal were likely just as partisan. The problem in Washington is systemic and transcends the personal flaws of any single politician.

In truth, the breakdown in bipartisanship was bound to happen, given that suspicion and distrust between the two parties and their leaders in Washington had become so deeply rooted in the destructive climate of the preceding decade. Blaming one party or suggesting that certain leaders or individuals are solely responsible for the divisiveness only makes the situation worse, tempting us to ignore the root causes of how we got to this point in our national political discourse.

GETTING TO THE TRUTH BEYOND the continual partisan sniping has become increasingly difficult for ordinary Americans. Partisans in Washington have become very sophisticated in the ways they murk it up with partial truths, political spin, misrepresentations, distortion, and an overall lack of intellectual honesty. And the media too often focus on who is winning and who is losing the latest skirmishes in the ongoing campaign rather than on the substantive issues involved and their effects on the lives of Americans.

But getting to the reasons why Washington is broken and dominated by partisan warfare and the culture of deception it spawns is not so difficult a task. Once people recognize that the problem with Washington is not the domain of one party or its leaders but rather a problem that afflicts both parties and their leaders, then we can begin to move beyond it and get Washington back on track to solving our most important challenges as a nation—and avoid some of the more destructive consequences of today's political hostility and verbal combat.

Some political observers—especially Democrats—blame Karl Rove for many of the excesses that characterize the era of the permanent campaign. Karl is a gifted, powerful practitioner of contemporary political warfare. But Karl Rove is not the problem. Karl Rove did not create the excesses of the permanent campaign. All you have to do is look back at the campaigns run by people like Lee Atwater, James Carville, and other past political masters to see that. Rather, the excesses of the permanent campaign created Karl Rove.

However, no political operative before Rove arguably had so much influence within a White House. As senior adviser overseeing political affairs and strategy, Rove controlled an inordinately influential power center in the White House. There were other influential power centers, but none had as much impact on White House governing, policy, and operations. Unlike Karen Hughes, whose goal was to help the president shape his message in ways that would appeal to ordinary Americans, particularly those in the vital center, and unlike Andy Card, the chief of staff who served as an honest broker among various political points of view, Rove was a central player who was anything but neutral in his political and ideological views.

Rove's role was political manipulation, plain and simple, which explains the machinations within the White House and their consequences, whether beneficial or detrimental.

As for the truth behind the accusation that "BUSH KNEW," it would take many months to sort out what had really happened in the months leading up to 9/11. The president's daily briefing, it would be learned in 2004, was based on the same intelligence reporting President Clinton received in the nineties. Unfortunately, the initial response of the Bush White House to demands by partisan critics in Congress and elsewhere for an independent investigation fueled the firestorm of anger. It was an early indication that the Bush administration did not sufficiently accept the necessity for transparency in its management of the public business.

The president and his senior advisers had little appetite for outside investigations. They resisted openness, and believed that investigations simply meant close scrutiny of things they would prefer to keep confidential. Not that anything they'd done had necessarily crossed a legal line; rather, some things done privately might not look so good if disclosed publicly, and might cause political embarrassment for the president.

Keeping the curtains closed and doors locked is never a good idea in government, unless it involves vital matters of national security. Secrecy only encourages people to do things they would prefer others not know about. Openness is critical for accountability.

The Bush administration lacked real accountability in large part because Bush himself did not embrace openness or government in the sunshine. His belief in secrecy and compartmentalization was activated when controversy began to stir. That secrecy ended up delaying but not preventing the consequences. Resistance to openness in times of controversy is ultimately self-defeating in the age of the internet, blogosphere, and today's heightened media scrutiny.

Andy Card knew from his service in two previous administrations that investigations have a way of taking on lives of their own. Control was something the White House always wanted, the more the better. But given the partisan nature of Washington, once a narrative had liftoff, it was hard to bring back to earth. Although the Bush White House was never willing to lead the charge in pursuit of potentially unflattering truths, the administration eventually concluded that an investigation of events leading up to the September 11 tragedy was inevitable. And so, in November 2002, the 9/11 Commission was born, as an impartial, bipartisan effort at transcending political warfare and uncovering the truth.

8

SELLING THE WAR

ON MONDAY, SEPTEMBER 16, 2002, I accompanied the president on a day trip to Davenport, Iowa. He planned to give a speech urging the Senate to pass the budget with full funding for important priorities while exercising fiscal restraint elsewhere. As deputy White House press secretary, I was filling in for Ari Fleischer, who had decided to take a break from the presidential road show.

While his "message of the day" was on fiscal discipline, the president continued to discuss Iraq, echoing what he had said before the United Nations General Assembly in New York four days earlier. The UN speech signaled the beginning of a stepped-up effort in the administration's carefully scripted campaign to win broad public support for a possible military confrontation. The president outlined the case against Saddam Hussein's regime—its brutal repression of Iraqi citizens, its deceptive and willful disregard of UN Security Council resolutions demanding elimination of its chemical and biological weapons, its interest in developing nuclear weapons, and its support for terrorism. Bush asserted that all these actions made the Iraqi regime "a grave and gathering danger" that could no longer be ignored in a post–9/11 world. Then he unambiguously stated his intentions, rooted in a policy that had been determined months earlier:

My nation will work with the UN Security Council to meet our common challenge. If Iraq's regime defies us again, the world must move deliberately, decisively to hold Iraq to account. We will work with the UN Security Council for the necessary resolutions. But the purposes of the United States should not be doubted. The Security Council resolutions will be enforced— the just demands of peace and security will be met—or action will be un- avoidable. And a regime that has lost its legitimacy will also lose its power.

In a White House that prided itself on message discipline, Bush's speech provided the new talking points for "educating the public about the threat" (as we described our campaign to sell the war). The president, his national se- curity team, and his other top advisers had used the UN forum as an opportu- nity to articulate the severity of the threat and the urgency of addressing it. They probably knew it was unlikely that international pressure could force Saddam Hussein to voluntarily come clean, which is why Cheney saw the UN route as needless. The only time Saddam had done so was in the face of an overwhelming military defeat after the Persian Gulf war of 1991. But most recognized the need to show the public that diplomatic efforts were exhausted before launching a war. Hence the ultimatum by Bush—either the UN act without delay and with zero tolerance for further deception by the Iraqi regime, or the United States would lead a military effort to do it his way.

The public opinion climate at the time favored the White House, since 9/11 remained fresh in the minds of Americans. A week earlier, in a prime-time address from Ellis Island, the president had commemorated the first anniver- sary of 9/11 in a magnificent display of stagecraft, with the Statue of Liberty over one shoulder and a waving American flag over the other. The president talked about answering history's call to spread freedom and alluded to Iraq, saying, "We will not allow any terrorist or tyrant to threaten civilization with weapons of mass murder. Now and in the future, Americans will live as free people, not in fear, and never at the mercy of any foreign plot or power."

Of course, not all Americans supported the idea of confronting Iraq. Sup- port for ousting Saddam Hussein militarily had peaked at 74 percent back in November 2001. By the end of summer 2002, amid expressions of concern among U.S. allies and military analysts about the potential cost of an invasion in terms of troops and money, that support had fallen to a slim majority, ac- cording to a Gallup poll sponsored by *USA Today*. But more than eight in ten

Americans believed the regime of Saddam Hussein supported terrorist organizations intent on attacking America, and more than nine in ten believed it possessed or was developing WMD. A majority also believed—erroneously—that Saddam Hussein had been involved in the 9/11 attacks.

Other elements in the political equation also strengthened the president's hand. Bush's public approval rating had declined from its unsustainable high of 90 percent immediately after the 9/11 attacks, but it was still strong, in the mid-sixties. The Bush campaign machine had a highly regarded team of national security advisers to call on in Cheney, Powell, Rumsfeld, and Rice, all of whom had seen their stature enhanced following the initial swift success in Afghanistan.

What's more, with the midterm elections less than two months away, members of Congress, particularly those in moderate- to conservative-leaning districts or states, would have been hard-pressed to oppose the Bush team's harder-line post–9/11 mind-set. For at least some Democrats, including those with future presidential aspirations, opposing efforts by the Bush White House to confront Saddam Hussein seemed to pose far greater political risk than going along with its approach, particularly in an environment where Americans, concerned about future attacks, supported a tougher approach on matters of national security.

So conditions looked favorable for the Bush team as it launched its campaign to convince Americans that war with Iraq was inevitable and necessary. The script had been finalized with great care over the summer, and now, September 2002, was the time to begin carrying it out. (As Andy Card had told the *New York Times* just days earlier, "From a marketing point of view, you don't introduce new products in August.") But on the day of the president's trip to Iowa, the administration's well-oiled message machine sputtered audibly.

That morning, the *Wall Street Journal* ran a story quoting Bush's chief economic adviser, Larry Lindsey, offering an analytical opinion as to the cost of a possible war with Iraq: somewhere between $100 and $200 billion. He added that this cost would probably have a relatively minor effect on the U.S. economy, since it would amount to only 1 to 2 percent of America's gross domestic product.

I saw the story as soon as I reached the office, since the *Journal* was one of the papers Ari had assigned me to read as part of a system he'd set up to make sure that someone on the press staff read each of the major national newspapers first thing each morning. It served in part as an early warning system so that the press secretary (or his deputy) would know what matters to discuss with senior staff at the morning meeting and nothing blindsided him at the briefing.

Lindsey's figures were eye-opening. It's a bit ironic. Looking at those numbers from today's perspective, with the Iraq war having lasted five years and counting, they look comfortably low (though Lindsey assumed the costs would be for a war of shorter duration). But at the time, when many—especially within the administration—expected a relatively quick and easy war, followed by a fairly smooth transition funded largely by Iraqi oil, they seemed high.

But Lindsey's biggest mistake wasn't the size of the figures he chose to cite. It was citing any figures at all. Talking about the projected cost of a potential war wasn't part of the script, especially not when the White House was in the crucial early stages of building broad public support. In fact, none of the possible unpleasant consequences of war—casualties, economic effects, geopolitical risks, diplomatic repercussions—were part of the message. We were in campaign mode now, just as we had been when Bush traveled the country leading the effort to pass tax cuts and education reforms. This first stage was all about convincing the public that the threat was serious and needed addressing without delay. Citing or discussing potential costs, financial or human, only played into the arguments our critics and opponents of war were raising.

Lindsey had violated the first rule of the disciplined, on-message Bush White House: don't make news unless you're authorized to do so. Lindsey's transgression could only make the war harder to sell. Coming on a day when Bush was focused on the importance of fiscal restraint, it also gave the Democrats a way to brand the president's message as hypocritical.

As soon as I read the paper, I knew that no one in the White House would be happy, least of all the president. I brought the story to the attention of others on the communications team and made sure that other senior staffers, including Andy Card, got the news as well.

The morning press gaggle aboard Air Force One en route to Iowa confirmed that Larry's estimates were drawing a lot of media interest. I brushed aside the questions by saying it was too early to speculate about a decision the president had yet to make, but I understood the story was being played as a big news item in Washington. I knew reporters would want Bush's comment if they could get it. I had to warn him.

Just ahead of his remarks in Iowa, Bush was scheduled to tour the facilities at Sears Manufacturing, which would serve as the backdrop for his speech. He wasn't scheduled to take any questions, but during the flight to Davenport I'd learned from advance director Brian Montgomery that the press pool would be just a few feet away during the tour. I needed to alert the president to the story and make sure he was prepared in case a reporter tried to shout out a question to him.

I cornered the president in a little holding area just outside the manufacturing area. "Mr. President, I need to talk to you," I said. Bush glanced at me a little impatiently. He was focused on the tour and, as always, eager to stay on schedule.

"Whadda you got?" he asked.

"Sir, there is no plan to take questions this morning, but the press will be pretty close to you on the tour. You need to know that they may try to ask you about Larry Lindsey's comments in today's *Wall Street Journal*."

"What did he say?" the president asked.

"He said that war with Iraq could cost between $100 billion and $200 billion," I replied.

Clearly irritated, the president turned his head to one side and grimaced. He was steamed, as I'd expected.

"Why did he say that?" the president asked rather pointedly, glancing back at me.

"I don't know," I said. "He was talking to a reporter, and I think he just blurted it out in response to a question. I already told the press it is too early to speculate about a decision that has yet to be made."

"Has anyone spoken to him?" the president asked.

"Yes sir," I said. "Andy was supposed to."

"It's unacceptable," Bush continued, his voice rising. "He shouldn't be talking about that. And let them know I don't plan on answering any questions." By "them" he meant the press.

"I already have," I responded. By then Bush was already exiting the holding area to begin the tour. I followed right behind.

The president managed to avoid any questions about Lindsey's loose-cannon comments that morning. Within four months, Larry was gone, having "resigned" from the administration as part of a reshaping of the president's economic team (his comments on the cost of the war did not help).

Larry, a highly regarded economist, had violated a basic principle of the Bush White House: the president doesn't like anyone getting out in front of him. It's his job to make the news, not anyone else's—unless authorized as part of the script. And making news by going off-message compounds the crime and makes it something close to unforgivable, particularly at that crucial early stage as we were just beginning the massive marketing campaign.

As a White House spokesman, I appreciated the need for a clear, controlled message. In a world of twenty-four-hour news cycles, the media bombard their audiences with thousands of competing messages conveyed in countless words and images. The chances of getting any single idea through that cacophony are slim. When you wield the bully pulpit of the White House and the giant megaphone of the presidency, it is easier to set the agenda and get your ideas covered. But it still requires a coherent message and repetition of it for any concept to sink in and be fully grasped. If an administration hopes to communicate with the public effectively, it has to develop simple, straightforward, and consistent messages that connect with people's interests, concerns, and needs. Then it must find a variety of ways to make those messages newsworthy so they can be hammered home to the public. Otherwise, what the president wants to say will get lost in the ether, and with it his chance to shape events, influence society, and (hopefully) make a positive difference in people's lives.

So, generally speaking, I not only understood and respected the Bush administration's emphasis on staying on message, but supported it and worked to help shape it and spread it as part of my job. But today, as I look back on the campaign we waged to sell the Iraq war to the American people—a campaign I participated in, though I didn't play a major role in shaping it—I see more clearly the downside of applying modern campaign tactics to matters of grave historical import. Reflecting on that period has helped crystallize my understanding of the permanent campaign, with its destructive excesses, and how Washington, in its current state of partisan warfare, functions on mutual deception. The picture isn't pretty.

The vast majority of our elected officials are good people. But they are caught up in an endless effort to manipulate public opinion to their advantage. Driven by partisan interests, they engage in deception, whether intentionally or not (and I believe in most cases the deception is, in fact, unintentional or subconscious). It is all part of the political propaganda effort to advance one's causes.

Then the media go to work. Focused on covering the conflicts and controversies, the winners and losers, of the perpetual campaign, the press amplifies the talking points of one or both parties in its coverage, thereby spreading distortions, half-truths, and occasionally outright lies in an effort to seize the limelight and have something or someone to pick on. And by overemphasizing conflict and controversy and by reducing complex and important issues to convenient, black-and-white story lines and seven-second sound bites, the media exacerbate the problem, thereby making it incredibly hard even for well-intentioned leaders to clarify and correct the misunderstandings and oversimplifications that dominate the political conversation. Finally, it becomes much more difficult for the general public to decipher the more important truths amid all the conflict, controversy, and negativity. For some partisans, that is fine because they believe they can maneuver better in such a highly politicized environment to accomplish their objectives. But the destructive potential of such excessively partisan warfare would later crystallize my thinking.

In the fall of 2002, Bush and his White House were engaging in a carefully orchestrated campaign to shape and manipulate sources of public approval to our advantage. We'd done much the same on other issues—tax cuts and education—to great success. But war with Iraq was different. Beyond the irreversible human costs and the substantial financial price, the decision to go to war and the way we went about selling it would ultimately lead to increased polarization and intensified partisan warfare. Our lack of candor and honesty in making the case for war would later provoke a partisan response from our opponents that, in its own way, further distorted and obscured a more nuanced reality. Another cycle of deception would cloud the public's ability to see larger, underlying important truths that are critical to understand in order to avoid the same problems in the future.

And through it all, the media would serve as complicit enablers. Their primary focus would be on covering the campaign to sell the war, rather than aggressively questioning the rationale for war or pursuing the truth behind it. The White House knew the national media would cover its arguments for war even if the underlying evidence was a little shaky. Questions might be raised, but the administration had the biggest platform, especially when something as dramatic and controversial as war was at stake. And the public is generally inclined to believe what the White House says, or at least give it the benefit of the doubt until the watchdog media proves it is unreliable.

But in this case, the media would neglect their watchdog role, focusing less on truth and accuracy and more on whether the campaign was succeeding. Was the president winning or losing the argument? How were Democrats responding? What were the electoral implications? What did the polls say? And the truth—about the actual nature of the threat posed by Saddam, the right way to confront it, and the possible risks of military conflict—would get largely left behind, at least until after Bush had gained the necessary support to begin the war, at which point public support for our troops in harm's way would kick in.

There were exceptions. A handful of reporters aggressively questioned the administration's chief rationale and focused on the necessity and realities of war. But they were unable to either change the primary focus of the media as the aggressive campaign to win public opinion raged or slow Bush's determined march to war.

DURING THE LEAD-UP TO THE WAR, I served as deputy White House press secretary. My role did not center on Iraq or even the effort to sell it. I spent most of my time tending to non-Iraq press issues. At times, however, I filled in for Ari Fleischer and consequently participated in the campaign to sell the war, or shape and manipulate sources of public opinion to our advantage.

Like many Americans at the time, I was uncertain about the necessity for war and the new doctrine of preemption that was being used to push us toward it. I wondered why we needed to move so fast toward military confrontation. But I trusted the president and the policymakers on his national security team. They'd received almost universal accolades for their swift yet measured response to 9/11, especially the war in Afghanistan. Now most of them believed the Iraq threat was serious, and that played a large role in my willingness to go along with, if not necessarily wholeheartedly embrace, the decision to confront Saddam militarily. After all, they had full access to the intelligence and an intimate knowledge of Saddam Hussein and his regime. I did not. So, also like most Americans, I was inclined to give them the benefit of the doubt unless and until they proved unworthy of it.

The campaign to sell the war didn't begin in earnest until the fall of 2002. But, as I would later come to learn, President Bush had decided to confront the Iraqi regime several months earlier. Cheney, Rumsfeld, and Wolfowitz all saw 9/11 as an opportunity to go after Saddam Hussein, take out his regime, eliminate a threat, and make the Middle East more secure. And Bush agreed.

As he told Bob Woodward in an interview late in 2003, he felt the United States first needed to take care of Afghanistan—to topple the Taliban and take away al Qaeda's safe haven there. It was a "first things first" approach, with Iraq always in the president's and his national security team's sights as part of their broad view of the war on terrorism.

When and why Bush made the decision to go to war in Iraq are probably the most fundamental questions to explore in order to understand the way his administration went about selling it to the American people.

Bush's foreign policy team had always held Saddam in low regard. They saw him as a destabilizing force in the Middle East, a region with vast oil reserves that represented a key national security interest of the United States. Even before 9/11, the Bush team advocated tougher measures against the Iraqi regime than those employed by the Clinton administration. That is why the administration had been pursuing smart sanctions through the UN and moving toward more robust military strikes if necessary to keep Saddam in line and perhaps even mortally weaken his regime.

But after 9/11, the president and his team took an even closer look at Iraq. They quickly came to view the war on terror as a broad war with many fronts, militarily and nonmilitarily—potentially including an invasion of Iraq. This was why Bush pulled Rumsfeld aside in a private one-on-one discussion in late November 2001, as author Bob Woodward confirmed with the president, and instructed him to update the Pentagon's war plans for Iraq. Bush made sure this initiative was closely held, known only by a few people who could be trusted not to leak it. But it meant that, in effect, Bush had already made the decision to go to war—even if he convinced himself it might still be avoided. In the back of his mind, he would be convinced on Iraq, as on other issues, that until he gave the final order to commence war the decision was never final. But as I would learn upon reflection, war was inevitable given the course of action the president set from the beginning.

President Bush has always been an instinctive leader more than an intellectual leader. He is not one to delve deeply into all the possible policy options—including sitting around engaging in extended debate about them—before making a choice. Rather, he chooses based on his gut and his most deeply held convictions. Such was the case with Iraq.

One core belief Bush holds is that all people have a God-given right to live in freedom. There was nothing I would ever see him talk more passionately about than this view, both publicly and privately. Another core belief is his deep disdain for tyrants like Saddam Hussein and his well-grounded belief that tyrants never give up their desire to possess the world's most deadly weapons. To the president, Saddam was an international pariah who was guilty of grave atrocities against humanity. This alone put Iraq on the president's radar screen from the start of his administration.

Bush also believes that America has an obligation to use its power to lead the rest of the world toward a better and more secure future. And he believes a leader should think and act boldly to strive for the ideal. Therefore, Bush believes it's important for his advisers to think about specific actions in terms of larger, strategic objectives—how they fit into the bigger picture of what the administration seeks to accomplish.

Finally, Bush was genuinely concerned about America being hit by terrorists again. The anthrax attacks had only heightened those concerns. Bush meant it when he said he would never forget the lesson of 9/11. He was determined to act before potential threats fully materialized.

When these beliefs were combined in the post–9/11 environment, the result was the most consequential decision of Bush's presidency. The line between the Bush national security team's preexisting desire to see Saddam gone and a new emphasis on acting against real and growing threats before they are imminent was quickly disappearing.

Did Bush's national security adviser, Condi Rice, fully calibrate for Bush's headstrong style of leadership or appreciate the need to keep his beliefs in proper check? That will be for historians to judge. But overall, Bush's foreign policy advisers played right into his thinking, doing little to question it or to cause him to pause long enough to fully consider the consequences before moving forward. And once Bush set a course of action, it was rarely questioned. That is what Bush expected and made known to his top advisers. The strategy for carrying out a policy was open for debate, but there would be no hand-wringing, no second-guessing of the policy once it was decided and set in motion.

That was certainly the case with Iraq. Bush was ready to bring about regime change, and that in all likelihood meant war. The question now was not whether, but merely when and how.

Although I didn't realize it at the time we launched our campaign to sell the war, what drove Bush toward military confrontation more than anything else was an ambitious and idealistic post–9/11 vision of transforming the Middle East through the spread of freedom. This view was grounded in a philosophy of coercive democracy, a belief that Iraq was ripe for conversion from a dictatorship into a beacon of liberty through the use of force, and a conviction that this could be achieved at nominal cost. The Iraqis were understood to be modern, forward-looking people who yearned for liberty but couldn't achieve it under the brutal, tyrannical regime of Saddam Hussein. The president and his leadership team believed that victory in Iraq could be achieved swiftly and decisively, and that the Iraqi people would then welcome and embrace freedom.

Once democracy was established in Iraq, the president and his advisers believed, it would serve as an example to other freedom-seeking reformers in the Middle East. They believed that this positive domino effect might impact neighboring Iran, which, like Iraq, had a significant number of well-educated, forward-looking citizens, particularly among younger people. Afghanistan was already on the verge of democracy. It bordered one side of Iran, and Iraq bordered another. A free Iraq would further help inspire and embolden reform-minded Iranians to rise up and change their country's governance, and a free Iraq and free Iran would remove two major threats to peace and stability in the heart of the Middle East—two parts of the "axis of evil" Bush had highlighted in his January 2002 State of the Union address. And this, in turn, would dramatically reduce global tensions and enhance a key national security interest of the United States by ensuring the long-term stability of the massive oil reserves of the Middle East. As President Bush likes to say, free countries are peaceful countries that don't go to war with one another. So bringing freedom to the Middle East would be a huge step toward building a more peaceful twenty-first-century world.

The president had long believed in advancing freedom and democracy around the world, including in the Middle East, and had articulated his commitment to this vision as early as his Warsaw speech of June 2001. At the time, however, no serious consideration was being given to a large-scale military invasion to coercively advance such thinking. But 9/11 led him to focus just such an idea on Iraq. Bush's belief in advancing liberty globally was one reason he favored a resolution of the Palestinian-Israeli issue through the creation of a free Palestinian state—another step that would be beneficial to building a freer, more stable Middle East that would be less likely to export terror. For Bush, a free Iraq became a greater priority post–9/11 because it was more quickly achievable than solving the Palestinian-Israeli dispute.

I recall a conversation I had with the president in the Oval Office a couple of years later when I was press secretary. At the time, the story line was first emerging among the media that the outcome in Iraq would determine his legacy more than anything else. I asked Bush about this. He quickly and confidently replied, "No. The war on terror will determine my legacy and how Iraq fits into that will determine my legacy." In his grand vision, a free Middle East would offer hope and opportunity to the citizens of a region that had seen too little of either. This in turn would diminish the ability of radical Islamic terrorists to foment hatred and violence, and to recruit followers from the downtrodden, poverty-stricken, and poorly educated people in the region. It would ultimately mean prevailing in the war on terror, and Bush's place in history would be cemented.

The president's dream of a democratic Middle East was shared by several key administration officials, such as Deputy Secretary of Defense Paul Wolfowitz and his neoconservative intellectual supporters. As for Dick Cheney and Donald Rumsfeld, my sense is that they were mainly interested in eliminating a threat to regional and global peace and greater economic security, and a little less enthralled by Bush's vision of a world transformed by freedom. But they didn't disapprove of the democratic vision, and if it helped strengthen the president's commitment to a military mission they supported for other reasons, they were happy to sign on.

But during the campaign for war, this transformational vision for the region was downplayed by both the president and other members of his administration. Instead, they emphasized the threat of WMD and the possible link between Iraq and terrorism. As Wolfowitz would tell *Vanity Fair* in May 2003, Bush and his national security team "settled on the one issue that everyone could agree on which was weapons of mass destruction as the core reason." Wolfowitz went on to say:

> There have always been three fundamental concerns [about Iraq]. One is weapons of mass destruction, the second is support for terrorism, the third is the criminal treatment of the Iraqi people. . . . Actually I guess you could say there's a fourth overriding one which is the connection between the first two. The third one by itself, as I think I said earlier, is a reason to help the

Iraqis but it's not a reason to put American kids' lives at risk, certainly not on the scale we did it.

He also acknowledged that the "issue about links to terrorism is the one about which there's the most disagreement within the bureaucracy."

So the decision to downplay the democratic vision as a motive for war was basically a marketing choice. Not until well into my time as press secretary did I realize that the dream of a democratic Middle East was actually the most powerful force behind President Bush's drive to war. Time and again I heard President Bush speaking with obvious passion about the blessings of freedom during his private discussions with world leaders and casual conversations we would have.

Every president wants to achieve greatness but few do. As I have heard Bush say, only a wartime president is likely to achieve greatness, in part because the epochal upheavals of war provide the opportunity for transformative change of the kind Bush hoped to achieve. In Iraq, Bush saw his opportunity to create a legacy of greatness. Intoxicated by the influence and power of America, Bush believed that a successful transformation of Iraq could be the linchpin for realizing his dream of a free Middle East.

But there was a problem here, which has become obvious to me only in retrospect—a disconnect between the president's most heartfelt objective in going to war and the publicly stated rationale for that war. Bush and his advisers knew that the American people would almost certainly not support a war launched primarily for the ambitious purpose of transforming the Middle East.

There has always been a strong isolationist streak in America, and a resistance among Americans to committing troops into combat unless absolutely necessary. Most citizens today understand that our superpower status, achieved through our great wealth, our global influence, our military might, and our role as the foremost democracy, means that the United States needs to play a responsible leadership role in the world. But by the same token, we are a peace-loving people who are not interested in global conquest or imperial might. Instead, we want to take care of our own interests and needs at home, engaging in peaceful trade and friendly competition with other nations, and using our military strength not to reform other nations but to protect our own interests and those of our closest allies when they are directly threatened.

President Bush understands this attitude and to some extent shares it. That is why he ran for president in 2000 promising a "humble" foreign policy that would avoid the temptation of nation building and instead focus on the immediate security interests of America.

The idea of transforming the Middle East coercively contradicted this promised humility, and it would be very difficult for the president and his administration to sell to the citizens. It would provoke all kinds of debates that might not be easy to win—and that in the aftermath of the invasion in Iraq have now received more attention. Was it realistic to think about transforming a country like Iraq with an entrenched regime from tyranny into democracy primarily through military force? Were the peoples and civic institutions of Iraq fully ready to support self-rule? What kinds of sustained military presence and intervention would be required to maintain stability during a time of governmental or civil upheaval? What role would Islamic fundamentalism play in the newly constituted regime? What about the long-standing ethnic and religious tensions just below the surface in this tightly controlled country in the region? And how could we be sure that the new democratically elected government in Iraq would be pro-American and ready to live in peace with its neighbor (and American ally) Israel? The answers to these questions are not easily addressed, and require careful consideration and thoughtful planning.

Rather than open this Pandora's box, the administration chose a different path—not employing out-and-out deception but shading the truth; downplaying the major reason for going to war and emphasizing a lesser motivation that could arguably be dealt with in other ways (such as intensified diplomatic pressure); trying to make the WMD threat and the Iraqi connection to terrorism appear just a little more certain, a little less questionable, than they were; quietly ignoring or disregarding some of the crucial caveats in the intelligence and minimizing evidence that pointed in the opposite direction; using innuendo and implication to encourage Americans to believe as fact some things that were unclear and possibly false (such as the idea that Saddam had an active nuclear weapons program) and other things that were overplayed or completely wrong (such as implying Saddam might have an operational relationship with al Qaeda).

When you mount a campaign, you aim at deploying your strongest arguments. It's a bit like the strategy a courtroom lawyer uses. He doesn't worry about acknowledging the holes in his case or the valid points against his own arguments. He leaves that to the lawyers on the other side. Instead, he focuses purely on his most compelling arguments, even if this means presenting a one-sided picture of the case. That's his job. The search for ultimate truth is in other hands—those of the judge and the jury.

And that is the spirit in which the Bush administration approached the campaign for war. The goal was to win the debate, to get Congress and the public to support the decision to confront Saddam. In the pursuit of that goal, embracing a high level of candor and honesty about the potential war—its larger objectives, its likely costs, and its possible risks—came a distant second.

IN PART TO LAY THE GROUNDWORK for broadening the war on terror beyond Afghanistan and pursuing coercive democracy in Iraq, the president outlined a new doctrine of preemption during his commencement address at West Point in early June. I accompanied him on the trip. Among other things, Bush said:

> The gravest danger to freedom lies at the perilous crossroads of radicalism and technology. When the spread of chemical and biological and nuclear weapons, along with ballistic missile technology—when that occurs, even weak states and small groups could attain a catastrophic power to strike great nations. Our enemies have declared this very intention, and have been caught seeking these terrible weapons. They want the capability to blackmail us, or to harm us, or to harm our friends—and we will oppose them with all our power.
>
> For much of the last century, America's defense relied on the Cold War doctrines of deterrence and containment. In some cases, those strategies still apply. But new threats also require new thinking. Deterrence—the promise of massive retaliation against nations—means nothing against shadowy terrorist networks with no nation or citizens to defend. Containment is not possible when unbalanced dictators with weapons of mass destruction can deliver those weapons on missiles or secretly provide them to terrorist allies.
>
> We cannot defend America and our friends by hoping for the best. We cannot put our faith in the word of tyrants, who solemnly sign non-proliferation treaties, and then systemically break them. If we wait for threats to fully materialize, we will have waited too long.
>
> Homeland defense and missile defense are part of stronger security, and they're essential priorities for America. Yet the war on terror will not be won

on the defensive. We must take the battle to the enemy, disrupt his plans, and confront the worst threats before they emerge. In the world we have entered, the only path to safety is the path of action. And this nation will act.

The *New York Times* described this address as "a toughly worded speech that seemed aimed at preparing Americans for a potential war with Iraq." It was. Just as we'd sought to shape and manipulate sources of public opinion to our advantage in order to pass tax cuts and education reform, and would later do the same in our attempt to transform Social Security, now we were setting the conditions for selling military confrontation with Iraq.

This doctrine of preemption would become a cornerstone of the White House's new national security strategy that would be released in mid- to late September of that same year. Bush was now lowering the bar for engaging in preemptive war, a step that might have been more widely viewed as radical had it occurred prior to 9/11. The doctrine unambiguously stated that while the United States would always proceed deliberately and carefully weigh the consequences of actions, it would not hesitate to use force if necessary to pre-empt not just an "imminent" threat but a "grave and gathering" one if need be. It was based on the assumption that waiting for a threat to become immi-nent before acting would likely mean that we would respond too late. And this new principle encoded in our new national security strategy was clearly aimed in part at paving the way to removing Saddam Hussein from power by force.

Over that summer of 2002, top Bush aides had outlined a strategy for carefully orchestrating the coming campaign to aggressively sell the war. As far as I know, no one objected to the plan; it had consensus support from the president's foreign policy team and senior advisers. In the permanent cam-paign era, it was all about manipulating sources of public opinion to the pres-ident's advantage.

Of course, I didn't see it that way at the time. Like most if not all of those involved, I viewed it as the way things were done to advance the broader agenda—simply part of the way Washington governed. I didn't pause to think about the potential consequences of our campaign to manipulate the public debate. When you are caught up in the intense day-to-day experience of the White House and Washington your focus is on winning the daily battles, which makes it extremely difficult to step back and have a clear-eyed perspec-tive on the broader meaning of it all.

In *The Permanent Campaign,* contributor Hugh Heclo writes about the danger of such an approach:

> Peace and prosperity can deceive, but wartime pressures distill into their clearest essence the dangers of conflating political campaigning and governing. Government-sponsored propaganda campaigns abound under modern conditions of total war. It is disastrous, however, to confuse the propaganda campaign with the realities of the war-making campaign. Failure to govern on the basis of the truths of the situation, as best they can be known, is a sure route to eventual disaster for the governed and rulers alike. History suggests that one major reason the Western democracies were better governed in World War II than their opponents was that their leaders brought their people into the truth of governing the war effort and did not merely campaign to raise morale. While fascist dictators fell into the trap of believing propaganda campaigns they conducted with their own people, leaders such as Roosevelt and Churchill—even if in very general ways—told citizens about the hard truths of their situation. In his first war report to the nation on December 9, 1941, for example, President Roosevelt not only told the people, "So far, all the news has been bad." He also told them, "It will not only be a long war, it will be a hard war." There would be shortages: "We shall have to give up many things entirely." FDR said that he would not tell the people that there would be sacrifices ahead. He said instead that there would be the "privilege" of suffering.

Today, the fatal flaws of the administration's strategy are apparent. Bush's team confused the political propaganda campaign with the realities of the war-making campaign. We were more focused on creating a sense of gravity and urgency about the threat from Saddam Hussein than governing on the basis of the truths of the situation.

As soon as Bush decided to confront Iraq, the groundwork for a public campaign began to be laid. The new doctrine on preemption was part of the elaborate effort. So was the gradual ratcheting up of the rhetoric from late 2001 into 2002. Before 9/11, our rhetoric about Iraq had focused on warning Saddam Hussein not to develop weapons of mass destruction, while the policy centered on containing him with enhanced sanctions. In the first few weeks after 9/11, advisers still talked about the need for Saddam Hussein to let inspectors back into Iraq. Vice President Cheney even told Tim Russert on *Meet the Press* on September 16, 2001, that "Saddam Hussein's bottled up at this point," and he acknowledged that there was no evidence linking Saddam to 9/11. But by late November, the president was not ruling out military action against Iraq and he was saying that Iraq would be held accountable if it was found to be developing WMD. When Cheney returned to *Meet the Press* in early December, he raised the possibility that Iraq had been involved in the 9/11 attacks by citing a report—later to be discounted—that a high-ranking Iraqi intelligence official had met with Mohamed Atta, the leader of the 9/11 hijackers, in April 2001. And Cheney now was saying unequivocally that Saddam "has aggressively pursued the development of additional weapons of mass destruction" since 1998.

At times, the media stoked the controversy. Before citing one of the terrorists involved in the 1993 World Trade Center bombing as an example, during the same December interview with Cheney, Tim Russert said, "What we do know is that Iraq is harboring terrorists." Then he asked Cheney, "If they're harboring terrorists, why not go in and get them?"

In the early months of 2002, the groundwork continued to be laid. By February, Condi Rice was citing the need for a serious response to a regime like Iraq that pursues WMD. Pushing the envelope of credibility, Cheney was asserting that Iraq had "a robust set of programs to develop their own weapons of mass destruction," that "we know [Saddam] has been actively and aggressively doing everything he can to enhance his capabilities," and raising Iraq's "links and ties" to terrorists. Cheney also suggested that if "aggressive action" were required, the public would support it.

In March, the president sent Cheney to the Middle East "to consult with friends and allies" in the region about Iraq. Before Cheney's return, the president asserted that Iraq was "a nation that has weapons of mass destruction. This is a nation run by a man who is willing to kill his own people by using chemical weapons; a man who won't let inspectors into the country; a man who's obviously got something to hide. And he is a problem, and we're going to deal with him. But the first stage is to consult with our allies and friends, and that's exactly what we're doing."

After meeting with Bush upon his return, Cheney said the leaders he met with "are as concerned as we are when they see the work that [Saddam] has done to develop chemical and biological weapons, and his pursuit of nuclear weapons; the past history that we all know about, in terms of his having used chemicals." Cheney added:

> If you haven't seen it, there's a devastating piece in this week's *New Yorker* magazine on the 1988 use by Saddam Hussein of chemical weapons against the Kurds. If the article is accurate—and I've asked for verification, if we can find it—he ran a campaign against the Kurds for 17 months, and bombed literally 200 villages and killed thousands and thousands of Iraqis with chemical weapons. That's not the kind of man we want to see develop even more deadly capacity—for example nuclear weapons.

Bush later added, "When we say we're going to do something, we mean it; that we are resolved to fight the war on terror; this isn't a short-term strategy for us; that we understand history has called us into action, and we're not going to miss this opportunity to make the world more peaceful and more free."

A few days later, Cheney pushed the envelope even more by bringing up the most fearful scenario of a madman seeking nuclear weapons. "This is a man of great evil, as the president said," Cheney said on CNN's *Late Edition*. "And he is actively pursuing nuclear weapons at this time, and we think that's cause for concern for us and for everybody in the region."

The heightened rhetoric on Iraq, including unequivocal statements that made things sound more certain than was known, continued into the fall campaign push, when it would be amplified to a much greater and sustained degree. In late August 2002, at the Veterans of Foreign Wars convention in Nashville, Cheney said, "Simply stated, there is no doubt that Saddam Hussein now has weapons of mass destruction. There is no doubt he is amassing them to use against our friends, against our allies, and against us."

The relationship between Vice President Cheney and President Bush has always been clouded in mystery to some extent. But it is a very close one. The two spend considerable time together in private meetings, their discussions largely kept confidential. But it's obvious that, back in 2002, Bush knew the increasingly strong language Cheney was employing on Iraq. The vice president can lean a little more forward in his rhetoric than the president. In the 2004 reelection campaign, for instance, Cheney would be the attack dog who went after Kerry a little more pointedly than the president could. It is clear to me now, looking back, that some of the same strategy was used in the Iraq campaign.

However, the strong language used by Cheney may also have been due to the vice president's habit of being unable to stay on message. At times, he simply could not contain his deep-seated certitude, even arrogance—to the detriment of the president. Such was the case at the VFW speech, when Cheney essentially said that having UN inspectors go into Iraq would be useless or even misleading. Such was also the case when Cheney said, just before the invasion, that "my belief is we will, in fact, be greeted as liberators." That was off script, and it helped suggest a rose-colored view of Iraq that would prove harmful to the president later.

As Bush prepared to make the case for war at the UN, Condi Rice alluded to the nuclear threat from Iraq in stark terms on September 8, 2002. "The problem here is that there will always be some uncertainty about how quickly [Saddam] can acquire nuclear weapons. But we don't want the smoking gun to be a mushroom cloud."

The rhetoric in our campaign to sell war would continue to grow more certain and more grave. The nuclear threat and Iraq's contacts with al Qaeda became increasingly central to the talking points, helping to create a needed sense of urgency for dealing with the grave and gathering threat from Iraq.

Contrary to Cheney's view of the UN route being useless, the president agreed with other advisers that it was important to show he was exhausting all diplomatic options. Pursuing a new UN resolution that included an immediate call for Saddam to come clean and let inspectors back in was vital to building public support. Even more important for the American public was to have strong, bipartisan congressional backing. It was all part of the campaign. Americans would be much more likely to support war if they felt Bush had pursued and exhausted diplomatic options and if Congress provided strong bipartisan approval.

Even the Cheney-driven White House effort to provide all Americans with the smallpox vaccine that was being pushed publicly in the latter weeks of 2002 played into the environment of fear about the Iraq WMD threat. It seems to me a little cynical to suggest that its timing was calculated, but it did not hurt the broader campaign to sell the war.

Since I was just the deputy press secretary at the time, I was neither integrally involved in nor fully briefed about all the plans for selling the war. But I would have a role at times during the buildup to war.

On Friday, September 20, the same week as the president's trip to Iowa and the news about Larry Lindsey's war costs estimate, Bush hosted a meeting with Republican governors in the State Dining Room at the White House. The governors had come to town for their association's annual fall fund-raising reception the night before. While Ari held the morning press gaggle, I represented him at the meeting. With the media excluded from the meeting, President Bush—just two years removed from being a governor himself—was conspicuously candid with his former colleagues, now trusted friends and political allies. His remarks focused on homeland security and, in particular, Iraq. And Bush's forthrightness about his thinking and approach on Iraq was revealing.

The president talked about the capture of Ramzi Binalshibh by Pakistani authorities nine days earlier. A key member of al Qaeda, Binalshibh had been on the FBI's top five list of wanted terrorists for his role in planning 9/11 and other terrorist attacks. "We'll knock them down one by one," Bush said. "As for bin Laden, we don't know where he is, but he has been diminished."

Then he turned to Iraq. "It is important to know that Iraq is an extension of the war on terror," Bush stated. "In the international debate, we are starting to shift the burden of guilt to the guilty. The international community is risk averse. But I assure you I am going to stay plenty tough." Bush said he was reaching out to world leaders to build support for war, noting he'd spoken to President Putin of Russia earlier that same day.

Bush went on to talk about his favorite theme, "the importance of promoting liberty and individual freedom around the world." He held out hope for a peaceful transition in Iraq: "I believe regime change can occur if we have strong, robust inspections. Saddam Hussein is a guy who is liable to have his head show up on a platter," if enough outside pressure was brought to bear on him.

Expressing how deeply he despised Saddam, Bush added, "He is a brutal, ugly, repugnant man who needs to go. He is also paranoid. This is a guy who killed his own security guards recently. I would like to see him gone peacefully. But if I unleash the military, I promise you it will be swift and decisive."

He warned the governors not to fall into traps set by the opposition. "Don't fall into the argument that there is no one to replace Saddam Hussein," said Bush. "And our planning will make sure there is no oil disruption; we are looking at all options to enhance oil flow."

"Military force is my last option, but it may be the only choice," Bush stated. "I'm gonna make a prediction. Write this down. Afghanistan and Iraq will lead that part of the world to democracy. They are going to be the catalyst to change the Middle East and the world."

One of the first questions from the governors was about recent comments by the German justice minister comparing Bush to Hitler. Germany was days away from national elections. And despite giving his word to the president previously that he would not stand in the way of Bush's plans or do anything to undermine them, German Chancellor Schroeder, along with his cabinet, had made speaking out publicly in opposition to the war in Iraq a central part of their party's strategy for winning.

"I won't put up with that crap," Bush replied tersely (being compared to Hitler). There was nothing that angered the president more than a world leader who violated private assurances he made. And I would later hear Bush say as much to a number of world leaders in private, sometimes using Schroeder as an example. If Bush gave his word to a foreign leader, that leader could take it to the bank—and Bush expected the same in return.

When asked about building public support for war, Bush said, "There is a case to be made, and I have to make it. Iraq is a threat we will deal with in a logical way. If we have to act, my choices are really three. One, someone kills him [Saddam Hussein]. Two, the [Iraqi] population rises up and overthrows him. Three, military action."

One governor asked Bush about the timing for military action. "If we are going to go in militarily, it will be as soon as possible. It may take a while to resolve at the UN. This is a dangerous time for us [on the political front]. I worry that time will dissipate the UN speech," he added, stressing the need to press ahead urgently so as not to lose any momentum. He also noted that the mission would be to topple Saddam and change the regime, stating that his two sons and top generals would be removed as well.

A few minutes later, Bush said, "If Saddam Hussein gets his hands on nuclear weapons, it will change the world. If he does it during my term, I will have failed."

"There is nothing more risky than letting Saddam Hussein develop weapons of mass destruction," Bush commented in response to another question. "We will deal with him. This is not about inspections. It is about weapons of mass destruction and disarming the regime of them. The inspections are a means to an end. He is an evil man. I have seen a video of Saddam Hussein himself pulling the trigger on a man who didn't like his policies. He killed his two son-in-laws."

The president concluded the meeting by stating that "it is a tough decision to commit troops. I assure you, though, if we have to go [into Iraq], we will be tough and swift and it will be violent so troops can move very quickly. During the Gulf War, it took ten sorties to destroy two targets. Now we can fly one sortie to destroy two targets. If we go, we will use the full force and might of the United States military. Now if it looks like he is losing his grip on power, I am confident he will be gone. International pressure could help get it done. You see I believe in the power of freedom." He also stressed that it was important for a leader to "speak clearly" and to be "tough, credible, strong, and forceful." Then he expressed his belief that "freedom is a universal principle. We believe everybody matters, not just Americans."

Later, at the press stakeout outside the main entrance to the West Wing, Governor John Rowland of Connecticut, then-chairman of the Republican Governor's Association, called the meeting a "heart to heart" on Iraq. But it was also a frank strategy powwow between the leader of a campaign and some important members of his team—a collection of local politicians who could play a crucial role in helping to generate popular support for the decision to invade.

In early October, Bush delivered a major speech outlining the threat in Cincinnati, Ohio. Later in October, Congress overwhelmingly and in strong bipartisan fashion passed a joint resolution authorizing the use of military force in Iraq. This strong congressional backing strengthened our public case and convinced many Americans of the necessity of using force against Iraq. If members of Congress supported the president so strongly, he must be on the right course.

In mid-November 2002, just before the start of debate on a new Iraq resolution at the United Nations, my predecessor, Ari Fleischer, got married and went on his honeymoon. I assumed his responsibilities while he was away. Two days later the UN Security Council passed Resolution 1441 stating that it was "a final opportunity" for Saddam Hussein to come clean fully and unconditionally or "face serious consequences." For twelve days, I would be on the front lines of the political propaganda campaign in the march to war—conducting press briefings, attending presidential meetings, and sitting in on some top-level discussions.

The White House Iraq Group (WHIG) had been set up in the summer of 2002 to coordinate the marketing of the war to the public. It would continue as a strategic communications group after the invasion had toppled Saddam's regime, and I would participate in it once I became White House press secretary. As deputy press secretary, I filled in a couple of times for my predecessor when he could not attend—including during that period in November.

Some critics have suggested that sinister plans were discussed at the WHIG meetings to deliberately mislead the public. Not so. There were plenty of discussions about how to set the agenda and influence the narrative, but there was no conspiracy to intentionally deceive. Instead, there were straightforward discussions of communications strategies and messaging grounded in the familiar tactics of the permanent campaign.

At the meeting I attended in November, shortly after passage of the new UN resolution, the discussion centered on one of the key messages we wanted to get across at the time—the need for a zero tolerance policy toward the Iraqi regime, accepting no evasion or deceptions by Saddam Hussein. The UN resolution had called for full and unconditional cooperation and compliance, and I would emphasize that message from the podium. It was a message the president had also emphasized during a meeting with UN Secretary-General Kofi Annan I attended at the time.

Though I sensed we were on the verge of war, I didn't fully appreciate how clearly yet subtly our messages demonstrated that Bush had been set on regime change from the earliest days of his decision to confront Iraq. The UN speech he gave in September had been an ultimatum—either the UN acts to disarm Saddam Hussein or the United States will. The zero tolerance message was a further sign of how determined the president was to topple the regime by force. Saddam was never going to come completely clean. His power was grounded in his brutality and in his ability to portray the regime as stronger than it was to intimidate the populace and potential enemies like Iran. The zero tolerance policy and the new "last chance" resolution gave Bush plenty of room to maneuver and plausible justification for his policy of regime change.

Of course, Saddam Hussein made it relatively easy for the Bush administration to argue that it had no choice but to invade. Although UN weapons inspectors were allowed into Iraq, their access to key sites was impeded, the records they were given were incomplete and inaccurate, and the inspectors themselves stated that, under the circumstances, it would take months for them to determine whether or not Saddam had complied with UN resolutions. Most people observing the situation soon concluded, "Saddam is playing his old tricks. He obviously has something to hide. He was given a final chance. It was time to act." And so we acted.

President Bush managed the crisis in a way that almost guaranteed that the use of force would become the only feasible option. He did this backing it with the ultimatum in his UN speech of September, and by ordering a massive buildup of American arms and military forces in the region, which, for logistical reasons, couldn't remain in the area indefinitely without being used. It's ironic. One of the most important rules that any press secretary must follow is, *Never tie the president's hands unnecessarily.* That is, never make any statement that restricts the president's freedom to change course or select a particular option in the future. But during the buildup to war, the president's advisers allowed his own hands to be tied, putting Bush in a position where *avoiding* conflict was more difficult than launching it.

By creating this enormous momentum for war, the president and his advisers achieved several things. He made the job of his political opponents extraordinarily difficult, putting those who opposed the war in the position of arguing against what was almost a fait accompli. He trapped Saddam Hussein in a shrinking box, making it less and less acceptable for the dictator to continue to temporize and play games with the inspectors. He forced other countries—including those, like Russia and France, that had sometimes sided with Iraq—to make hard decisions as to whether or not they would permit a U.S.-led invasion absent a clear imminent threat.

Most important, the White House forestalled any debate about the fundamental goals and long-term plans for such an invasion. By pushing so hard on the WMD issue, reducing the larger issue of the future of the Middle East into a short-term emergency threat that must be dealt with *now*, the president and his advisers avoided having to discuss the big issues of what would happen after the invasion. Who would rule Iraq? How would the region respond? How long would the United States have to remain on the ground? How would tensions among the nation's ethnic and religious groups be resolved?

Few of these questions ever appeared on the national radar screen during the run-up to war. But they would come back to haunt the president, and the nation, in years to come, when it became clear that the stated rationales for war—the WMD threat and Iraq's link to terrorism—were less than convincing.

The lack of candor underlying the campaign for war would severely undermine the president's entire second term in office.

WHEN BUSH WAS MAKING UP his mind to pursue regime change in Iraq, it is clear that his national security team did little to slow him down, to help him fully understand the tinderbox he was opening and the potential risks in doing so. I know the president pretty well. I believe that, if he had been given a crystal ball in which he could have foreseen the costs of war—more than 4,000 American troops killed, 30,000 injured, and tens of thousands of innocent Iraqi citizens dead—he would have never made the decision to invade, despite what he might say or feel he has to say publicly today.

And though no one has a crystal ball, it's not asking too much that a well-considered understanding of the circumstances and history of Iraq and the Middle East should have been brought into the decision-making process. The responsibility to provide this understanding belonged to the president's advisers, and they failed to fulfill it. Secretary of State Colin Powell was apparently the only adviser who even tried to raise doubts about the wisdom of war. The rest of the foreign policy team seemed to be preoccupied with regime change or, in the case of Condi Rice, seemingly more interested in accommodating the president's instincts and ideas than in questioning them or educating him.

An even more fundamental problem was the way his advisers decided to pursue a political propaganda campaign to sell the war to the American people. It was all part of the way the White House operated and Washington functioned, and no one seemed to see any problem with using such an approach on an issue as grave as war. A pro-war campaign might have been more acceptable had it been accompanied by a high level of candor and honesty, but it was not. Most of the arguments used—especially those stated in prepared remarks by the president and in forums like Powell's presentation at the UN Security Council in February 2003—were carefully vetted and capable of being substantiated. But as the campaign accelerated, caveats and qualifications were downplayed or dropped altogether. Contradictory intelligence was largely ignored or simply disregarded. Evidence based on high confidence from the intelligence community was lumped together with intelligence of lesser confidence. A nuclear threat was added to the biological and chemical threats to create a greater sense of gravity and urgency. Support for terrorism was given greater weight by playing up a dubious al Qaeda connection to Iraq. When it was all packaged together, the case constituted a "grave and gathering danger" that needed to be dealt with urgently.

Some of Bush's advisers believed that, given Saddam Hussein's history, it was only prudent to suspect the worst. And some, like Cheney, Rumsfeld, and Wolfowitz, were evidently pursuing their own agendas.

The most significant of these personal agendas was probably Cheney's, given his closeness to the president and his influence over him. It is also the agenda that is most likely to remain unknown, because of Cheney's personality and his penchant for secrecy. He may have been driven by a desire to finish the job he started as defense secretary in 1991, when the United States defeated Saddam Hussein and pushed his troops out of Kuwait but stopped short of advancing to Baghdad to end his rule. Cheney was also heavily involved in economic and energy policy. He might well have viewed the removal of Saddam Hussein as an opportunity to give America more influence over Iraq's oil reserves, thereby benefiting our national and economic security.

In any case, it's obviously a problem when forceful personalities like Cheney, Rumsfeld, and Wolfowitz pursue their individual interests and push them on the president. As the president's top foreign policy adviser, National Security Adviser Condi Rice should have stood up to those more experienced, strong-viewed advisers rather than deferring to them. However, my later experiences with Condi led me to believe she was more interested in figuring out where the president stood and just carrying out his wishes while expending only cursory effort on helping him understand all the considerations and potential consequences.

It goes to an important question that critics have raised about the president. Is Bush intellectually incurious or, as some assert, actually stupid? The latter accusation seems to me a sad reflection on today's political climate, where name-calling and emotional rhetoric get more attention than reasoned and civil discourse. Bush is plenty smart enough to be president. But as I've noted, his leadership style is based more on instinct than deep intellectual debate. His intellectual curiosity tends to be centered on knowing what he needs in order to effectively articulate, advocate, and defend his policies. Bush keenly recognizes the role of marketing and selling policy in today's governance, so such an approach is understandable to some degree. But his advisers needed to recognize how potentially harmful his instinctual leadership and limited intellectual curiosity can be when it comes to crucial decisions, and in light of today's situation, it has become reasonable to question his judgment. The fact that he has been portrayed as not bright is unfortunate, but it's a result of his own mistakes—which could have been prevented had his beliefs been properly vetted and challenged by his top advisers. Bush's top advisers, especially those on his national security team, allowed the president to be put in the position he is in today. His credibility has been shattered and his public standing seemingly irreparably damaged.

The permanent campaign mentality bears some of the blame. Throughout the campaign, building public support by making the strongest possible case for war was the top priority, regardless of whether or not it was the most intellectually honest approach to the issue of war and peace. Message discipline sometimes meant avoiding forthrightness—for example, evasively dismissing questions about the risks of war as "speculation," since the decision to go to war supposedly had not yet been made. In Washington's hyperpartisan atmosphere, candor was viewed as too risky; critics could easily twist and manipulate words to their advantage, undermining the well-planned strategy.

In the end, of course, President Bush bears ultimate responsibility for the invasion of Iraq. He made the decision to invade, and he signed off on a strategy for selling the war that was less than candid and honest. An issue as grave as war must be dealt with openly, forthrightly, and honestly. The American people, and especially our troops and their families, deserve nothing less.

The controversy over how Bush took the nation to war was soon to explode. A permanent state of suspicion and partisan warfare would start to take hold. An enormous effort had been put into selling the war and the detailed planning for toppling the regime of Saddam Hussein. But the same kind of energy and resources were not invested in planning for the postregime occupation period. The insufficient planning and preparation would only become visible in the aftermath as an insurgency took hold, terrorists seized the opportunity to inflict terrible harm, American military casualties rose, and the Iraqi people suffered a seemingly endless cycle of violence.

The war would become an increasingly challenging problem for the administration. Having created an atmosphere of suspicion and partisan warfare, the White House would be unable to call on bipartisan support when it was needed most—for the sake of the war and our troops who were called to carry it out. Questions of deliberate deception about the case for war would hover over it all. And the truth would be caught in the political crossfire.

But as we entered May 2003, with the initial phase of the war having been conducted successfully and the president standing tall with the American public, from inside the bubble I was unable to foresee the coming political wars. Nor did I realize that I was about to be offered the experience of a lifetime that would place me on the front lines of the coming battles.

9

BECOMING WHITE
HOUSE PRESS SECRETARY

THE CALL THAT WEEKEND CAME as a surprise. Ari phoned me at home to let me know that he would be announcing that Monday—May 19, 2003—that he would be resigning his position as press secretary effective the middle of July. The reason was simple: burnout.

Only a few months earlier, Ari had volunteered in one of our casual conversations that he was planning on staying put for a while. At the time, he still seemed full of energy and enthusiasm for the job. I know he really enjoyed conducting briefings, and sparring with the press under the klieg lights. But he had served in the position through 9/11, the war in Afghanistan, and what at that moment appeared to be a war in Iraq headed toward a successful conclusion. Standing in front of a "Mission Accomplished" banner on board the USS *Lincoln* off the coast of San Diego, the president had only a couple of weeks earlier declared, "Major combat operations in Iraq have ended. In the battle of Iraq, the United States and our allies have prevailed." Ari had already been through a lot, serving as the administration's chief spokesperson during some very tumultuous times.

Ari was also a newlywed, having been married the preceding November. I couldn't fully appreciate it then, but in subsequent years I would come to learn just how quickly the continual daily wear and tear can sneak up on a press secretary. We all have a limit on the number of times we can recharge our batteries, and Ari had reached his.

During our conversation, Ari said he'd recommended that I replace him. I told Ari he'd served the president well and would be missed, and I expressed my deepest appreciation to him.

After we hung up, it started to sink in that I might soon be thrust into the spotlight Ari had occupied. I didn't know for sure, of course. But I felt I'd shown myself to be completely loyal to Bush. He trusted me. Our relationship was strong. I'd demonstrated that I knew the tone the president liked to set, and I had a keen understanding of the way he thought and the principles on which he made decisions—all reasons Karen Hughes had thought I was a good complement to Ari, with his Washington experience. I'd also shown I could do the job the president wanted me to do on and off the podium. I'd filled in for Ari seamlessly at various times, and when he was away, getting married, I'd assumed all his duties and conducted several back-to-back briefings over an extended period.

And I had shown I knew how to handle tragedies and crisis situations, most recently on Saturday, February 1, 2003. Ari was out of town that weekend when the space shuttle *Columbia* broke apart upon reentry into the earth's atmosphere, killing seven courageous astronauts, six Americans and one Israeli. At such times, I understood it was especially important to provide the press with facts and information for history's sake and so they could report the news fully and accurately to the American people.

After receiving the phone call from the situation room that morning, I immediately headed into the office. I was there to meet the president when he returned from Camp David to address the nation, and I shadowed his movements, taking careful notes. I will never forget standing in the Oval Office as he spoke by phone to the families of the astronauts, who were all gathered in a conference room at Kennedy Space Center. None of us could imagine what they were going through, but we knew it was beyond painful. All I could do was pray for them in my own personal and private way, as I am sure many others in the room and across the country were doing.

The president offered the family members his sincerest condolences and prayers, calling it "a tragic day for America." When the call concluded, the president had to step out of the Oval Office into his private area ever so briefly. He was greatly pained by the call to the families and needed a few seconds to gather himself before heading into a briefing on the tragedy in the nearby Roosevelt Room.

Later that afternoon, following the president's remarks to the nation, I gaggled with reporters and provided the press with facts and information from the president's day. Just as on 9/11, all I could think was, why?—why did it have to happen?—and how much I would have preferred never to have had to deal with it. But this was the reality of White House life: we always had to be ready for the unexpected.

Everything seemed to happen fast after Ari announced his departure. By the middle of the week of May 19, I had met with Chief of Staff Andy Card to discuss expectations on both sides. On Sunday, I spoke with the president. Bush had hosted his close ally, Japanese Prime Minister Koizumi, at his home in Crawford on Thursday and Friday and then spent the weekend there. During the return flight aboard Air Force One, he officially offered me the job.

"I told everyone there was no need to consider anyone else," the president said. "We had our man as far as I was concerned."

"I am honored, sir," I responded. "I will do my best to serve you and the country well."

"You should feel honored," the president agreed. "There are not very many people who get to say they were White House press secretary. It is a pretty small fraternity."

It had been a whirlwind week for me. My life had changed so quickly, and with my regular duties to tend to I had little time to let it all sink in completely and to think through all the necessary, longer-term considerations I should be exploring. The president and I knew each other well enough. I knew what the president expected, I knew what the job entailed, and I knew how he wanted me to do it. But I did want to make sure of a couple of things.

One was access to Bush. When I asked the president about that, he reassured me. "Absolutely," the president said. "I know you need that to do your job. You will have access to me anytime you need to see me."

The second was access to important meetings. I wanted to make sure I was included in all the presidential meetings—from policy briefings to world leader meetings—that Ari had attended. That, too, was not a problem, the president said. I had thought about going further and asking about a couple of meetings that Ari had not been included in. I probably should have asked, but I didn't, deciding that those might be more effectively pursued gradually through Andy or other avenues.

I knew the president's mind-set when it came to the press secretary. He did not want his spokesman stepping beyond the talking points or making news unnecessarily or unexpectedly. Part of it was based on Bush's personal preference of making the news on his own time frame, not letting the media control the agenda. Part of it was based on his distrust of the national media, which he believed harbored a liberal bias against Republicans. Knowing how closely the press secretary has to interact with the press all day, the president wanted him to have access to necessary information. But his definition of "necessary" would keep the press secretary on a relatively short leash.

Early in his presidency, in a comment noted by the White House press corps, the president had unintentionally undermined Ari by saying there would be times when he would tell Ari he was *not* going to let him know something. When that occurred, he added, he would expect Ari not to question it. Eventually, many of the president's key advisers would come to share the same attitude.

But everything was happening at once and I had little time to think about the job offer from a selfish perspective—to consider whether accepting the job was in my own best interest. I'd long ago fully committed myself to serving Bush. My first instinct, as a strong believer in public service, was to view his latest call for me to serve as his chief spokesman not just as a great personal opportunity but as a duty. I've also always been one who believes that God opens doors for a reason. That, I felt, was happening now. I had never plotted out a course to become the White House press secretary. I had simply stepped through the doors that had been opened to me, and now they had led to this moment. The reason for the invitation to enter this particular door might be beyond my comprehension, but my faith in God and His plan for me was strong.

But it's a natural human tendency to question things, and in fact, my view of faith teaches me to do so. Once I had time to catch my breath, soon after accepting the job, my reservations about going through with it became so serious that I delayed the formal announcement until the latter part of June. My excuse was that I wanted time to prepare quietly outside the glare of the spotlight. Once it was known publicly that I would be the new press secretary, that opportunity would be gone. But I also used this time to consult with some of my most trusted advisers—my political mentor, my mother, my wise older brother Mark (who has good common sense despite his dual doctoral status as a Ph.D and M.D.) and the newest member of my inner circle, my fiancée Jill (I had proposed at the end of March).

They all encouraged me to go forward, calling it a great opportunity. They advised me to do it for a couple of years and see how it went; in any case, the experience would be extraordinarily beneficial.

But my doubts persisted. I wondered whether I really wanted to move into the spotlight of Washington, with all its ugliness and pettiness. Having grown up with a mother in politics, I'd never cared for the bitterness that crept into the discourse, nowhere more so than in Washington. Did I really want to put myself—and now Jill—under the political microscope? The insults and name-calling wouldn't bother me as much as the barbs aimed at Mom when I was a kid. Maybe because of that boyhood experience, I knew that even the most hate-filled, mean-spirited attacks wouldn't faze me. But would it really be worth it? Something about the situation nagged at my gut.

The big question was whether I would have enough freedom, flexibility, and access to do the job effectively and be the kind of press secretary I hoped to be. Would I be privy to the *real* rationales behind *every* important administration decision? Would I be permitted to witness the interplay between political pressure and the national interest that helped to shape policy decisions—or would I simply be presented with the final product and told to sell it, willy-nilly? Would I be able to consistently help shape the administration's message and influence it in the direction of transparency and candor, or would I be kept in the dark at times?

At the time it was hard to explain this to the people I looked to for personal advice. You had to have lived these issues inside the Bush White House. Only today do I fully appreciate it and realize I should have done more to change it at the time—not gradually, *after* I started, but *before* I accepted the offer.

I was assured I'd have necessary access to the president and to most presidential meetings, which meant I'd witness the shaping of many of the policies I'd be expected to defend. This was standard treatment for a White House press secretary, and it was important. A press secretary had to be in the know to be effective.

But it was also clear that there would be limits to my access. Like Ari, I would probably not be included in some key decision-making discussions, particularly some informal, very small meetings when Bush wanted information compartmentalized and restricted to as few people as possible—and not made public until later. The press secretary was excluded from "strategery" meetings. In addition, Bush did not feel the press secretary needed to be a regular invitee to National Security Council meetings. And the daily "communications meeting" in the Oval, which included the president, the vice president, Andy Card, Karl Rove, Condi Rice, and Karen Hughes (and later Dan Bartlett) also excluded the press secretary.

There were some ways for getting around some of the exclusions, though not the primary ones specifically mentioned above, although I made some effort to be included in those. Sometimes, it meant just showing up at a meeting you hadn't been invited to. Other times, it was possible to get complete and timely information from others who'd attended the meeting. And still other times, I could go directly to the president, who would either tell me what I needed to know himself or, if necessary, make a phone call to the necessary adviser. These workarounds would almost always get me the information I needed.

I also felt I might have a leg up on Ari when it came to being informed. I had a longer-standing relationship with the president grounded in our shared Texas roots. I felt well regarded and trusted by everyone else in the inner circle—perhaps more so than Ari had been. For example, when Condi Rice learned that Ari had been reading the notes from the president's calls with world leaders, she immediately took away his authority to do so. (The way around it was to just show up to the Oval during important calls and listen in to them live.) My impression was that Karen Hughes sometimes regarded Ari as a little too freewheeling at the podium. For example, there was the time Ari created a mini-press firestorm when he suggested the Clinton White House's attempt to "shoot the moon" on Middle East peace had actually resulted in more violence. I walked into the Oval to hear Karen complaining about Ari to the president in front of Condi. Ari was forced to issue a retraction later that day.

But, as I gradually came to understand, more troubling than the press secretary's access limitations was the overall mind-set of secrecy within the administration, its negative attitude toward the national media, and the limited support given to the press secretary as a result of such thinking.

For example, the president liked to compartmentalize information within the White House. There were regular meetings between the president and the vice president or Andy Card or Karl Rove that were strictly private. That was understandable—when a president and his closest advisers meet, they want to be able to speak with utmost freedom and frankness, and any third party, even a trusted member of the team, might limit that freedom. But in the Bush White House, that closed door was a little troubling. Cheney had greater power and influence than any other vice president in history, and no one really knew how extensively he wielded it. Being shut out from his thinking and from the ways he advised the president left a large black hole in my understanding of what was really going on inside the administration. The same thing happened when I wasn't filled in on some relevant decision-making that had occurred in a private one-on-one or small group setting. And being kept in the dark is an uncomfortable position for any press secretary to be in.

More broadly, I had a sense that the Bush administration gave minimal support to the role of press secretary. Few among the president's top policy advisers took a proactive stance when it came to keeping the press secretary informed about behind-the-scenes policy changes and the reasons behind them. Worse still, at times even after the press secretary got wind of an important development, getting details about it from some key advisers involved a game of twenty questions. No one charged with keeping the press and the public informed about the workings of the government should have to play such frustrating games.

Ari's frustration over the difficulty of getting information was part of the reason he'd burned out sooner than I anticipated. The job of press secretary, like other senior-level White House positions, is incredibly demanding and time-consuming. There are plenty of challenges to deal with on any given day without having to spend an inordinate amount of time trying to stay on top of things or play catch-up when the clock is ticking and a live session on camera with the press corps is just moments away. And no press secretary should have to worry about getting blindsided by the press finding out what has happened inside the White House before he does.

Over time, I realized that the reason the press secretary was treated this way had nothing to do with who occupied the position but rather was rooted in distrust of the national media. Neither the president nor most of those in his inner circle of advisers placed any great value on the national media, including the White House press corps. Andy Card once remarked that he viewed the Washington media as just another "special interest" that the White House had to deal with, much like lobbyists or trade associations. I found the remark stunning and telling.

Like many presidents, Bush regarded the press as a necessary evil or nuisance. They were a cadre of intermediaries that stood between him and the

American people, often excessively filtering the clear transmission of his messages and, at times, actively working to sabotage his administration and weaken its link to the citizenry. Decades of conservative complaints about "the liberal media," going all the way back to Spiro Agnew's diatribes against "nattering nabobs of negativism," had reinforced the assumption that the press would never give a Republican president a fair break. In part because of that sentiment, most members of the Bush White House didn't believe in providing the media with much information beyond a bare minimum of data that had been carefully scrubbed to support the president's positions and give the opposition no foothold for criticism.

To this day, I'm often asked about the "liberal media" critique. Is it true? Is the problem with Washington in part a result of the fact that left-wing journalists are, in effect, at war with conservative politicians and trying to bring them down?

My answer is always the same. It's probably true that most reporters, writers, and TV journalists are personally liberal or leftward leaning and tend to vote Democratic. Polls and surveys of media professionals bear this out. But this tilt to the left has probably become less pronounced in recent years, with the ascendancy of a wider variety of news sources, including Fox News, demonstrating the popularity and therefore the commercial viability of conservative views. And more important, everything I've seen, both as White House press secretary and as a longtime observer of the political scene and the media, suggests that any liberal bias actually has minimal impact on the way the American public is informed.

The vast majority of reporters—including those in the White House press corps—are honest, fair-minded, and professional. They try hard to tell all sides of the stories they report, and they certainly don't treat information or statements coming from a conservative administration with excessive harshness or exaggerated skepticism. And even when a bit of bias does seep through, I believe the public sees it exactly for what it is. We in the Bush administration had no difficulty in getting our messages out to the American people.

If anything, the national press corps was probably *too* deferential to the White House and to the administration in regard to the most important decision facing the nation during my years in Washington, the choice over whether to go to war in Iraq. The collapse of the administration's rationales for war, which became apparent months after our invasion, should never have come as such a surprise. The public should have been made much more aware, before the fact, of the uncertainties, doubts, and caveats that underlay the intelligence about the regime of Saddam Hussein. The administration did little to convey those nuances to the people; the press should have picked up the slack but largely failed to do so because their focus was elsewhere—on covering the march to war, instead of the necessity of war.

In this case, the "liberal media" didn't live up to its reputation. If it had, the country would have been better served.

I'll even go a step further. I'm inclined to believe that a liberal-oriented media in the United States should be viewed as a *good* thing. When I look back at the last several presidential administrations—the two Bushes, Bill Clinton, Ronald Reagan, Jimmy Carter, Gerald Ford—I see a succession of conservative/centrist leaders, either right of center or *just* left of center, who pursued mainstream policies designed to satisfy the vast bulk of middle-class American voters. All of these presidents were at least moderate on economic policy, generally pro-business in their orientation, and within the mainstream on most other issues, from foreign policy to education to the environment. And the congressional leaders they worked with were, generally speaking, from the same mold—conservative or centrist. Over the past forty years, there have been no flaming liberals in positions of greatest power in American politics.

Under these circumstances, a generally liberal or left-leaning media can serve an important, useful role. It can stand up for the interests of people and causes that get short shrift from conservative or mainstream politicians: racial and ethnic minorities, women, working people, the poor, the disenfranchised. As the old saying goes, a liberal reporter ought to take up the cause of "comforting the afflicted and afflicting the comfortable," speaking out on issues that otherwise would be neglected or ignored, exposing wrongdoing, and helping to keep the powerful in government and business honest.

Furthermore, I welcome media that are skeptical and untrusting. The more so the better—as long as they are honest and fair. Those who are in positions of power should have to continually earn the trust of the governed. They should be constantly challenged to prove their policies are right, to prove they can be trusted, and to prove they are accountable. That is the way we are more likely to get to the important, sometimes hard truths. In today's information-based society, if a media outlet or journalist goes overboard they will pay the price. I witnessed up close just how that can happen when some within CBS News let their preconceived biases infect their coverage (most notably in the scandal over Dan Rather's use of dubious documents to charge Bush with having received special treatment over his National Guard service). The handful of news people who overzealously sought to bring down the president instead brought themselves down.

So I don't agree with those who excoriate the "liberal media." As long as they do their job professionally, I have no problem with liberal reporters, and I certainly dealt with them happily enough as press secretary. The real problem with the national media is the overemphasis on controversy, the excessive focus on who is winning and who is losing in Washington, and the constant search for something or someone to pick on and attack. These bad habits too often cause the larger truths that matter most to get lost in the mix.

Most in the Bush White House, however, do not share my view about the benefit of a liberal-oriented media. And I think the concern about liberal bias helps to explain the tendency of the Bush team to build walls against the media. Unfortunately the press secretary at times found himself outside those walls as well.

Despite all these misgivings, I agreed with the advice from my circle of counselors about accepting the position of press secretary. The president had always been fully accessible and open enough with me. And I felt my relations with the rest of the inner circle were such that I could overcome the extra obstacles placed in front of me doing my job. I believed I could gradually work to remove the few obstacles I felt were particularly unnecessary. If these obstacles had been the only problem I would face on the job, it might have turned out differently.

However, by Tuesday, July 15, 2003, the day I assumed my duties as White House press secretary, I was just beginning to realize how difficult it would be to help the president overcome the biggest challenge—reversing the downward trend of his credibility and public standing.

The doubts about weapons of mass destruction in Iraq were becoming harder to suppress, not only outside the administration but also inside it. Yet many of us, including the president, were anxiously, in hindsight wishfully, clinging to the false hope that, in due time, the U.S.-led inspection team, with its large staff and vast resources, would discover Saddam's weapons—the weapons we *knew* he must have—hidden in bunkers or buried under Iraq's desert sands. The intelligence could not have been so far off the mark. Saddam had to be hiding at least some WMD somewhere in Iraq. Anything would do. This wishful thinking was why the president jumped the gun and declared that we had found the weapons in the form of two mobile biological weapons labs—only for our intelligence to conclude later that they weren't weapons labs at all.

My own doubts had begun to grow a little more acute a couple of weeks before I took center stage in the briefing room. I well remember a turning point in my own psychological evolution—a moment when the tables were turned and a press secretary received a valuable insight from a reporter.

One day, Ann Compton, a respected veteran Washington correspondent now covering the White House for ABC News Radio, popped her head inside the office I occupied as deputy press secretary, located directly behind the podium of the press briefing room and just down a hallway ramp from the press secretary's office. Because the lower press office was conveniently connected to the briefing room and its adjoining booths where beat reporters worked, they would frequently drop in on me and my fellow deputy, Claire Buchan, for comment or information. The official press areas—an upstairs space where the small offices provided for the network correspondents and wire reporters were packed with two to four journalists each during the working day, a basement area where cable, radio, and other print journalists were housed, and the down-at-the-heels briefing room itself (it hadn't been remodeled in years) where camera crews and sound people working for the networks usually hung out—were cramped and not as private, so my office was a better place to talk.

I was always happy to speak with Ann. She seemed to thoroughly enjoy being a reporter. She'd been a member of the press pool on 9/11 and had provided on-the-spot reporting about the president's day between his departure from Sarasota, Florida, on Air Force One and his return to Washington that evening.

On this late June day, Ann had come to ask me something about the war in Iraq, which was in its third month. With major combat operations declared over, coalition forces appeared to be engaged in mopping-up operations after a quick and easy victory over the armies of Saddam Hussein. But the dictator himself remained at large, unguarded caches of weapons and ammunition had been looted in the aftermath of the invasion, and the American military was beginning to notice a disturbing uptick in the number of attacks being mounted by a growing Iraqi insurgency, particularly in the area known as the Sunni Triangle. Unalloyed optimism—even glee—over our swift conquest was beginning to give way to concern about the long-term prospects for Iraq.

When the conversation veered into the issue of WMD, I repeated the White House's standard position at the time, which I shared: "We believe that weapons of mass destruction will eventually be found. The inspectors are still in the early stages of their work."

Ann's response was blunt. In a matter-of-fact tone, she declared, "They're not going to find any weapons. If there were any, they would have found them by now." She spoke with an air of confidence as someone who had worked in Washington long enough to anticipate a story's likely end.

I was a bit shaken for a moment, but as Ann left my office, the sense of hard-nosed reality she brought with her departed as well. I quickly found myself repeating in my head yet again the logical arguments we'd been making for days about why Saddam's WMD surely existed, even though they were difficult to find—arguments about his history of owning and using them, about his record of deceiving and outwitting UN inspectors, about the solid judgment of intelligence analysts not only in our own intelligence community but among our allies as well. The weapons inspection team, known as the Iraq Survey Group and headed by David Kay, we reminded ourselves, was still scouring through miles of Iraqi government documents, translating them from Arabic, and searching the more barren parts of the country, following leads on underground bunkers and possible burial sites for the elusive weapons. Saddam was a deceitful, defiant ruler who had played rope-a-dope in the desert with inspectors over the years.

For all those reasons, we still suspected the weapons existed. These were the same arguments some of us would continue to make for several more months—though we would eventually start emphasizing weapons of mass destruction "programs" over weapons of mass destruction, even as more and more people outside the White House bubble came to believe that the primary justification for the invasion had been badly off the mark.

But deep inside, Ann Compton's words haunted me. They were on my mind as I visited with Karen Hughes, the president's former counselor, in my new office on day one of my stint as White House press secretary.

I had run into Karen shortly after my first briefing in my new role. "I caught some of the briefing," she remarked with a smile. "How'd it feel?"

"I thought it went fairly smoothly, all things considered," I replied. We were already embroiled in the sixteen words controversy about the president's State of the Union claim—later determined to be unfounded—that Iraq had tried to obtain nuclear materials from Africa. Under the circumstances, with the White House press corps increasingly emboldened to challenge the White House, I knew there would not be much of a honeymoon period for the new press secretary. But the assembled reporters had gone somewhat easy on me on my first day on the job. They knew they'd have plenty of opportunity to verbally swing away at me in the months to come.

"You looked pretty comfortable at the podium," Karen replied.

"Thanks," I said. "We haven't had a chance to talk in a while. If you have a minute, I'd be interested in visiting with you and getting your thoughts about the job."

"Sure, I can come down to your office in a little while," she said.

Karen had left her position as counselor to the president just over a year earlier, in June 2002, having wearied of the countless hours in the White House and longing to spend more time with her husband and teenage son, Robert. She still served as a part-time adviser to the president, Dan Bartlett (her successor), and other senior White House staff, visiting Washington every few weeks to participate in big-picture strategy discussions. With the president moving into reelection mode, we'd be seeing more of her.

We sat down at the small round conference table in my office, near the fireplace. Outside the window was the entryway at the end of the driveway to the main entrance of the West Wing, where a marine often stood guard in dress blues. Four thirteen-inch TV screens flickered silently on one wall, typically set to the three cable news stations and C-Span, except on some working weekends when Texas Longhorn sports on ESPN or one of the networks would get a little playing time. Against another wall stood a comfortable couch underneath large photographs of the president—one of him visiting troops, another at the ceremony commemorating the first anniversary of 9/11, and a third enjoying a laugh with his father the first time they stepped foot in the Oval together as president and former president on inauguration day, 2001.

Karen got straight to her most important advice. It was about credibility. "Your most important job, in my view, will be to make sure the president maintains his credibility with the American people," she said. "It's one of his greatest strengths. People trust him. His 'honest and trustworthy' numbers in polls have always been very high."

She went on to say, "I think you have a real opportunity to be a very effective press secretary. The press likes you. They know they can trust you. If you handle the job the way you're capable of, you can go down as another Mike McCurry."

This was a very gratifying (and bipartisan) bit of flattery. Mike McCurry had been Bill Clinton's longest-serving press secretary. What's more, he had managed to build and sustain a strong personal reputation based on his own credibility among White House reporters and in Washington circles, despite serving at a time when the president's personal approval and own reputation for integrity was plummeting due to revelations about his private peccadilloes.

But my gratitude for Karen's words was tempered by concern. I couldn't forget Ann Compton's comments from a couple of weeks before. Nothing had happened in the interim to improve matters. As it became increasingly clear that our chief rationale for justifying military action in Iraq might well be entirely wrong, I knew it would be increasingly difficult to diminish the corresponding tension and contentiousness of the briefing room. The sixteen words controversy was an early indication, and it was still under way. I'd begun catching myself thinking, a bit ruefully, that Ari got out just in the nick of time—even lightheartedly teasing him about it. "You picked a good time to leave," I said.

Disaster was not imminent. In the short term, most members of the public would take the rising level of attacks on the president with a big grain of salt. An election was on the horizon, and voters understood that the rhetoric would be heating up. When voters perceive attacks as partisan mudslinging, they tend not to be influenced by them, reserving judgment until the criticisms are proved to be valid. And many Americans who'd begun to accept the notion that WMD might not be found in Iraq were remaining steadfast in their support of the war—at least for now. "Saddam fooled Bush," they shrugged. "So what? He fooled everybody else too. That doesn't change the fact that he was a brutal thug and a dictator. Good riddance to him."

But the factors that worked to our advantage in the short term were also working against us in the long term. The buoyant opinion polls clouded our judgment. We assumed that public patience with the president and the war would be sustained as we continued to show forward progress toward a democratic Iraq. The gradual but consistent increase in the number of American troops killed or wounded would prove us wrong. Having gotten this far by vigorously seeking to manipulate public approval to our advantage—most notably in our political propaganda campaign to sell the war—we assumed the same approach would continue to work in our favor and help us overcome any challenges ahead. And having turned away from an open and forthright approach in the buildup to war, whether consciously or not, it would become increasingly difficult as we entered the reelection campaign to alter that course we had set.

The biggest mistake I made as press secretary was in failing to challenge this kind of ingrained thinking within the Bush White House. But in retrospect, it would have been exceedingly difficult for me to do so. The cards I had to play were dealt even before I accepted the job, meaning that the unsatisfying outcome of my years as press secretary may have been preordained the moment I stepped to the podium for the first time that morning in July.

Whatever the full dynamic behind the insular, secretive, combative nature of the Bush White House, it was well established by the time I was asked to become press secretary. I could see that it was unlikely to change in any significant way during my tenure, especially with the reelection campaign already taking shape. This was not a time when anyone was looking to change the way things were done. In the end, I decided to accept the job because of my affection for the president, commitment to public service, and my realization that this was the opportunity of a lifetime.

Having resigned myself to accepting the restrictions and difficulties that went with the job of press secretary in the Bush White House, I suspected there might be a price to pay. While I didn't know exactly what it would be, I didn't expect it to be too severe. Nor did I anticipate how painful some of the lessons learned in my new job would turn out to be.

10

DENIABILITY

THE IDENTITY OF CIA AGENT Valerie Plame was leaked in the days and
weeks before I assumed my new responsibilities as White House press secretary on July 15, 2003. Two years later, I began learning who was involved in the
leak, and another nine months after that, I learned about the secretly declassified NIE information—at the same time the news media disclosed it to the
whole world.

To anyone unfamiliar with life in Washington, the tightly compartmentalized world of the Bush White House may seem difficult to understand. But the
president's key advisers believed there were good reasons for keeping the nature of the campaign against Joe Wilson under wraps. The president and those
around him agreed that, in Washington's permanent campaign environment,
the president was always to be shielded from the unsavory side of politics and
any potential fallout resulting from it. He would stay above the fray, uninvolved
in the aggressive, under-the-radar counterpunching of his advisers. He purposely chose to know little if anything about the tactics they employed.

For this reason, Howard Baker's famous question from the Watergate era,
"What did the president know, and when did he know it?" may not be the most
relevant in judging the ethical behavior of the Bush administration or, indeed,
of any recent administration. White House staffs have learned the importance
of shielding presidents from guilty knowledge. Under these circumstances, the

fact that a president "didn't know" may not be a meaningful defense but just another regrettable fact about how things are done in Washington.

In June 2003, the campaign to undermine Joe Wilson's credibility as a critic of the White House's use of intelligence to bolster the case for war was beginning. As noted earlier, Nicholas Kristof had just published an opinion piece in the *New York Times* that cited an anonymous source (later identified as Joe Wilson) who accused the Bush administration of ignoring evidence that called into question some of its claims about Iraqi WMD. Then longtime *Washington Post* reporter Walter Pincus published a truth-seeking follow-on story that offered details contradicting Kristof's one-sided Niger article, while still challenging the administration's credibility on the broader issue of prewar intelligence.

In early June, while making inquiries about what Kristof wrote, Pincus had contacted Cathie Martin, who oversaw the vice president's communications office. Martin went to Scooter Libby to discuss what Pincus was sniffing around about. The vice president and Libby were quietly stepping up their efforts to counter the allegations of the anonymous envoy to Niger, and Pincus's story was one opportunity for them to do just that. The vice president dictated talking points to Libby, who used them when responding to Pincus.

On June 12, 2003, in "CIA Did Not Share Doubt on Iraq Data," Pincus reported that while a CIA-directed mission to Niger had indeed challenged the uranium claim used by the president in his State of the Union speech, this information had never been given to White House officials. Instead, the CIA had failed to "share what it knew" and thereby helped "keep the uranium story alive" until ElBaradei's report to the UN Security Council. The CIA, Pincus wrote,

> ... did not include details of the former ambassador's report and his identity as the source, which would have added to the credibility of his findings, in its intelligence reports that were shared with other government agencies. Instead, the CIA only said that Niger government officials had denied the attempted deal had taken place, a senior administration official said.

An unnamed "senior intelligence official" reminded Pincus that the uranium intelligence was "only one fact and not the reason we went to war. There was a lot more." But on the broader issue, a "senior CIA analyst" suggested that the whole uranium matter was "indicative of larger problems" about the intelligence regarding Iraq's chemical, biological, and nuclear weapons programs as well as its reputed links to al Qaeda. In the lead-up to war, this analyst suggested, "information not consistent with the administration agenda was discarded and information that was [consistent] was not seriously scrutinized."

Pincus's column fueled the growing controversy. Even as it suggested that the White House might be blameless in regard to the specific Niger claim, it strengthened the spreading belief that the administration's claims about Iraq's WMD had been based on faulty intelligence or, even worse, deliberately hyped and manipulated to mislead the nation into war.

In this atmosphere of growing controversy—and with no WMD in sight anywhere in Iraq—Kristof's anonymous source, Joe Wilson, decided to go public.

On Sunday, July 6, Wilson published an opinion piece in the *New York Times*, "What I Didn't Find in Africa." It openly accused the administration of manipulating the intelligence about Iraq's nuclear weapons program to justify military action by exaggerating or hyping the threat.

After meeting with dozens of former and current government officials and people involved in the uranium business in Niger, Wilson wrote in the *Times*, "it did not take long to conclude that it was highly doubtful that any such transaction had ever taken place." He further expressed "every confidence" that the information he "provided was circulated to the appropriate officials within our government."

Questioning how it was used by "our political leadership," Wilson said that if "the information was ignored because it did not fit certain preconceptions about Iraq, then a legitimate argument can be made that we went to war under false pretenses."

That same day on *Meet the Press*, Wilson told guest host Andrea Mitchell that he was "absolutely convinced" that the vice president's office had received "a very specific response" based on his trip because it was the "standard operating procedure" in the case of a question raised by such a senior-level office.

Judging that the administration knew full well that the uranium information was "erroneous" if it referred specifically to Niger, Wilson suggested that the administration had selectively used it along with other intelligence "to bolster a decision" to go to war that had already been made, and that the use of weapons of mass destruction was a "cover" for some other reason to invade Iraq.

Wilson's performance turned the spotlight squarely on the charge being leveled by Kristof and other critics that the Bush administration had knowingly misled the public. It further riled the vice president. It also provided the national media with a full-fledged controversy to cover, involving a colorful, outspoken character ready to level explosive charges against high-ranking officials.

For the Bush administration, the timing of Wilson's assault was bad. The president was scheduled to make a major diplomatic journey to Africa (ironically, the very continent where the uranium controversy had originated). What's more, the first half of July marked the prearranged transition from Ari Fleischer to me as White House press secretary. But we all knew that even a president can't always choose how and when to respond to issues. Sometimes events outside his control demand action at inopportune times. This was one of those times.

Since the president was departing that Monday, there would be only one morning briefing at the White House, an off-camera press gaggle. But the Wilson article, coupled with persistent questioning from the press that morning, would cause the White House to admit a serious mistake—something rare in any administration, and possibly more so under President Bush.

Armed with updated talking points from the vice president's office, Ari Fleischer sought during the gaggle to portray the Wilson article as offering nothing new other than Wilson's identity as the envoy to Niger. Fleischer disputed the notion that Cheney and others in the administration must have known about Wilson's findings. "The vice president's office did not request the mission to Niger," Fleischer said. "The vice president's office was not informed of his mission and he was not aware of Mr. Wilson's mission" until news about it had been published recently.

But then Fleischer inadvertently dropped a small bombshell: "Now, we've long acknowledged—and this is old news, we've said this repeatedly—that the information on yellowcake did, indeed, turn out to be incorrect." For those following the story closely, this was far from being "old news." It was true that, since the January State of the Union address, the CIA had publicly acknowledged that the Niger intelligence was based on forged documents and inaccurate. But Fleischer now appeared to suggest for the first time that the president's sixteen words in the State of the Union had been based primarily on the Niger documents. Up until that point, the White House had maintained that the president's language had been deliberately broad so as to include African countries other than Niger.

The reporters caught the nuance and jumped all over it. After repeated questioning led by veteran *New York Times* reporter David Sanger, Fleischer punted, saying he would issue a statement on "the specific answer on the broader statement on the speech" later in the day. Admitting that something the president had said was wrong was big news, and it would need to be discussed among senior advisers and approved by the president.

Throughout the day, there was much discussion among the president's advisers on whether or not to acknowledge the obvious. National Security Adviser Condoleezza Rice emerged as one of the chief advocates for acknowledging a mistake, and her point of view prevailed. The White House later in the day said, "There is other reporting to suggest that Iraq tried to obtain uranium from Africa. However, the information is not detailed or specific enough for us to be certain that attempts were in fact made." The NIE on Iraq's weapons of mass destruction was still not formally declassified for public consumption (although, as I was later to learn, it had secretly been declassified for the vice president's use). Although two other African countries were mentioned in the NIE as possible sources of uranium for Iraq, the only detailed or specific intelligence about Iraqi attempts to acquire uranium from Africa was related to Niger, and this was clearly the primary basis for the president's sixteen words.

Authorized by the president, "senior officials" were quoted as elaborating on this concession. In the *Washington Post*, Walter Pincus published a story headlined, "White House Backs Off Claim on Iraqi Buy," which included a quote: "Knowing all that we know now, the reference to Iraq's attempt to acquire uranium from Africa should not have been included in the State of the Union speech." The *New York Times* also quoted a senior official who said, "We couldn't prove it, and it might in fact be wrong."

It was the first public acknowledgment that the president should not have made the uranium allegation in his State of the Union address and that the information on which it had been based was incomplete or inaccurate. At the White House, everyone hoped the acknowledgment would put the sixteen words controversy to rest. The reality was the opposite.

As deputy press secretary, I was supposed to go on the Africa trip with the larger White House press corps aboard its chartered plane. But with Ari's departure imminent, I decided instead to do some preparation for my new job. So, while the controversy was beginning to boil and the president was traveling in Africa, I took a little time off to clear my head, get advice from some of my predecessors from previous administrations, and receive overviews from the senior directors in the National Security Council on their foreign policy priorities. Since my background was in communications and Texas politics and not foreign policy, I wanted a thorough rundown of the focus areas abroad, with top priority on the high-profile ones.

I already had good relations with Condi Rice and her deputy, Stephen J. Hadley, and the meetings would help establish or strengthen relations with key NSC people whose expertise I could call on in times of need.

My self-education efforts proved invaluable. But meanwhile the Niger controversy, having reached critical mass, was expanding. In Washington, it's never enough to simply acknowledge a mistake. The press focus then shifts to follow-up questions: How could the mistake happen? Who was responsible? What are the consequences? The questions don't stop until the hungry media beast is satisfied that it has hunted down all the facts.

As the news circled the globe, Prime Minister Tony Blair's team was privately furious with the White House. The British government—which staunchly supported Bush in Iraq—was standing by the Niger claim, maintaining that their intelligence was based on information other than the forged documents. This made the White House concession a serious embarrassment that would cause Prime Minister Blair much media blowback in the near term.

Democrats kept the controversy brewing by calling for a congressional investigation. Carl Levin, the ranking minority member of the Armed Services Committee, questioned how the "bogus" uranium claim had become part of the case for war, and Ted Kennedy suggested it was "deliberate deception." Whether legitimate expressions of concern or grandstanding for political gain, their efforts to raise more suspicion about the White House were a natural part of the ongoing partisan warfare that President Bush had promised to end. Now, the way the president had chosen to sell the war to the American people and his reluctance to discuss openly and directly how that case had been made were ensuring his promise would not be kept.

The uranium controversy overshadowed Bush's trip to Africa, including his efforts to triple relief funds for combating the AIDS pandemic, fight the malaria scourge, and give Africans hope by promoting development. It was a foretaste of things to come, as the Bush administration would find all its accomplishments increasingly overshadowed by persistent controversies over Iraq.

THE WHITE HOUSE FOUGHT BACK against its critics in the media and on Capitol Hill on several fronts. To defend itself against the accusations of deliberate dishonesty leveled by Joe Wilson, Vice President Cheney and his staff were leading a White House effort to discredit Joe Wilson himself. On a broader front, the White House sought to dispel the notion that the intelligence had been "cooked" by showing that it had been provided and cleared by the CIA. Most observers—war critics and supporters, Democrats and Republicans—had shared the assumption that Saddam had WMD programs and likely possessed at least some chemical and biological weapons. Only now, after the fact, were some prominent critics disavowing or downplaying their earlier belief, and the partisan tone of their attacks provided us with the gist of our counterattack.

But that still left open the emerging question, How and why did our intelligence about Iraq go so badly wrong? And how did the now discredited Niger claim make it into the most heavily vetted speech of the year, the State of the Union address?

In a July 11 briefing with the traveling press pool aboard Air Force One on the way to Uganda, Condoleezza Rice was peppered with questions—forty in all—about the infamous "sixteen words." While noting that the British continued to stand by the uranium claim and that the October NIE had referenced efforts to "acquire yellowcake in various African countries" and not just Niger, Rice added, "We have a higher standard for what we put in presidential speeches. We don't make the president his own fact witness. That's why we send them out for clearance."

Was it true, Rice was asked, that the CIA had expressed doubts about the Niger claim to the White House well before the State of the Union? "The CIA cleared the speech in its entirety," Rice replied. "If the CIA, the director of

Central Intelligence, had said, take this out of the speech, it would have been gone, without question. What we've said subsequently is, knowing what we now know, that some of the Niger documents were apparently forged, we wouldn't have put this in the president's speech." (Rice would find out several days later that the National Security Council, which she oversaw, bore primary responsibility for the error.)

Was Rice blaming the Niger error on the CIA? So some newspapers would report after the briefing—not unfairly. Rice denied that was the case. But within hours, CIA director George Tenet publicly took the blame for the intelligence failure—at the request of the White House. "I am responsible for the approval process in my agency," Tenet said, loyally moving to deflect responsibility from the president and those around him.

Could the yellowcake citation in the October NIE be declassified, so the American people could judge for themselves whether or not the administration had exaggerated it? Reflecting public policy, Rice replied that the White House did not "want to try to get into [a] kind of selective declassification, but we're looking at what can be made available." At the time, she was unaware of the fact that President Bush had already agreed to "selective declassification" of parts of the NIE so that Vice President Cheney or his top aide Scooter Libby could use them to make the administration's case with selected reporters.

Republican congressional leaders didn't like seeing the chief rationale for war being undermined as the 2004 election year loomed. Some seized on Tenet's mea culpa as an opportunity to distance themselves—and the Republican president—from the blame. Pat Roberts, chairman of the Senate Intelligence Committee, blasted Tenet and was described in the *New York Times* as being "disturbed by extremely sloppy handling of the issue from the outset by the CIA." Roberts also expressed displeasure at a "campaign of press leaks by the CIA in an effort to discredit the president," a reference to CIA officials defending themselves over the Iraqi WMD intelligence by suggesting that policymakers had selectively edited the intelligence to make a stronger case for war.

The squabbling would leave the self-protective CIA lying in wait to exact revenge against the White House. And the approaching election year would provide a convenient opening.

The press loved it all. There are few things reporters enjoy covering more than controversy over internal administration squabbling and the opportunity it provides for gossip, score settling, and backdoor machinations. And within days, another shock from the media would drive the intensity of the coverage even higher.

This time, the bombshell was launched not by members of "the liberal press" but by a noted conservative reporter, pundit, and commentator, the feisty, beetle-browed Robert Novak. In a July 14, 2003, column titled "Mission to Niger," Novak probed how Wilson's trip had come about and what it concluded. An easily overlooked revelation buried near the bottom of the article started the ball rolling toward a full-fledged Justice Department investigation. "Wilson never worked for the CIA, but his wife, Valerie Plame, is an agency operative on weapons of mass destruction," Novak disclosed. "Two senior administration officials told me that Wilson's wife suggested sending him to Niger to investigate the Italian report [about yellowcake sales]."

The point of mentioning Wilson's wife, of course, was to dispel once and for all the notion that Vice President Cheney had somehow arranged Wilson's mission to Niger. The fact that Wilson's wife was involved also carried with it a whiff of nepotism, a vague sense that perhaps there was something improper in the assignment—as if Wilson had been sent by his wife "on a junket," to quote the words scrawled in the margin of his own copy of Wilson's op-ed column by none other than Vice President Cheney himself.

But the charge of possible nepotism wasn't the reason Novak's column caused an explosion. Rather, it was the first time the name Valerie Plame had appeared in print along with the words "agency operative." By revealing Plame's status, Novak inadvertently elevated the Niger controversy into a full-blown scandal.

Intentionally disclosing the name of a covert CIA officer (which Plame was, despite some later controversy over that point in the press) to an individual not authorized to know it, such as a reporter, is a felony. Novak evidently didn't recognize the seriousness of publishing Plame's identity. Months later, when the Justice Department investigated the leak, Novak wrote that CIA spokesman Bill Harlow had requested that Plame's name not be used in Novak's column because, while "she probably never again will be given a foreign assignment ... exposure of her Agency identity might cause 'difficulties' if she travels abroad." This struck Novak as an inadequate reason to withhold relevant information from the public. Novak defended his actions by asserting that Harlow had not suggested that Plame "or anybody else would be endangered," and that he learned Plame's name (though not her undercover identity) from her husband's entry in the well-known reference book *Who's Who in America.*

And where did Novak get the information about Plame's CIA role in the first place? It would be years before the answer to that question would come to light. In his column, Novak attributed it only to "two senior administration officials."

It was a reference echoed in a story by Matt Cooper of *Time* magazine published three days after Novak's column, on July 17, 2003. Cooper wrote that "some government officials" had told *Time* about "Wilson's wife, Valerie Plame," and speculated about the administration's motives for spreading the word about Plame: "Has the Bush administration declared war on a former ambassador who conducted a fact-finding mission to probe possible Iraqi interest in African uranium? Perhaps." Cooper also quoted Joe Wilson, who had no doubts about what he believed the administration was doing: "This is a smear job," Wilson insisted.

Whether war, smear job, or PR offensive gone haywire, the CIA took the leak of Plame's name very seriously. A couple of weeks later, around the end of July, in an undisclosed letter to the Criminal Division of the Department of Justice, the CIA reported "a possible violation of criminal law concerning the unauthorized disclosure of classified information," and informed Justice that its office of security was investigating the matter.

Already battling attacks about its offensive tactics (the Niger claim and the hyping of prewar intelligence generally), the Bush administration would soon have to answer questions about its defensive tactics—leaking Valerie Plame's identity in an effort to beat back her husband's assaults.

And in the midst of all this—on July 15, just one day after Novak's column—neither aware of the leaks nor previously involved in the effort to discredit Wilson, I took over Ari Fleischer's job as White House press secretary. If I'd been expecting a honeymoon, I quickly learned otherwise.

ON MY SECOND DAY AS PRESS SECRETARY, presidential counselor Dan Bartlett, my fellow Texan and the man in charge of overall communications for the White House, conducted an important planning meeting for relevant staff under his purview. Its purpose was to make sure that the White House communications team was intently focused on the need to "win every news cycle" and make sure we were contributing to the "broader strategic plan" during the upcoming reelection effort. This directive was coming directly out of the White House strategey meeting that had just been held around that time.

As we met, the sixteen words controversy was continuing to dog us. And now that we'd acknowledged that the uranium claim was probably false, we were stuck defending the indefensible—not a good place for the president and his White House team to be.

We needed to refocus the debate on the larger strategic framework—the big picture of national security that the president would relentlessly push during the reelection campaign against his eventual opponent, Senator John Kerry.

At the meeting, Bartlett outlined the winning message: the president's most important obligation, particularly in a post–9/11 world, is to protect the American people from terrorists and outlaw regimes. The way to win this war on terror is to stay on the offensive, ending threats by confronting them. And a peaceful, freer, and more stable Middle East is key to our own safety and security. Our job was all about keeping the focus on national security and specifically the war on terrorism, which would become the central theme of the president's reelection campaign.

In this context, the war in Iraq was not only justifiable but essential. Saddam Hussein's regime had been a threat before the invasion, whether it had WMD or not. Now we were dismantling al Qaeda, and we were fighting a broad war on terror in both Afghanistan and Iraq.

For the next ten weeks, every significant opportunity on the president's schedule would be used for pushing this message. Republicans in Congress and allies in the media, such as conservative columnists and talk radio personalities, would be enlisted in the effort and given communications packets with comprehensive talking points aimed at helping them pivot to the message whenever they could. Daily talking points and regular briefings for members and staff would be provided, and rapid, same news cycle response to any attacks or negative press would be a top priority—an effort Bartlett had spearheaded during the 2000 campaign.

It was a determined campaign to seize the media offensive and shape or manipulate the narrative to our advantage. But the sixteen words controversy refused to go away. How had the apparently mistaken claim about uranium from Africa found its way into the State of the Union address? If Tenet's CIA was responsible, shouldn't Tenet suffer some consequences? If not, who should? Questions like these came up in almost every press gaggle and briefing.

And as the days went by, it became increasingly clear that they had to be dealt with decisively—and the sooner the better.

It was White House chief of staff Andy Card and presidential counselor Dan Bartlett who ultimately took charge of resolving this dilemma—Andy, by directing everyone on the White House staff to provide all relevant recollections and documents tracing the genesis and handling of the uranium claim, and Dan by organizing the information and developing a clear, forthright presentation that showed how such an egregious error occurred.

For people like Dan and me, charged with handling communications on behalf of a complex organization like the White House, tension between us and our "clients" in the news media is a basic part of the job description. When the people in charge, from the president on down, are secure in their roles and committed to maximum openness, that tension is diminished. We're permitted to share information with relative freedom, and we're usually able to overcome resistance to openness from those (especially the lawyers and some other top advisers) who tend to be overly cautious or prefer secrecy. But when our leaders choose not to embrace openness and erect roadblocks in the path of full disclosure, the tension is aggravated. This can make our job almost unbearable. More important, it may ultimately undermine an administration and even the president himself.

In most organizations, including the Bush administration, there are people on both sides of this issue—those who favor disclosure and those who abhor it. Artfully managing the tug-of-war between different factions is also part of our job. And in today's world of the twenty-four-hour news cycle, time pressures complicate the challenge enormously.

Speed is always desirable when releasing information, but getting all the facts can take time. When the information is incomplete, the media may fill the void with emotion-rousing partisan rhetoric that provides conflict, controversy, and negativity, and too often—whether deliberately or unconsciously—jumps to oversimplified, black-and-white conclusions that define a story line before the whole, nuanced truth can be uncovered.

The story behind the sixteen words controversy was a complicated one, and because we at the White House were a little slow in getting important facts together and sharing them, it kept burning into my second week as press secretary. On July 18, two days after our communications meeting, Bartlett provided some facts about the controversy on background to reporters. Part of the October NIE, including the paragraphs related to Iraqi attempts to ob-

Getting an early political lesson at age four by participating in a mock election Mom held for neighborhood kids in our front yard in 1972.

Results show Mom, surrounded by her four sons and arm around her mother, Madge Keeton, wins re-election to an unprecedented third term as Austin mayor in 1981. I am to her right, plaid shirt. Oldest brother Mark on her direct left. Brother Brad, face partially visible, in far background center. Brother Dudley not pictured.

I hold the Bible as Granddad, W. Page Keeton, the former dean of the University of Texas School of Law, administers the oath for statewide office to my mother in 1994.

I listen as the president confers with press secretary Ari Fleischer and communications director Dan Bartlett in a classroom at Booker Elementary School in Sarasota, Florida on September 11, 2001, prior to his first public statement upon learning that America was under attack. —WHITE HOUSE PHOTO/ERIC DRAPER

Visiting with the president just before he threw out the first pitch of game three during the World Series in October 2001, the first game in New York during an emotional time in the city's history.

—WHITE HOUSE PHOTO/ERIC DRAPER

Discussing with the president the questions the press was likely to ask following his meeting with Gen. Tommy Franks (center) in Crawford, Texas, in December 2001 during the war in Afghanistan.

—WHITE HOUSE PHOTO/SUSAN STERNER

I talk to the president aboard Marine One in 2002. —White House Photo/Eric Draper

On Ari Fleischer's last day as press secretary, July 14, 2003, National Security Adviser Condoleezza Rice and I attend the president's meeting in the Oval Office with UN Secretary-General Kofi Annan.
—AP Photo/Charles Dharapak

Walking into my first briefing as press secretary in July 2003 as Assistant Press Secretary Reed Dickens closes the door behind me.
—WHITE HOUSE PHOTO/ERIC DRAPER

Enjoying a laugh with the president in October 2003.
—WHITE HOUSE PHOTO/TINA HAGER

Gaggling with reporters in my office at the White House the morning following news of Saddam Hussein's capture in December 2003; Deputy Press Secretary Claire Buchan and Chief National Security Council Spokesman Sean McCormack listen to my far left.
—WHITE HOUSE PHOTO/SUSAN STERNER

Conferring with Condi Rice, Dan Bartlett (to her left), and CIA Director George Tenet, 2003.
—WHITE HOUSE PHOTO/TINA HAGER

With the President, Vice President, Dan Bartlett, and Al Gonzales in the Oval Office in 2004.
—WHITE HOUSE PHOTO/PAUL MORSE

With Secretary of Defense Donald Rumsfeld in the Oval staff area in 2004.

—WHITE HOUSE PHOTO/ERIC DRAPER

Visiting with Bush, Colin Powell, and Andy Card at the president's house in Crawford, April 2004; Joe Hagin and Blake Gottesman are in the background.
—WHITE HOUSE PHOTO/ERIC DRAPER

Gaggling with White House reporters aboard Air Force One in 2004; Press Assistant Peter Watkins listens behind me while stenographer Greg North records the briefing.
—WHITE HOUSE PHOTO/ERIC DRAPER

A lighthearted moment with Karl Rove as we await a meeting with the president outside the Oval in March 2005.
—WHITE HOUSE PHOTO/KRISANNE JOHNSON

A version of the infamous "flyover" photo: President Bush surveys the damage from Hurricane Katrina while flying over New Orleans en route to the White House, August 31, 2005.

—AP Photo/Christopher Morris/VII

The president and I walk down the Colonnade in April 2006.   —White House Photo/Paul Morse

tain uranium from Africa, were officially declassified through CIA channels and released at the same time. But our internal investigation was incomplete at that time, and the meager facts Dan shared didn't satisfy the media.

Over the next few days, more documents were unearthed, and the full story of the uranium claim gradually came into focus. On July 21 there was a late-night gathering among select senior advisers in Andy Card's office to discuss our communications strategy for dealing with the issue. Present were Card, Bartlett, Condi Rice and deputy Steve Hadley, White House counsel Alberto Gonzales, staff secretary Harriet Miers, and myself.

One topic of discussion was a detail that had turned up in a story by White House correspondent Richard W. ("Dick") Stevenson in the *New York Times* eight days before. According to that story, a claim that Saddam Hussein had tried to buy 550 tons of uranium ore from Niger had been dropped from a speech given by President Bush in Cincinnati back on October 7, 2002. CIA director George Tenet, the story said, had personally warned deputy national security adviser Steve Hadley that the claim couldn't be supported by solid intelligence. If true, this raised an obvious question: Why would a claim deemed too flimsy for a speech in Cincinnati be given a place in the president's most prominent message to the American people, the State of the Union address?

Most people on the outside are not familiar with Hadley, but those of us who work with him know him to be an honorable man. His behavior that evening only reaffirmed the fact.

Hadley confirmed having the conversation with Tenet. But three months later, when the State of the Union address was being finalized, he'd forgotten about it. On reflection, he felt that he should have recalled the conversation and Tenet's warnings about the Niger claim. "Signing off on these facts is my responsibility," Steve said. "And in this case, I blew it. I think the only solution is for me to resign."

Hadley had been particularly upset that Tenet had been made to look like the scapegoat, since he believed it was nobody's fault but his own. Intra-administration squabbling and finger-pointing among agencies was one of the few things that visibly disturbed Hadley's calm, deliberate, and thoughtful demeanor. The offer to resign was his notably selfless attempt to clear the name of someone he felt had taken an unfair degree of blame, and to accept his own responsibility for an honest mistake whose consequences were now playing out before a worldwide audience.

As I sat considering Hadley's words, his proposal was rejected almost out of hand by others present. Hadley was one of the most loyal members of the Bush team and a valued adviser, and his mistake had hardly been a hanging offense. But we agreed that an approach of openness, forthrightness, and honesty was now essential. Bartlett and Hadley, the two White House staffers most directly familiar with the speech-vetting process and the facts in this case, would be the best ones to inform the world as to what had happened and why. And only Hadley could correct the record about where responsibility rested for the sixteen words getting into the president's address.

The next day, in the Roosevelt Room of the White House, Bartlett and Hadley briefed reporters about how the sixteen words had been permitted to appear in the State of the Union address. As the White House communications director, Bartlett had overseen the speechwriting process. As the number two NSC official, Hadley was the point person for signing off on the factual content of speeches in his area of expertise. Acknowledging Tenet's earlier request not to include the Niger claim, Hadley told the assembled reporters he had "failed" in his responsibility for vetting the speech: "The fact is that given the October 5 and 6 CIA memorandum, and my telephone conversation with the DCI Tenet at roughly the same time, I should have recalled at the time of the State of the Union speech that there was controversy associated with the uranium issue."

The Bartlett-Hadley briefing lasted an hour and twenty-three minutes. I imagine it felt longer for Steve. But it accomplished our goal of putting the sixteen words controversy behind us.

Yet this was only one of the battles we in the White House faced. The broader question about prewar intelligence continued to loom. Why had the Bush administration, along with so many other well-informed experts from many nations, been so badly mistaken about the status of Saddam's WMD and WMD programs? What's more, the new conflict over the apparent leak of Valerie Plame's identity by administration officials bent on discrediting Joe Wilson would soon heat up.

ON SEPTEMBER 16, THE CIA informed the Justice Department about its completed investigation into the disclosure of Valerie Plame's name and undercover status and requested that the FBI "initiate an investigation of this matter." Justice advised the CIA on September 29, 2003, that its counterespionage section supported the request for an investigation. The clear implication was that there was good reason to believe a crime had been committed in the leaking of Plame's name. The White House would be informed about the Justice Department decision later that evening.

The made-for-Washington scandal was now fully grown. It was taking place against the backdrop of a high-stakes presidential reelection campaign. Partisanship permeated the controversy, even to the name of the story. We at the White House referred to it simply as the "leak investigation," while our critics called it "Plamegate" in an effort to make it sound as sinister as the best-known political scandal of all. Perhaps the hottest question surrounding the leak investigation was whether Karl Rove—arguably the Bush administration's most controversial official—had been involved.

I was first asked specifically whether Rove had been involved in the leak late in the briefing on September 16, 2003. Russell Mokhiber, editor of the advocacy newsletter *Corporate Crime Reporter*, a Ralph Nader associate and liberal White House critic, asked a pointed question. It came out of the blue, but that was normal for the gruff Mokhiber, who usually wasn't interested in the news of the day. He was interested in gotcha reporting, plain and simple, to damage an administration he held in low regard.

"On the Robert Novak-Joseph Wilson situation," Mokhiber said, "Novak reported earlier this year—quoting—anonymous government sources telling him that Wilson's wife was a CIA operative. Now, this is apparently a federal offense, to burn the cover of a CIA operative. Wilson now believes that the person who did this was Karl Rove. He's quoted from a speech last month [at an August 21 public forum in suburban Seattle] as saying, 'At the end of the day, it's of keen interest to me to see whether or not we can get Karl Rove frog-marched out of the White House in handcuffs.' Did Karl Rove tell that ..."

I wasn't prepared for the question in the sense that I had not spoken to Rove about it yet, but it was phrased in such an emotionally off-putting way, referring to Rove deliberately "burning the cover" of a CIA operative, that I confidently interrupted Mokhiber. "I haven't heard that. That's just totally ridiculous." Mokhiber followed up by asking if Rove had disclosed Plame's name to Novak, and I again said it was "totally ridiculous." It was the stance I would maintain as the scandal blossomed.

I saw Rove shortly after the briefing in the Roosevelt Room and spoke with him quietly near the doorway to the hallway separating the Roosevelt Room from my office area. I wanted to make sure I hadn't climbed out on a limb. Rove had known Novak for years and spoke with him from time to time, and of course he was known for playing hardball politics. But surely even he knew that leaking classified national security information would cross a line.

"I was asked in the briefing today about Joe Wilson's comment that he wanted to see you frog-marched out of the White House in handcuffs," I said to Rove. "A reporter asked me if you were one of Novak's sources and 'burned the cover' of Wilson's wife. I said it was totally ridiculous. You weren't one of Novak's sources, right?"

"Right."

"Just wanted to make sure," I said.

"You're right," Rove said.

The second time I checked with Rove was on Saturday, September 27, 2003. Mike Allen, a tireless, thirty-something *Washington Post* White House correspondent who'd covered the 2000 presidential campaign, was working on a piece about the leak investigation along with veteran *Post* reporter Dana Priest, who covered intelligence matters for the paper.

According to Mike, a senior administration official had told them that two senior White House officials had spoken to at least six reporters about Wilson's wife. Mike did not know the names of the aides alleged to have been involved in the leak, but he and Priest viewed their source as credible and planned to run with the story.

I was at Camp David that day, where the president was meeting with President Putin and holding a press availability at which each would make statements and then take a couple of questions from their respective press corps. Rove got in touch with my trusted deputy Claire Buchan, letting her know he'd received an email inquiry from Mike for the story.

The implication of the *Post* story was clear: the White House had disclosed Plame's identity to discredit or even punish Joe Wilson. The story would put the leak of her identity right at the White House's doorstep. Before, it was just "two senior administration officials" in a Novak column. But now the *Post* was reporting that two senior aides specifically in the White House had disclosed her identity to multiple reporters, implying the possibility of a concerted effort by the White House to reveal Plame's role and her involvement in her husband's trip to Niger.

Claire spoke with Rove before I returned to the White House in the staff vans. I arrived back at my office sometime after 1:00 P.M., and a short time later got the rundown from her.

She informed me that Rove had volunteered to her that Novak had called him about Plame. He hadn't confirmed Plame's CIA status because he didn't know about it.

I replied in some bewilderment, "Karl spoke to Novak?"

Claire said he had. I was taken aback that Rove hadn't mentioned the contact to me the first time we talked. Claire and I discussed how that fit with what I had previously said in the briefing on September 16. It was consistent with what Karl was saying to Claire now: he had not been one of Novak's sources because he could not confirm what he did not know.

I felt that Rove should have disclosed this conversation to me previously, so I decided to call him. He repeated to me what he had told Claire earlier in the day: "He [Novak] said he'd heard that Wilson's wife worked at the CIA. I told him I couldn't confirm it because I didn't know."

Then, knowing where the story line was headed with the coming *Post* article, I asked Karl an unambiguous, unqualified catch-all question, "Were you involved in this in any way?" I was clearly referring to the leaking of Valerie Plame's identity—information that was believed to be classified—to any reporter.

Karl replied categorically, "No. Look, I didn't even know about his wife."

There was no mention of a phone conversation Karl had on July 11, 2003, with *Time* magazine's newest White House correspondent, Matt Cooper, which would remain under "double super secret" anonymity (Cooper's wit, not mine) for nearly two more years. That is when it would be revealed publicly and to me that Rove had disclosed Plame's identity to Cooper during that call.

Rove's categorical "no" gave me the assurance I needed to defend a fellow member of the Bush team and fellow Texan I had known for more than a decade, who was invariably a prime target of our most partisan critics.

By Monday morning, September 29, Joe Wilson, appearing on ABC's *Good Morning America*, was backing away from his previous assertion that Rove had been responsible for leaking his wife's identity. However, Wilson also asserted during the interview that he believed Rove "at a minimum con-doned the leak."

I checked with Rove that day to confirm that he'd neither leaked nor con-doned leaking Plame's identity. He assured me that was correct. That day would be the last time I would talk to or hear from Karl about anything specifically related to the leak.

As I walked into the Oval Office on the morning of September 29, it could have been any other day at the White House.

As I frequently did, I touched base with the president in the morning be-fore facing the press corps that day. It was an opportunity to get his thoughts on how to respond to a particular issue, to make sure I was keeping him fully abreast of what was on reporters' minds, or just to confirm that my thinking on how to handle a topic was in line with his own. The Oval shortly after 7:00 A.M. and just before the daily senior staff meeting at 7:30 A.M. was a good opportu-nity to catch him. Other times it would be after his daily intelligence and FBI briefings, or when he was leaving the Oval to head down to the Situation Room for a secure conference call or a meeting of his National Security Council.

But today was not like any other day at the White House. The dark cloud of scandal was casting its shadow over us this late September morning.

"Good morning, Mr. President," I said as I walked into the Oval, past the couches, across the blue presidential seal in the center of the light beige carpet. His desk was located in front of three tall windows hung with long, golden drapes that could stop bullets but not the cheery sunlight that filled the office. The elegant desk was made from timbers of the HMS *Resolute*, the British Arctic exploration ship once recovered by an American whaler. The desk had been used by nearly every commander in chief since the British, in a gesture of appreciation, donated it to President Rutherford B. Hayes. Andy Card, the White House chief of staff, stood to the left of the president.

"Hey, Scott," the president said good-naturedly. "What's on the press's mind today?"

"The reports of a Justice Department investigation into the leak of Valerie Plame's name," I said, knowing his question was just pro forma since he, like all of us, was well aware of the topic *du jour*. "I want to talk to you about it before I gaggle."

"Karl didn't do it," the president reflexively said, referring to his senior adviser and chief political strategist, Karl Rove. The "it" clearly meant disclosing Plame's identity to reporters. He was holding on to the armrests and leaning back in his chair behind his desk. He seemed to be in fairly good spirits.

"I know …" I began, not realizing the president had more to say.

"He told me he didn't do it," the president continued, cutting me off midsentence.

It was just two months since Bob Novak had written his article outing Plame and quoting two "senior administration officials" as his sources for the leak. Rove had already denied to me that he'd leaked Plame's name, and now I was learning that he had also told the president that he was not involved.

Then the president glanced toward Andy, who had raised his hands above his waist and was now gesturing down with both to indicate to the president that he should keep quiet and stop talking about what was fast becoming a sensitive subject.

"What?" the president said, looking at Andy with a slight hint of irritation in his voice. "That's what Karl told me."

"I know," Andy said. "But you shouldn't be talking about it with anyone, not even me." Andy was ever cautious. That morning the *Washington Post* was reporting that the Justice Department had opened a criminal investigation into the disclosure of Plame's identity.

Andy felt his first responsibility as chief of staff was to protect the president: his time, his reputation, and his legacy. He had served in two previous administrations and knew how scandals can take on a life of their own in Washington. In Andy's view, looking out for the president sometimes meant standing between him and other senior aides, including the chief spokesman.

But the president and I had our own unique relationship, shaped in our home state of Texas. And, in this instance, he paid little attention to Andy's not so subtle effort to keep him from talking to me about what Karl had said. His face showed a bit more irritation as he grimaced with a "Fine, whatever" expression and looked straight ahead away from Andy and me. It was an expression the president showed from time to time when someone on the staff tried to tell him what he should or should not be doing.

"I talked to Karl too," I continued, as I looked back to the president. "He said the same thing to me."

"Does the press think he did it?" the president asked.

"I've already told them he didn't," I responded. "But I'm sure they will ask again today." I mentioned the Sunday story in the *Washington Post*, which said that two top White House officials had called at least six Washington journalists to disclose Plame's name and current position at the CIA.

I didn't delve further into the president's conversation with Karl, in part because of Andy's unease. But I assumed from his comments that he had asked Karl earlier that morning whether or not he was one of the two sources. It seemed to be fresh on his mind, and I felt confident about defending Karl, since the president too had received assurances from him. My impression was that Andy was fully aware of what Karl had told the president.

Then I looked at Andy and asked, "Do we know anything more about an investigation?"

Andy replied that he had not heard anything new, and as far as he knew we had yet to hear anything from the Justice Department.

The discussion in the Oval that morning—the day we would learn that an investigation was indeed under way—was a moment Andy would later recollect for prosecutors, and that I would be asked to confirm under oath before a federal grand jury.

I then turned the conversation to the approach I was planning to take with the White House press corps later in the morning at the gaggle and in the afternoon briefing. The primary White House response to the looming press feeding frenzy would come from me. The president had two public events scheduled at the White House that day, but he was not planning on taking questions from reporters at either one. No one on the staff saw anything to gain from having him do so, since they would likely focus solely on the leak investigation.

"I plan on saying you believe the leaking of classified information is a serious matter, and that it should be looked into and pursued to the fullest possible extent," I said to the president. "And that the Department of Justice is the appropriate agency to look into it. And I don't plan on going too far beyond that."

"Yeah, I think that's right," the president replied. "I do believe it's a serious matter. And I hope they find who did it."

"And Andy, I am still good to say that nothing has been brought to our attention to suggest White House involvement, beyond what we have read in the papers, right?" I asked.

"I do not know of anything," Andy responded. "And last I heard from Al, he did not either," he added, referring to Al Gonzales, the White House counsel and a longtime Bush loyalist from Texas. We were all on the same page.

The president offered some words of encouragement as I headed out the door. I knew it was likely to be a contentious gaggle and briefing. This was the first major scandal to hit the Bush White House, and the press corps was ready to pounce. The president was up for reelection next year, and Democrats saw an opportunity to put us on the defensive and potentially deal a serious blow to the president's chances at reelection. I was at the center of the brewing storm—the first line of defense for the White House.

Just over two months into the job as White House press secretary, I was about to go through my first real test in the briefing room. There would be plenty of the inherent tension between press and press secretary at play today. Half the time during the daily White House briefing the press corps is trying to get under the press secretary's skin or catch him in a mistake or contradiction—a "gotcha" moment. It is a rite of passage for any press secretary, one way reporters try to crack through the wall when only carefully selected information is being provided publicly.

I had a pretty good idea of what I was walking into, which gave me an opportunity to prepare. Many of my colleagues at the White House would be watching the briefing closely today, in part to see how I handled myself under pressure.

There were some eighty-five questions during the informal, off-camera morning gaggle with reporters, seventy of them about the reported leak investigation. Reporters talked over one another as they fired away with their questions, and that was fine by me. I wanted to make sure I had a good feel for the specific questions the press would be asking, including at the daily briefing later in the day. I intentionally let the gaggle run a little longer than the normal fifteen minutes. It confirmed what I already knew: there was going to be a feeding frenzy at the briefing, focused almost exclusively on the investigation into the leak of Valerie Plame's identity.

Since Novak had quoted "two senior administration officials" in his article and the *Washington Post* had cited "two White House officials" as spreading

information about Plame's identity, the media assumed that White House officials must have been responsible for the leak.

Rove, the lightning rod for White House critics who viewed him as the
president's Machiavellian mastermind, was the usual suspect of speculation in
the Washington rumor mill. His name was invoked repeatedly by reporters
during the day's gaggle and briefing. Each time I dispelled any notion he was
involved.

By tradition, the daily press briefing ends when the senior wire correspondent on the front row, whichever of the two present from the Associated
Press and Reuters has covered the White House longer, says "thank-you." So
the duration of the briefing can range from a minimum of twenty minutes to
an average thirty or thirty-five minutes to a maximum of forty-five to fifty-
five minutes. Today would be at the high end of the range. On most days, the
official White House briefing transcript, which is made public each afternoon, lists about ten or so different topics. Today, it would list just two: the
leak investigation and Iraq.

Neither the press nor I took the briefing room contentiousness personally.
We were just doing our jobs. Mine was to help the president advance his
agenda and to faithfully and accurately articulate his views and policies in the
way that he preferred. Theirs was to report the news about the president and
his administration, hold us accountable for his decisions and policies, and
question his governance and that of his staff and advisers. Journalists who
cover the White House tend to be some of the best in their profession.

So there we were that Monday afternoon a little past noon, less than three
months into my tenure as press secretary, ready to engage in verbal combat.
There was a high press turnout in the briefing room. Some "stills" (photographers) were ready to click the one or two pictures that could fit with the front-
page stories to be printed in the nation's newspapers the following day; if the
press got the better of me, the picture would likely be unflattering. The cut-
away cameras were set, four or five people each shoulder-harnessing or
tripoding their respective networks' cameras, three or four feet at most to my
left with one always rotating in and out about two feet behind my left shoulder. The cable networks were preparing to go live to cover one of the top news
items of the day: a White House under investigation for the reported leak of
classified information about a covert official—a potential felony offense if
done intentionally and knowingly.

I felt well prepared. The prebriefing prep session, a mini "murder board" (a simulated, though very informal briefing with my deputy and assistant press secretaries that gave me a chance to practice answering questions and fine-tune my responses) had been helpful. Card and Gonzales had already assured me they knew of no White House involvement in the disclosure of Plame's identity.

Since the subject had come up in the morning gaggle, I'd visited with the president before the briefing to make sure he was fine with my saying in response to questions that he would fire anyone involved in the leaking of classified information, specifically the identity of Valerie Plame. I told him I intended to say that anyone involved in this would no longer be in the administration.

The president had agreed, saying firmly, "I would fire anybody involved." I had his full, unequivocal approval. He also asked whether I had urged reporters to come forward if they knew who the leakers were. I said I would make that point. He said, "Good, I think you should."

I could feel the adrenaline flowing as I gave the go-ahead for Josh Deckard, one of my hard-working, underpaid press office staff assistants, to give the two-minute warning, so the networks could prepare to switch to live coverage the moment I stepped into the briefing room.

When visitors see the White House briefing room, they usually say, "It looks a lot bigger on TV." It was a cramped, dingy space, particularly on days when most of the forty-eight assigned seats are occupied and other reporters are standing in the narrow aisles. Throw in the glare of the klieg lights, numerous microphones hanging from the ceiling, some still photographers and network camera crews so close they could almost knock the podium over, and you get quite a set.

I pushed back aggressively on assumptions embedded in the questions, and challenged reporters to produce information suggesting that White House aides were responsible for the leak. I reiterated that the president expected everyone in his administration to adhere to the highest standards of conduct, and that no one would have been authorized to leak the identity of Wilson's wife.

Terry Moran, the chief White House correspondent for ABC News, tried to pin me down on the assertion I'd made in the morning gaggle that the president knew Karl Rove was not involved in the leak. It had been fresh in my mind from the meeting with the president, and I'd unintentionally let it slip in response to questioning about why the president was neither directing the White House to get to the bottom of the controversy nor interested in knowing whether or not his senior adviser was involved. It immediately prompted questions about how the president "knew."

The follow-up had been easier to brush off in the gaggle. In the on-camera briefing, I danced around the question a little before repeating a line I used at times: "We are not in the habit of discussing conversations the president has with his senior advisers."

In response to a question from Dana Bash of CNN about why the president was not looking at this as an ethical matter, since he'd committed himself as a candidate to restoring honor and integrity to the White House, I replied, "The president has set high standards, the highest of standards for people in his administration. He's made it very clear to people in his administration that he expects them to adhere to the highest standards of conduct. If anyone in this administration were involved in it, they would no longer be in this administration."

Those last words would get plenty of media play over the next few years, particularly as important information came to light. With the president's approval and his oft-stated commitment to honor and integrity embedded in my mind, I could not have been more confident in what I said.

When he announced that he was running for president in June 1999, Bush had said, "We will show that politics, after a time of tarnished ideals, can be higher and better. We will give our country a fresh start after a season of cynicism."

On January 22, 2001, our first full day in office, the president had reminded all of us in his administration at the public swearing-in ceremony for senior White House staff to adhere to "the high standards that come with high office" and avoid "even the appearance of problems."

His commitment to high ethical standards had made many of us who served proud to answer the call to be a part of his team. We believed this president was uncompromisingly committed to something better than what Americans had seen from some elected leaders. And he had established his reputation in part on saying what he meant and doing what he said.

Now, two and a half years later, the question of whether the administration still adhered to those high standards was on everybody's mind.

Forty-five minutes after it began, the briefing was over. It was time for me to come down from the adrenaline rush of a contentious session and enjoy the moment. The feedback in the postbriefing critique with my deputies and assistants was very positive.

The official White House transcript was thirty-two pages long. The first twenty-four were about the leak investigation. More than 110 questions and 33.5 minutes elapsed before we turned to topics other than the leak investigation.

I received many accolades that afternoon for the way I conducted the briefing under fire. Praise came from colleagues in the White House and the administration, and even a number of White House reporters. Bill Plante, a cynical veteran CBS News White House correspondent, even said to me, "I've seen a lot of press secretaries in tough spots. That was not easy today. I just wanted to say you did a good job."

When I saw the president later in the day, he similarly said, "Good job today." I expressed appreciation, not knowing whether he had actually caught any of the briefing or was simply told by my colleagues on the senior staff that I'd held my own.

I don't know whether this was my finest performance in the briefing room, but I felt pretty good about it, and even better after receiving kind words throughout the day. At least I'd shown that I was ready to do my part to help navigate the Bush White House through the troubled waters to reelection. For the second night in a row, the network newscasts all headlined their broadcasts with the leak story, as did the morning shows and newspapers the following day.

It wouldn't be the last time. Like the war at the root of the scandal, it was not going away anytime soon.

11

BETTING
THE PRESIDENCY

The leak episode was just one offshoot of Bush's most consequential decision and the predominant issue in Washington as I assumed my new responsibilities as White House press secretary: the Iraq war. Many other aspects of the war would come into play over the remainder of Bush's first term, especially in the run-up to Election Day.

Throughout the second half of 2003 and into 2004, with the Iraq occupation gradually becoming more controversial, Democrats saw an opening for attacking Bush's credibility, judgment, and competence. Had the president and his team exaggerated or distorted the intelligence on WMD to deliberately mislead the nation to war? How was the war in Iraq part of the war on terror when it had no connection to 9/11 and no relationship with al Qaeda? Why did Bush rush to war with no plan to win the peace? How did the administration miscalculate the strength of the insurgency so badly? Either Bush and his advisers had distorted the truth (in which case they were less than honest), or they had failed to recognize the truth in a rush to topple Saddam Hussein (in which case they were less than competent).

In either case, the president appeared vulnerable. It was quite a change from the period right after the 2002 midterms, when Bush had been riding high in the opinion polls and many experts foresaw an easy reelection bid.

The Washington media were enlivened and energized by the prospect of a hotly contested political duel. With the president's credibility being questioned, an increasingly costly war and an economic recovery yet to show any job creation, his popularity was beginning to sag, and the number of Americans who viewed him unfavorably was growing. This in turn affected the tenor of media coverage, a common occurrence in the era of the permanent campaign. When a president is up in the polls, he tends to be lionized in the media; when he is down or trending downward, he tends to be attacked. And in the case of George W. Bush, the media had more reason than usual to change its tune in harmony with public opinion. Having failed to be sufficiently skeptical and assertive in the lead-up to war, they would seek to remedy their shortcomings by challenging a now vulnerable president ever more aggressively.

Bush and those of us on his team remained confident. We still boasted the bully pulpit of the White House, a formidable campaign machine headed by the famous and widely feared Karl Rove, an energized Republican base, and a national network of supporters among cable news commentators, newspaper pundits, and radio talk show hosts who could be counted on to defend the president. Every political calculation would be made within the context of the overall campaign strategy, which was calculated to ensure that national security—especially the war on terrorism, Bush's perceived strength—would remain at the core of the public debate.

What's more, even as Bush's personal popularity sagged, the president and his political team recalled the old truth that "you can't beat somebody with nobody." Bush was still a formidable "somebody," while the Democrats had yet to settle on a nominee for 2004—a "somebody" with weaknesses and vulnerabilities of his own. As soon as the Democratic opponent was named, Karl Rove would direct the assault on him, drawing contrasts in ways that would be favorable to the president and unfavorable to the challenger. As everyone knew, few if any in politics could do it better.

The president would firmly stand his ground on Iraq. There would be no give on his part about the necessity of war. There would be no second-guessing the decision. There would be no doubting the eventual outcome.

Changing the tone and ending the partisan warfare in Washington was no longer a consideration. As far as the spirited political competitor Bush was concerned, it was a time to stand firm and starkly clarify the choice facing the American people ahead of the coming election. His presidency was on the line. His legacy was at stake. He would bet it all on Iraq.

In retrospect, this was the defining period for Bush's presidency. And it revealed much about him as a leader.

As PRESS SECRETARY, I WAS participating regularly in most of the president's key meetings: policy deliberations, congressional outreach, cabinet meetings, and world leader visits. As a Texas loyalist, I was a trusted member of the president's senior-most team of advisers, frequently conferring with him and a select group of insiders that included Card, Rove, Rice, and Bartlett.

World leader meetings at the White House usually included small delegations, equal in number, representing each side. The president's delegation would typically include the U.S. ambassador to the country in question, the national security adviser, the secretary of state (or one of his deputies or assistants), an NSC director for the region, the vice president's chief of staff or national security point person (if not Cheney himself), and the press secretary. The secretary of defense would sometimes attend, too. In the Oval, Bush and the foreign leader would sit in the light blue and gold striped chairs in front of the fireplace. Our delegation would sit to Bush's left, usually three on the couch followed by two or three in chairs. The visiting delegation would be situated similarly on the other side the room.

Bush's strategic vision of changing the Middle East by establishing a free and democratic Iraq was one he emphasized in virtually every world leader meeting. These meetings early in my tenure as press secretary underscored for me that Bush's thinking on democratic transformation was the driving reason for our invasion of Iraq. It was a strategic mission much more grandiose than the one emphasized publicly of eliminating a "grave and gathering danger" in Iraq. As the chances of uncovering WMD in Iraq dwindled, the dream of transforming the region became more and more prominent in the president's rhetoric—and mine.

The day before I officially assumed my duties as press secretary, I attended the president's meeting in the Oval with UN secretary-general Kofi Annan. It started with a discussion about the president's recent trip to Africa and the unprecedented support the United States was offering that beleaguered continent, including HIV/AIDS relief, expanding trade, combating hunger, and supporting African-led peacekeeping efforts in areas of civil unrest.

Then the conversation turned to Iraq, a topic fraught with tension. Before the invasion, Annan had urged Bush not to act without UN support, advice that Bush had rejected. The president viewed Annan as a weak leader who epitomized the ineffectual body he served. Ever the soft-spoken, low-key diplomat, Annan did not inspire confidence in the assertive, action-oriented, results-centered Bush. Nevertheless, their relationship was cordial and respectful.

The president thanked Annan for sending the widely respected special representative Sergio Vieira de Mello to help in Iraq's transition. Bush and his foreign policy team felt it was important to have a UN presence in Baghdad. The more the United Nations and other countries were involved in Iraq—including countries that had opposed the original decision to go to war—the lighter the burden for the United States. Of course, this position was a bit of a contradiction, given the president's willingness to preemptively wage war without the explicit approval of the UN (though he viewed Security Council Resolution 1441 as providing him authority to do so). Hence Bush's delicate encouragement for the UN in Iraq and his constant diplomatic niceties with Annan and other skeptical leaders, both in private and in public.

Tragically, Vieira de Mello was killed on August 19, 2003, in a terrorist bombing that targeted the Canal Hotel in Baghdad, which had been used as the UN's local headquarters since 1991. Twenty-one other staff members were killed at the same time. As a result, the UN dramatically reduced its involvement and presence in Baghdad for the immediate future.

In speaking with Annan, Bush emphasized his view that a free, democratic Iraq was essential to peace in the Middle East. He acknowledged that the situation there was tough going but asserted that the coalition was slowly getting the upper hand. He said he felt that Paul Bremer was doing "a hell of a job" in overseeing the early days of Iraq's fledgling democratic transition. Annan stressed the need to show that there was a "light at the end of the tunnel" to the American-run Coalition Provisional Authority led by Bremer, and called the just announced Iraqi Governing Council, a broadly representative body appointed by the CPA, a "very positive step" toward putting Iraq on the path toward sovereignty. The Bush themes would become increasingly familiar to me as I attended world leader meetings in my new role as press secretary.

My first day in my new post, the president met with Prime Minister Vladimír Špdila of the Czech Republic. Bush began by thanking the prime minister for his "strong support in the face of tough criticism" on Iraq, and let him know his administration would not forget his "strong leadership." This was typical of the president, I would learn. He tended to judge the character and "strength" of a world leader more favorably if he had supported the decision to invade Iraq. Špdila, like some other leaders who had lived under communist rule, shared Bush's passion for freedom and stood firmly with him on Iraq.

Špdila said he believed what the United States was doing in Iraq would "help bring peace and stability" to the Middle East. "You make a very important point," Bush responded. "It's important to keep in mind the big picture, our vision. The action we took in Iraq will bring peace and stability. I truly believe a free and peaceful Iraq will have a long-term effect [on the Middle East]. Freedom is powerful."

In late October 2003, the president visited Canberra, Australia, following the Asian-Pacific Economic Summit in Bangkok, Thailand, with stops in Japan, Singapore, and Indonesia. Bush met with Prime Minister John Howard, a good ally and friend. I attended the meeting in the Cabinet Room at Parliament House. Howard, despite deep division among Australians, had stood strongly behind Bush's decision to topple Saddam Hussein, persuading the Australian parliament to commit troops in support of the American-led invasion and occupation. Bush and Howard, as usual in such a meeting, discussed a number of pressing priorities, including Iraq and transformation of the Middle East.

"Thank you for being tough," Bush said to Howard. "And for your friendship. It is important to have the courage to do what is right. You've done that, John. Iraq will change the Middle East. Iran will change" because of what we are doing in Iraq.

Later in the meeting, one of Howard's advisers asked Bush if he thought Islamic cultures could really adopt democracy.

"I think so over time," Bush replied. "I believe Iraq is the place" that will help make it happen. "It will evolve into a democratic, free" country like Turkey or like Bahrain is "moving to."

"I believe freedom is the deepest hope of every human heart," Bush added. "I think there are enough Muslim leaders committed to freedom to move Islamic states in that direction. I believe it is going to happen."

In early November, the president welcomed Prime Minister Ranil Wick-remesinghe of Sri Lanka to the White House. Bush began by thanking the prime minister for "standing strong" on Iraq at the most recent UN General Assembly meeting in September. Ranil had stated that the United States had "no choice but to intervene" militarily, leading to heavy criticism of him in the media at home. "The decisions I made were for the security concerns of America," Bush stated. "I also believe free societies are peaceful societies." He added that by dealing with Saddam Hussein, other rogue nations like North Korea knew how serious the United States was about addressing threats. "Fifty years from now people will say thanks" for what we are doing in Iraq, Bush said. "You have stood rock solid in the face of critics. I assure you one thing: a free and peaceful Iraq will help achieve peace in the Middle East."

The consistency and prominence of the president's rhetoric in these meet-ings with foreign leaders was striking. It convinced me of the sincerity of his passion for the idea of implanting democracy coercively as a way of bringing peace to the Middle East. One could question the wisdom or the practicality of this plan, but not the genuineness of the personal vision that drove it. At the time it was something powerful and hopeful I could embrace, which helped quell the uncertainties I harbored about the original decision.

COMMUNICATING WITH THE AMERICAN people about the situation in Iraq was more challenging. Having been sold on the necessity of war by the argument that Saddam represented a direct and growing threat to the region, the United States, and the world, the public and the media were growing more and more skeptical as the summer wore on and no WMD were found. So we felt relieved near the end of July when the killing of Uday and Qusay Hussein, the ruthless and much-hated sons of the dictator, afforded us a brief change of focus in the media coverage. It came just in time for the president's usual midsummer news conference. This was an event typically held at the end of July just before the president and some of us on his team headed to Crawford, Texas, for the month of August. It would be Bush's first formal news conference since the invasion.

The tone set by the president in discussing Iraq was always something we, his team of advisers, struggled to properly calibrate. We didn't want him to sound pessimistic, of course, but we also didn't want him to sound disconnected from the painful reality on the ground being reported by the media. With events in Iraq changing daily and unpredictably, and with frequent attacks occurring against American troops—despite the president's declaration in May that major combat operations had ended—this was a tricky line to walk.

In preparing for the July press conference, we agreed that Bush would have to accept responsibility for the flawed "sixteen words" in the State of the Union address. This would get headline attention, since it was news. But we hoped we could also draw attention to some of the positive developments of recent weeks in Iraq. The president preferred a more informal briefing before the press conference. With the help of my deputy press secretaries, I would prepare questions and suggest responses so Bush could review them the evening before. Communications Director Dan Bartlett would focus on broader message points Bush should emphasize and work with the speechwriting team to get the opening statement down. There would usually be two sessions the day of the news conference where we could go through likely questions. The first would be in the Oval shortly after the president arrived or after his morning intelligence briefings. It tended to be shorter, in the twenty to thirty minute range, while the final one closer to the scheduled time of the news conference in the Oval would be a half hour to forty-five minutes. Andy Card, Condi Rice, and Karl Rove would usually attend at least one of the sessions. Bush would sit at his desk for these "murder board" sessions where we'd throw the tough or killer questions at him. Bush liked bringing a little levity to the sessions, ridiculing some questions with playful responses he would never utter in public. It was a way for him to relax and get his mind focused, in much the same way that a world-class athlete might ease nervousness ahead of a crucial contest.

When the game began, the president was ready. One by one, he hit all the points he'd planned to cover. On Iraq, he pointed to progress while acknowledging difficulties and calling for patience. Most of Iraq was growing more peaceful, he noted, although "remnants of Saddam Hussein's regime, joined by terrorists and criminals," were "making a last attempt to frighten the Iraqi people and undermine the resolve of the coalition."

"The rise of a free and peaceful Iraq," Bush emphasized, "is critical to the stability of the Middle East, and a stable Middle East is critical to the security of the American people. The success of a free Iraq will also demonstrate to other countries in that region that national prosperity and dignity are found in representative government and free institutions. They are not found in tyranny, resentment, and . . . support of terrorism. As freedom advances in the Middle East, those societies will be less likely to produce ideologies of hatred and produce recruits for terror."

Bush alluded to the killing of Uday and Qusay, saying, "As the blanket of fear is lifted, as Iraqis gain confidence that the former regime is gone forever, we will gain more cooperation in our search for the truth in Iraq." And he expressed his confidence that the truth about WMD would confirm his decision to go to war. "We know that Saddam Hussein produced and possessed chemical and biological weapons, and has used chemical weapons. We know that. He also spent years hiding his weapons of mass destruction programs from the world. We now have teams of investigators who are hard at work to uncover the truth."

Bush also touched on some other issues Americans were concerned about. Remembering that his father's reelection campaign had faltered in large part because of his apparent indifference to people's economic woes ("It's the economy, stupid") and thinking about the current criticism of a "jobless" recovery, Bush made a point of emphasizing his administration's economic accomplishments in the form of additional stimulus for taxpayers and small businesses. And for the first time he signaled openness to the idea of a constitutional amendment to ban same-sex marriage, a hot-button topic for Christian conservative leaders.

The president had done a good job, we felt. But in the Washington game, once the press senses a politician is on the defensive, a peculiar quirk in the rules rears its head: the referees and the opposing team can appear indistinguishable. The media headlines coming out of the news conference focused on Bush's shrinking credibility, noting his denials on the charge of having oversold his case for war in Iraq. As the old political adage says, when you're defending, you're losing—and that was the uncomfortable spot Bush now found himself caught in.

NBC News followed its coverage of the news conference with updated poll numbers showing that the president's approval rating had dropped from

71 percent in April to 56 percent now, while his disapproval rating had risen from 23 percent to 38 percent over the same period. On the other hand, he still held strong on the war on terrorism, with 66 percent approving of his handling of it. And 56 percent said that they felt the Democratic attacks on Bush were just "playing politics."

Still, the trends weren't good. If problems in Iraq continued to fester—and particularly if the human and financial costs continued to soar and the chief rationale for the war continued to unravel—it was only a matter of time before Americans began to abandon the war in droves, and with it the administration that had staked its credibility on that war.

DURING THAT SUMMER, WE HAD not yet abandoned hope of finding WMD. David Kay, a respected scientist and experienced weapons inspector, provided some assurance to us privately and publicly that there was every reason to believe that damning evidence of Saddam's quest for WMD would eventually be uncovered in Iraq. Kay headed the Iraq Survey Group, a 1,400-plus-person fact-finding mission set up by the Pentagon and the CIA to search for WMD in Iraq. Based on what we were being told, we sensed that, while large stockpiles were unlikely to be discovered, some small stocks of chemical or biological weapons still might be found, along with evidence of WMD research and development programs. If that happened, it would greatly weaken Democratic attacks asserting that the Bush administration had exaggerated the threat or deliberately misled the American people to sell war.

NBC News anchor Tom Brokaw interviewed Kay in mid-July about the effort. He introduced the interview by saying, "Kay, a cautious professional who is well aware of the political pressure, is confident he can make the case against Saddam Hussein on WMD." Kay then told Brokaw that within six months he expected to find "a substantial body of evidence" to demonstrate that Saddam had a WMD program.

Kay's optimism provided some comfort to us in the White House—false comfort, as it turned out. But at the time, his ongoing efforts allowed us in the administration to fend off questions about the intelligence used to justify war. Lacking evidence to support what we'd confidently convinced ourselves to believe, we could still defer—or evade—getting drawn into acknowledging any definitive judgments about the rationale while the Iraq Survey Group continued its work.

In early October, Kay released an interim progress report. He cautioned that it was still too early to reach final conclusions. The study group had "discovered dozens of WMD program-related activities," but no weapons of mass destruction. We quickly pounced on the report as proof that Saddam Hussein had been in material breach of Resolution 1441, which had given him one final opportunity to comply with UN disarmament demands or face serious consequences. The report showed that the president had been "right to eliminate the danger his regime posed to the world," as Colin Powell stated. Our talking point had now shifted from focusing on WMD to WMD programs, though if asked we would say we continued to believe weapons would eventually be found.

War critics and some Democrats used the Kay report to again raise the possibility that the administration had at a minimum hyped the WMD threat from Iraq. It was a theme that Diane Sawyer pressed Bush to address during an interview at the White House a couple of months later, in December 2003. Citing a poll showing that 50 percent of Americans believed the administration had exaggerated the evidence in the buildup to war, Sawyer asked if the president felt they were wrong or misguided.

Bush declined to take the bait. He said the intelligence had been sound and that "there was no doubt that Saddam Hussein was a threat." Sawyer sought to pin him down, saying that before the war he and others had asserted there was no doubt that Saddam Hussein had weapons of mass destruction. The president returned to his oft repeated assertion that he'd made the right decision regardless of the presence or absence of WMD. "Saddam Hussein was a danger and the world is better off because we got rid of him," he said.

Sawyer pressed again, focusing on the distinction between WMD and WMD programs. The administration, she pointed out, had previously asserted "that there were weapons of mass destruction, as opposed to the possibility that he could move to acquire those weapons still."

Bush's response was telling, much more so than I stopped to contemplate at the time. "So what's the difference?" Bush asked. After all, if Saddam had acquired WMD, he would still have been a danger. Bush declined to say whether the administration could have been more precise in laying out the evidence prior to the war and dismissed criticism that it might have been misleading. He asserted again that everyone had seen the same intelligence and come to the same conclusion—Saddam Hussein was a threat that needed to be dealt with.

The president's response received quite a bit of media attention and criticism from Democrats, some of whom noted that the rationale had been that the Iraqi regime posed an urgent threat that required preemptive action. But at the time, it did not have an immediate negative impact on public opinion. Just before Sawyer's interview our troops had captured Saddam Hussein, pulling him out of the "spider hole" in which he'd hidden. The good news gave us a temporary bump in support for the war. Still, the narrative of exaggeration or deliberate deception had been established at least as far back as the sixteen words controversy.

Our lack of candor and slowness in doing something to address the problem, even by investigating why it was wrong, only allowed it to take hold. The president was right that (virtually) everyone had the same intelligence to review and believed Saddam Hussein was a danger. But he was the one who rapidly pushed the country toward war, based on the way his advisers packaged the intelligence to sound more certain, grave, and urgent than it was turning out to be.

Because of our continuing lack of openness and forthrightness about the case for war, the president was boxing himself in, deepening suspicion and fueling partisan combat. It allowed some critics and partisan Democrats to raise questions and insinuate deliberate deception about how Bush's team of policymakers had used intelligence to sell the war. But since we avoided discussing it or fully examining the truth of how the case was made, we could only counterattack by questioning (though not completely dispelling) the honesty or fairness of their arguments. So the verbal warfare would only accelerate.

The media, in such an instance, might fairly be accused of overemphasizing the controversy and allowing deceitful attacks against us to receive too much attention. But our spin and evasion were leaving lingering questions unaddressed and opening the administration to growing criticism. It was a narrative that could only be changed through candor and a willingness to accept some short-term political pain by acknowledging our own mistakes. In hindsight, we missed our opportunity to put that narrative to rest for good. To do so, the president would have had to fully investigate the selling of the war, openly accept responsibility, and then hold top people accountable. Instead, the president was on a course that would ultimately lead to a much heavier price being paid in terms of his credibility and legacy.

That course led in January 2004 to another major setback in the struggle for public support. David Kay resigned as head of the Iraq Survey Group that month and testified before Congress that there were no WMD stockpiles to be found. "It turns out we were all wrong, probably, in my judgment," Kay stated. Along with prominent Democrats, Kay called for an independent outside inquiry into the apparent failure of U.S. intelligence. But Kay stated he did not believe the administration had pressured intelligence analysts to exaggerate the threat. (In the summer of 2004, the Senate Intelligence Committee would reach similar conclusions, stating that policymakers had been misled by faulty intelligence and putting off any examination of how the intelligence was used by policymakers.)

Bush and his advisers feared outside investigations. However, as momentum built for yet another independent probe, we saw the benefit of acting quickly and on our terms. Bush soon announced the creation of a bipartisan independent commission to look into our intelligence on WMD, including Iraq. Its members were appointed by the president, and its scope set by his team. It would not include looking at how the intelligence had been used to make the case for war. That was something Bush and his top advisers sought to avoid, concerned at a minimum—particularly in an election year—that it would prove politically fatal. They were willing to allow things to become more politicized, some considering it a battle that could be fought to a draw or even used to motivate the base, and believed that the short-term political cost could be minimized.

In Bush's mind, how the case for war had been made scarcely mattered. What mattered now was the policy and showing success. The public tends to be more forgiving when the results are promising. If the policy was right and the selling of the policy could be justified at the time, then any difference between the two mattered little. In this view, governing successfully in Washington is about winning public opinion and getting positive results.

To this day, the president seems unbothered by the disconnect between the chief rationale for war and the driving motivation behind it, and unconcerned about how the case was packaged. The policy is the right one and history will judge it so, once a free Iraq is firmly in place and the Middle East begins to become more democratic.

Bush clung to the same belief during an interview with Tim Russert of NBC News in early February 2004. The *Meet the Press* host asked, "In light of not finding the weapons of mass destruction, do you believe the war in Iraq is a war of choice or a war of necessity?"

The president said, "That's an interesting question. Please elaborate on that a little bit. A war of choice or a war of necessity? It's a war of necessity. In my judgment, we had no choice, when we look at the intelligence I looked at, that says the man was a threat."

I remember talking to the president about this question following the interview. He seemed puzzled and asked me what Russert was getting at with the question.

This, in turn, puzzled me. Surely this distinction between a necessary, unavoidable war and a war that the United States could have avoided but chose to wage was an obvious one that Bush must have thought about in the months before the invasion. Evidently it wasn't obvious to the president, nor did his national security team make sure it was. He set the policy early on and then his team focused his attention on how to sell it. It strikes me today as an indication of his lack of inquisitiveness and his detrimental resistance to reflection, something his advisers needed to compensate for better than they did.

Most objective observers today would say that in 2003 there was no urgent need to address the threat posed by Saddam with a large-scale invasion, and therefore the war was not necessary. But this is a question President Bush seems not to want to grapple with.

I SAT STONE-FACED AND MOTIONLESS in the elegant White House East Room, trying hard not to show any outward concern in front of the assembled inquisitors. But I could feel the muscles in my body tensing up as I listened to the president's tortured response to a straightforward question.

It was near the end of a prime-time press conference in April 2004. The president had called on John Dickerson, a White House correspondent for *Time* magazine. Having covered Bush since the 2000 campaign, Dickerson was a comfortingly familiar face. Risk averse by nature, the president hesitated to call on reporters he did not recognize, preferring to stick largely to the recommended names highlighted with a Sharpie on the seating chart resting on the podium. The list always included the most prominent journalists from the major networks, wire services, and newspapers, as well as at least one radio and one news magazine reporter.

The advantage of this approach was that the questions from traditional media correspondents predictably focused on the week's current headlines. Rarely was a question asked that we hadn't prepared the president for ahead of time. Bush was hardly ever thrown completely off his game, unable to either fall back on his broad philosophical views or find a way to segue to a few familiar talking points he could recite in his sleep.

This night, I'd highlighted the name of a different news magazine correspondent, primarily because Dickerson had been called on more recently. But I also knew his probingly clever questions had a way of knocking the president off script. The result might be to change the next day's news coverage from what we sought the focus to be or even—worse yet—create some actual news. For example, in one previous press conference, Dickerson had asked the president about whether he thought Muslims worshiped the same God as Christians. In another, he'd asked whether he agreed with "many" of his supporters that homosexuality is immoral. These controversial social topics were too far outside the president's comfort zone to elicit expansive public comment. When Bush had responded by saying that, yes, Muslims worshiped the same God as Christians, some evangelical leaders were dismayed. And when he answered the question about homosexuality by referring to tolerance for all individuals, his initial remark that "we're all sinners" caused some critics on the left to cry foul (because Bush was implying that homosexuality was sinful).

But Dickerson had a disarmingly easygoing, down-to-earth manner not unlike the president's, and this made Bush partial to him. His question would be the next to last one asked, and it was deceptively simple.

"Thank you, Mr. President," the clean-cut, golden-haired reporter began as he was handed the wireless microphone and rose to ask his question. "In the last campaign, you were asked a question about the biggest mistake you'd made in your life, and you used to like to joke that it was trading Sammy Sosa. You've looked back before 9/11 for what mistakes might have been made. After 9/11, what would your biggest mistake be, would you say, and what lessons have you learned from it?"

The president began with a lighthearted quip: "I wish you would have given me this written question ahead of time, so I could plan for it." The assembled reporters chuckled. "John, I'm sure historians will look back and say, gosh, he could have done it better this way, or that way. You know, I just—I'm sure something will pop into my head here in the midst of this press conference, with all the pressure of trying to come up with an answer, but it hadn't yet." His response was followed by an agonizingly long pause.

Have you ever experienced seconds that felt like minutes? A hundred thoughts flowed through my brain while that terrible silence hung embarrassingly in the air. I found myself thinking, *Come on, sir, this one is not difficult! Just say something like, "I am sure I have made plenty of mistakes, and history will judge them. But I've got a job to do and, while some would like me to look backward (you can even use your favorite expression, "navel gaze"), I believe it's important to keep looking forward, thinking about the important objectives we are trying to accomplish. That's what the American people expect me to do, and that's what I intend to do."*

The assembled reporters stirred uneasily in their seats as the silence continued. When someone is struggling in public, everyone around feels uncomfortable. No American wants to see our president look awkward or embarrassed on a national platform. Yet that is what we were witnessing now. As President Bush continued to agonize over a response, I blamed myself. *Why didn't we throw that one at him in the murder board session beforehand? We used it before, without specifying "after 9/11." It's such an obvious one—what is wrong with me?* But then a counterreaction kicked in. *Wait a second! We're talking about the president of the United States here! He didn't get to be president without being able to bat down a simple question. We've talked about mistakes. We've talked about 9/11. We've talked about the invasion of Iraq. Why can't he pull up some of those talking points?* And all the while, as the debate raged in my head, the president continued to stumble, while I wanted desperately to scream out an answer for him. The pauses lasted only a few seconds but at the time, it seemed much longer than that.

Finally the president came out with a rambling, rather incoherent, ultimately unsatisfying response to Dickerson's question:

> I would have gone into Afghanistan the way we went into Afghanistan. Even knowing what I know today about the stockpiles of weapons, I still would have called upon the world to deal with Saddam Hussein. See, I happen to believe that we'll find out the truth on the weapons. That's why we've sent up the independent commission. I look forward to hearing the truth, exactly where they are. They could still be there. They could be hidden, like the 50 tons of mustard gas in a turkey farm.

One of the things that [UN arms inspector] Charlie Duelfer talked about was that he was surprised at the level of intimidation he found amongst people who should know about weapons, and their fear of talking about them because they don't want to be killed. There's a terror still in the soul of some of the people in Iraq; they're worried about getting killed, and, therefore, they're not going to talk.

But it will all settle out, John. We'll find out the truth about the weapons at some point in time. However, the fact that he had the capacity to make them bothers me today, just like it would have bothered me then. He's a dangerous man. He's a man who actually—not only had weapons of mass destruction—the reason I can say that with certainty is because he used them. And I have no doubt in my mind that he would like to have inflicted harm, or paid people to inflict harm, or trained people to inflict harm on America, because he hated us.

I hope I—I don't want to sound like I've made no mistakes. I'm confident I have. I just haven't—you just put me under the spot here, and maybe I'm not as quick on my feet as I should be in coming up with one.

In desperation, he turned and called for another question, relief obvious on his features as he said, "Yes, Ann?"

Watching Bush struggle with the simple question, I sensed, as many others in the room did, that he was hung up on what he thought the press still sought to extract from him: an acknowledgment, one year after the fact, that his decision to go into Iraq was a mistake. That's why, unwilling to make any such admission, his response had morphed into yet another justification of the invasion, even though this was exactly the opposite of what Dickerson had asked.

As we were walking out of the East Room at the end of the press conference and moving briskly to catch up with the president, Dan Bartlett and I conversed in muted tones. We both agreed that the Dickerson response had not gone well.

The president, his tie now loosened, was waiting for us just inside the main entrance to the unlit State Dining Room. The only light came from the cracks of the sliding doors, the two openings to the dimly lit Red Room, and the opening to the Old Family Dining Room nearby.

Dan and I knew the drill. It was the president's bedtime, and he didn't care for an in-depth critique of his performance right after leaving the media pressure cooker. So we began by complimenting the president on hitting the right tone and getting his message across on questions about what the government had been doing pre–9/11 to combat terrorism and Iraq. Then Dan tactfully broached the awkward response to the Dickerson question. We had to bring it up in the little time we knew we could hold the president's attention.

"Yeah, I know," Bush said. "I kept thinking about what they wanted me to say—that it was a mistake to go into Iraq. And I'm not going to. It was the right decision." His tone was cocksure and matter-of-fact, not testy. I heard him assert such certitude about the decision often in casual conversation. He felt pretty good about his performance that evening, despite stumbling on the Dickerson question.

"I thought you were on the right track," I said, "when you mentioned how historians would look back and judge your decisions. All you needed to add was to say that you plan to stay focused on the future."

"Yeah, that's right," Bush agreed. "All right, guys. Thanks for your good work," and he headed around the corner in his usual swift manner to join the butler who was holding the elevator to his private residence above, followed by a Secret Service agent.

There were many other times, in private and public, when the president defended the most fateful decision of his administration. But few will be remembered as vividly as the one he made that night. It became symbolic of a leader unable to acknowledge that he got it wrong, and unwilling to grow in office by learning from his mistake—too stubborn to change and grow.

My knowledge of George W. Bush suggested several reasons for his inability to admit a serious mistake on his part. One was his fear of appearing weak. A more self-confident executive would be willing to acknowledge failure, to trust people's ability to forgive those who seek redemption for mistakes and show a readiness to change.

Another likely reason was the personal pain he would have suffered if he'd had to acknowledge that the war against Saddam may have been unnecessary. It would have been very difficult for anyone, much less the president, to confront the realization that his own decision was a mistake. An honest statement of the facts would have served Bush better—something like, "We now know that Saddam was a less serious threat than we believed. Still, the war was just and justified. Saddam was a brutal dictator, guilty of many crimes against humanity. He had an opportunity to come clean, but chose continued defiance.

What is important now is that we continue to work together on a consensus way forward to a successful outcome—one we can all agree on. That is how we, here at home, will best serve our troops fighting abroad and honor the sacrifices that so many of them have made and are making."

But Bush was not one to look back once a decision was made. Rather than suffer any sense of guilt and anguish, Bush chose not to go down the road of self-doubt or take on the difficult task of honest evaluation and reassessment. Rather than look back, he would always look forward, focused on the challenges of the future rather than the regrets of the past. That was especially true when it came to a decision as irrevocable and consequential as war in Iraq.

But at times, Bush had no choice but to face those doubts. He believed one of his most important responsibilities as a war-time president was to visit the wounded and comfort the families of the fallen. He did so frequently, in Washington and during his travels around the country. I would shadow him in such settings.

He visited the wounded at Walter Reed Army Medical Center a number of times. It was always moving to see the spirit and courage of those who had suffered terrible sacrifice—from traumatic head injuries to lost limbs. Most just wanted to return to Iraq to rejoin their band of brothers though their injuries would prevent it. Modern-day medical care thankfully is able to save many more lives than in past wars. One of the most memorable images that stands out to me took place during one of the president's visits to Walter Reed. He would go from room to room, visiting with the wounded soldiers and their loved ones. I entered a room just ahead of him and stood by the doorway. The room was dimly lit. A young mom from Texas and her seven-year-old son were seated next to their husband and father. He sat upright in a wheelchair, motionless. His head was covered in white gauze and bandage from the top down to his eyes. He was clearly not aware of his surroundings; the brain injury was severe.

The president entered just after me. He walked over to the mom and hugged her. He put his hand on the son's shoulder and told him, "Your dad is a very brave man." After visiting briefly, Bush turned back to the soldier, placed his hand gently on the wheelchair, bent down, and softly kissed the top of his head before whispering in his ear, "God bless you." Then he turned and walked toward the door. Looking straight ahead, he moved his right hand to wipe away a tear. In that moment, I could see the doubt in his eyes and the vivid realization of the irrevocable consequences of his decision.

Many a time, I would see the president walk into a room or area where the family of a fallen soldier was gathered. He would hug the mom or wife. He would visit with them and the dads and children, listening to them share stories of their loved one. Often a mom would look the president in the eye and say, "You finish the job. You make sure my son did not die in vain."

These visits had a way of reinforcing the president's resolve to successfully complete the mission—to press ahead. The momentary doubt became, in the end, another reason for his unshakable determination.

Still another motive for Bush to avoid acknowledging mistakes was his determination to win the political game at virtually any cost. Bush was not about to give the establishment Washington media anything critics could use to damage him and his reelection effort. He knew that, in today's political climate, if he admitted error on a consequential matter like the decision to go to war, partisan critics would seize on it and use it to tear him down. On this, he probably wasn't wrong, but I believe that embracing openness and forthrightness could have redeemed him, transcended partisanship, and brought together leaders of both parties to chart a consensus way forward on Iraq. It may not have been on Bush's exact terms or to his preferred way of achieving a successful outcome, but it would have served our country and those we asked to defend it a lot better.

Finally, there was Bush's insistence on remaining true to his base. Wary of replicating any of his father's political errors, Bush feared that his conservative base would begin to fracture if he appeared to back away from his commitment to Iraq. Bush and Rove believe that the base wants a leader that is strong, decisive, and firm in his beliefs above all. Since holding the base and keeping it energized was an absolute must in their view, Bush's reluctance to admit error was at least understandable—if not wise.

As far as Bush and his advisers (especially Karl Rove) were concerned, being open and forthright in such circumstances was a recipe for trouble. And perhaps they were right—for the short term. In the long run, the president's inability to face the reality of his own decisions, as illustrated by that emblematic moment in the press conference, would become a large and steadily growing barrier between him and the American people. It would also help erode any remaining opportunity for bipartisanship and a diminution of the partisan warfare crippling Washington and the American political system—all happening while our men and women in uniform abroad could have used the opposite from Washington.

But in May 2004, Bush and Rove were focused on the short term—the fall election. The president had promised himself that he would accomplish what his father had failed to do by winning a second term in office. And that meant operating continually in campaign mode: never explaining, never apologizing, never retreating. Unfortunately that strategy also had less justifiable repercussions: never reflecting, never reconsidering, never compromising. Especially not where Iraq was concerned.

The first grave mistake of Bush's presidency was rushing toward military confrontation with Iraq. It took his presidency off course and greatly damaged his standing with the public. His second grave mistake was his virtual blindness about his first mistake, and his unwillingness to sustain a bipartisan spirit during a time of war and change course when events demanded it.

I imagine that my views about Iraq have evolved in parallel to those of many Americans. Before the invasion, I was uncertain about the necessity of waging a new kind of preemptive war. Few people like the idea of going to war. If we are attacked, of course, then we must respond forcefully. But Iraq was different. No attack was imminent, Iraq was not known to be involved in any attack on America (other than firing on our planes in the no-fly zone), and the threat was not urgent.

But 9/11 had affected our thinking in a profound way. The shock and anger we all experienced left many of us resolving to avenge the attacks in any way necessary. And our quick military success in toppling the Taliban in Afghanistan solidified broad public support for the president and his administration. Trust in Bush and his tested advisers was extraordinarily high, and so was public deference toward their judgment.

I shared that sense of deference. As a Texas loyalist who followed Bush to Washington with great hope and personal affection and as a proud member of his administration, I was all too ready to give him and his highly experienced foreign policy advisers the benefit of the doubt on Iraq. Unfortunately, subsequent events have showed that our willingness to trust the judgments of Bush and his team was misplaced.

Today, my views on Iraq probably still track those of most Americans. Although I've been forced to conclude that we should never have rushed to war in the first place, I want us to succeed. But that success should be defined with a consensus of bipartisan leaders who are focused on doing what is best for the nation. It's clear that our troops have been there too long and been called on, as have their families, to do far more than should have been required. We need to find a way—sooner rather than later—to significantly reduce our troop presence in the heart of Iraq so that our forces can focus on terrorist activity and rapid deployment to assist the Iraqis as necessary. My concern is the same as that of so many other Americans. What is the end game? Where is the light at the end of the tunnel? If more outside support is needed, we need to somehow build a broader coalition, perhaps under the auspices of the United Nations, perhaps with the help of a regional coalition of powers, so that other countries can help bear the burden.

Can such a solution still be attained at this late date, with so many people and so much treasure already lost? I hope so. But, sadly, it almost certainly will not be achieved by this president. His credibility, with Americans and people around the world, has been damaged by his refusal to talk honestly about his war and its costs. All he can do now is prepare to pass along the problem to his successor.

It didn't have to be this way. Even after the initial mistake of rushing to war in Iraq had been made, the situation was far from irretrievable. But no one in the president's inner circle—myself included—had the wisdom or courage to press him to be more open and honest with the American people.

Instead, throughout 2003 and 2004, as the bad news about Iraq slowly emerged, the president and top advisers clung to the belief that the war he had wagered his presidency on would somehow turn out right. As the trickle of bad news turned into a torrent, the president could only double down.

In May 2004, the horrific pictures from Abu Ghraib prison surfaced, shaming many Americans and causing a worldwide revulsion that severely damaged our efforts to win the hearts and minds of people in the Muslim world.

As the number of U.S. military dead and injured rose beyond expectations (we would reach the 1,000 killed mark shortly before the election), I watched the president grapple with the painful toll up close and in person during those private hospital visits and meetings with the families of the fallen. Just as Vietnam had come to haunt two administrations forty years earlier, so Iraq haunted both the Bush presidency and George W. Bush the man. I saw time and again how the sight of a combat veteran gravely injured in battle, or the wife and child of a young soldier who would never come home again, caused Bush deep personal distress, even anguish. But the one reaction Bush would never allow himself was self-doubt. If anything, the painful moments he spent

trying to comfort those who had lost loved ones in Iraq—losses caused, ultimately, by Bush's decision to go to war—only strengthened his determination
to prove that the choice to invade had been the right one and that their sacrifice would be for a noble cause.

There were moments of hope mixed in with the gloom. The official transfer of sovereignty to an interim Iraqi government on June 28, 2004, helped
buoy American spirits. The transfer spoke to Bush's most heartfelt rationale
for invading Iraq—to spread democracy in the Middle East—and bolstered
the hope that, despite its growing toll, the war in Iraq would ultimately seem
both just and justified in the eyes of history.

As the 2004 election campaign unfolded, and with it the hyperpartisan atmosphere that has become standard for a national election year, other issues
took their turn in the spotlight, including the economy, the 9/11 Commission's investigation, a furious controversy over Bush's National Guard service
back in the 1970s, and a debate over Bush's plan for providing prescription
drug coverage to seniors under Medicare.

But three core issues at the heart of the Iraq debate kept dogging Bush
and his presidency: whether the rationale for war was deliberately misleading;
whether the decision was right or worth it, even without WMD; and whether
the administration's handling of the situation on the ground was satisfactory.
The permanent campaign battle to manipulate public opinion and shape the
narrative to our advantage over each would play a central role in determining
the outcome of the election.

12

BRUSH FIRE

Meanwhile, as the chief rationale for our war in Iraq gradually unraveled against the backdrop of a looming presidential race, one piece of the Iraq drama continued to unfold—the story of how the identity of CIA agent Valerie Plame had been revealed as part of the growing partisan battle between the Bush administration and its critics on Capitol Hill and in the media. It was a saga that would increasingly come to affect me personally.

Tuesday, September 30, 2003, the day after I explicitly asserted that Karl Rove had not leaked classified security information—Valerie Plame's identity—was a travel day. No White House briefing, just a gaggle aboard Air Force One en route from Andrews Air Force Base, where the world's best-known plane is based, to Chicago.

The president was doing the usual VIP photo-ops and speaking at a Bush-Cheney luncheon to raise money for the fast approaching 2004 reelection campaign. Then he'd be meeting with area business leaders to highlight what he was doing to address economic concerns and help create jobs.

About 8:30 P.M. the night before, the Justice Department had informed White House counsel Al Gonzales that officials there had opened a criminal investigation into the Valerie Plame leak. The White House, he'd been told, should preserve all records that might be relevant. At Al's request, the department would send a formal letter to this effect on Tuesday. Al asked whether the White House needed to inform staff that evening, or if it could wait until the morning. The Justice Department said morning would be fine.

Since rumors of a criminal investigation had been circulating during the previous few days, I had been staying in close contact with Al and his deputy, David Lietch, including the morning before I departed the White House with the president. I wanted to make sure I was up-to-date on any contacts from Justice, and I needed advice from Al and David about how to respond to questions from the press.

Al informed the entire senior staff of the investigation shortly after 7:30 A.M. during our daily meeting, as we were all seated in our assigned leather chairs around the wooden conference table stretching the length of the Roosevelt Room. He instructed us to tell members of our respective staffs to preserve "all materials that may be related" to the leak, and said that "the president has directed that we fully cooperate with this investigation." Al also said a memo to all White House staff would be emailed at 8:30 A.M. with specific instructions.

Andy Card made it clear that the president wanted to get to the bottom of the matter and that staff should report relevant information to the Department of Justice. The room was eerily silent as all present listened intently to Al and Andy.

The president and I chatted about this new development in the leak case that morning in the Oval, as well as during the short Marine One chopper flight from the south lawn of the White House to Andrews. The president, Dan Bartlett, and I all agreed that he should comment on the investigation, now that we officially had been notified about it.

During the gaggle on Air Force One, I updated the press pool about the Justice Department notification to Al. I had already spoken with some reporters earlier that morning before leaving the White House, and they had already been given a copy of the memo Al had sent to all staff.

The press pool is a small group of journalists that covers the president when there is insufficient space for the entire press corps or when other logistical reasons require it. There are usually about fifteen in the pool, and that is the number of seats they have on Air Force One. They sit in the far back left of the plane, directly behind a section for Secret Service agents. Three spots are reserved for the print wire services, including the AP, Reuters, and Bloomberg News. One spot is held for the rotating print pooler, who comes from one of the major newspapers on the beat. One spot is for a radio correspondent and one for a news magazine journalist (from *Time, Newsweek, U.S. News,* or *National Journal*); one for a broadcast correspondent or producer; two for the same network's camera person and sound person; and the rest for various still photographers. Anything they cover must be shared at the earliest possible time with the larger White House press corps.

Based on what the president and I had agreed to earlier in the morning, I ended my opening comments to the pool by saying, "The president wants to get to the bottom of this as much as anyone, and believes it should be pursued to the fullest extent, as I said yesterday. The president has always expressed his concern that leaking classified information is a serious matter and it should be taken very seriously. The president expects anyone in the administration to adhere to the highest standards of conduct." I added that the president believes "anyone who has information relating to this investigation should report that information to the Department of Justice."

Following the president's Chicago meeting, the unruly, elbowing mob of the combined White House and local press pool was escorted into the small room where a roundtable discussion was to take place. The president, seated in the center surrounded by local business leaders and next to Mayor Daley, with whom he'd gradually developed a good relationship, started by making some comments about the economy. Then he said he would take a couple of questions. I had recommended two reporters and briefed him on the likely questions he would be asked.

Deb Reichman, a White House reporter for the Associated Press, got the first crack. "Do you think that the Justice Department can conduct an impartial investigation, considering the political ramifications of the CIA leak, and why wouldn't a special counsel be better?"

"There are too many leaks of classified information in Washington," the president said. "And if there is a leak out of my administration, I want to know who it is. And if the person has violated law, the person will be taken care of." He added that he had confidence in the career Justice Department officials who were assigned to work on such investigations, and that he'd directed his administration to cooperate fully.

Then the president called on Bob Kemper, since we were in his newspaper's home town. Bob covered the White House for the *Chicago Tribune* and had covered the president since the 2000 campaign. "Yes, let's see, Kemper— he's from Chicago," the president said. "Where are you? Are you a Cubs or

White Sox fan?" There was laughter from those in the room. "Wait a minute. That doesn't seem fair, does it?"

Kemper, undeterred by the president's good-natured needling, said, "Yesterday we were told that Karl Rove had no role in it . . . "

"Yes," the president interrupted.

"Have you talked to Karl and do you have confidence in him?" Kemper interjected.

"I don't know of anybody in my administration who leaked classified information," he said. "If somebody did leak classified information, I'd like to know it, and we'll take the appropriate action."

Mission accomplished. The president had made clear how seriously he took the investigation, how much he disliked leaks of classified information, and how much he wanted to get to the bottom of the matter. And he'd made clear that if anyone in his administration had been responsible for the leak, he or she would have to leave.

The next morning's gaggle back at the White House signaled that the press was now turning toward a new rumored suspect in the leak, the vice president's chief of staff—Scooter Libby.

Here's how it started. Just as I was ending the gaggle, John Roberts, CBS News chief White House correspondent, said, "One more question. You said the other day, emphatically, that you had received assurances from Karl Rove that he had nothing to do with this. Have you since then received similar assurances from the vice president's chief of staff?"

"John, I'm not going to go down—I made this clear the other day—I'm not going to go down a list of every single member of the staff in the White House," I said, as I started moving away from the podium.

"That's just one name," Roberts pleaded, a little sarcastically, to some laughter.

I continued, "And there was a specific accusation made, and I responded to that. But I'm not going to go down the list from this podium."

"It's a short list, though," Roberts said, garnering a few more laughs as I headed out the sliding door to the lower press office.

I did not have much time to sit and critique the gaggle session with my staff that morning. President Uribe of Colombia would be meeting with the president shortly. Knowing the president's penchant for punctuality, I grabbed my notepad, told my staff that we would talk more before the briefing, and walked the twenty feet or so over to the Oval for the NSC prebrief with the president and his meeting with Uribe.

As I entered the Oval staff area, I ran into Scooter Libby. He frequently represented the vice president in world leader meetings when Cheney did not attend, and we often sat next to each other. Since we were both early, I asked if I could talk to him for a minute. We both stepped back into the small entryway connecting the Oval support staff area with the waiting area in the hallway.

"You need to know," I said, "the press is starting to ask more questions about you and whether you might have leaked Plame's name."

Scooter listened carefully. "I told them that I was not going to go down a list of White House staff and answer whether every staffer was involved in the leak," I continued. "I want you to know why. Now that there's an investigation under way, I can't put myself in that position. I want you to know I'm not trying to leave you hanging out there to dry."

Scooter expressed his appreciation for the heads-up but said little more. He seemed to be okay with my strategy, although neither he nor anyone in his position would be happy about it. But I felt I had at least done my part to make sure he got the news directly from me rather than from the media.

That Saturday, October 4, was a relaxed, casual morning for me as I lounged around my single-bedroom, downtown apartment reading the *Washington Post* and the *New York Times*. I hadn't yet shaved or showered, having slept in until 7:00 A.M., a couple of hours later than on a weekday, and I was thinking about hitting the gym downstairs. I typically tried to enjoy my Saturday mornings from home, unless I had to go into the office. I tended to go in Sunday afternoons to get some work done ahead of the coming week. Of course, with a twenty-four-hour news cycle, I was always on call and worked from home on weekends even if I did not go into the office.

The call from Andy Card came around 8:30 A.M. "The president and vice president spoke this morning. They want you to give the press the same assurance for Scooter that you gave for Karl."

I am not a coffee drinker. I drink diet Coke for my morning caffeine fix. I was still sipping on one, but what Andy just said jolted me more than the soft drink did.

"Okay," I said, not really indicating my instinctive disinclination to do what he was directing me to do. I told him that I would head into the office and talk to him more when I got there.

As I showered and dressed to go to the White House, I asked myself why Scooter hadn't talked to me first if he had a problem with the approach I was taking. Based on Andy's comments, it was clear to me Scooter had enlisted the vice president to personally appeal to the president to have me publicly deny his involvement. Now that the investigation was fully under way, I didn't like the idea of singling out staff members to defend. Earlier in the week, I had spoken with Al and David, who'd advised me pretty strongly against commenting any further on matters pertaining to the investigation, including the names of individuals. I had already told the press I would not do it. And I knew if I opened the door for one, it would be virtually impossible to close it if other names started to surface. And the press would be curious why I'd asked Scooter about his involvement, and why the White House wasn't asking every staff member the same question.

But this was an order coming from on high. As a result, I was about to cross the line I'd drawn publicly once the investigation had gotten under way earlier in the week.

After dropping my briefcase in my office, I headed over to Andy's. He was standing in front of his assistant's desk in the waiting area that his office shared with his deputy's on the opposite side.

I knew from Andy's terse comments on the phone that what he was saying was not really up for debate, nor did I expect him to offer any additional information about the president's telephone discussion with the vice president.

To this day, I do not know what the two discussed. I am confident from knowing the president and from our previous conversations that he did not have any knowledge about Libby, Rove, or anyone else involved in disclosing Plame's identity to reporters. President Bush would not have deliberately misled me. While I wish I could say the same about the vice president, I simply don't know for sure. Information that would become public in future legal proceedings would raise questions about the vice president's actions that he has never publicly addressed.

I told Andy I would make the same public statement about Scooter as I had for Karl, provided I received the same assurance from Scooter. Andy asked what statement I had given about Karl, and I told him I had said he was neither involved in leaking Plame's identity, nor did he condone it. I told Andy that once I'd spoken with Scooter, I would call a few reporters to make sure it got out.

When I got back to my office, I called a White House operator to track down Scooter. As he often did, he was traveling with Cheney, who was spending the weekend at his place in Jackson Hole, Wyoming.

The conversation was short. Scooter was never one for many words anyway. He knew why I was calling since he had instigated what I was being instructed to do. "Were you involved in the leak in any way?" I asked him.

"No, absolutely not," Scooter replied.

"All right," I said. "I plan to tell reporters that you did not leak the classified information, nor would you condone doing so. Is that correct?"

"Yes," he replied. Then we talked about which reporters I planned to call. Scooter hung up and I set about my disagreeable task.

I called reporters for *Newsweek*, which I'd heard was working on a story focusing on Scooter, the AP, and the *New York Times*. That same day, I happened to run into *Washington Post* correspondent Mike Allen outside on the White House grounds, and I told him as well. That made four reporters from four top national media organizations—plenty to get the news out, especially with it getting on the AP wire for all media to see. I told each that Scooter had assured me "he neither leaked the classified information, nor would he condone it," and made sure the press duty officer for the day was aware so as not to be caught blindsided if other media outlets called seeking to match their competitors.

Sure enough, pretty soon it was on the Associated Press newswire as part of a larger story on the leak investigation. I was glad to see it handled that way. It meant I'd managed to get the news about my "official" defense of Scooter out without drawing too much extra attention to it.

A short time later, I learned from Sean McCormack, another of my deputies and the chief spokesman for the National Security Council, that Elliott Abrams, a senior National Security Council staffer, had denied any involvement to a reporter who had contacted him directly because of "rumors." It's a sadly typical tactic used by some of the less scrupulous partisan activists in Washington during a time of scandal: Float a rumor in the media and see if it sticks. There was zero information to suggest Elliott was involved in the disclosure of Plame's identity, but he was considered a leading neoconservative foreign policy hawk and was an early advocate of regime change in Iraq. He'd also been pardoned by the first President Bush for two misdemeanor pleas for withholding information from Congress during the infamous Iran-Contra scandal. For these reasons, he was always an easy target for unsubstantiated allegations.

As far as I was concerned, Elliott was a seasoned foreign policy expert and helpful colleague who always shot straight with me, including that day. I contacted him and got the same assurances, and thought I'd better go ahead and get his denials out to the same reporters I'd spoken to about Scooter, since Elliott had already spoken to one anyway. Better to get it all out at once in the same news cycle, as opposed to one today, one tomorrow, and so on. So I called the same reporters back.

I was becoming increasingly frustrated, as this was exactly what I didn't want to happen. I was putting myself in the middle of the investigation by publicly vouching for people, against my own wishes and against the sound advice of White House counsel.

The following week, the press questions were back to the usual wide range of topics in the gaggles and briefings, but the leak investigation remained in the mix. Meanwhile, White House aides, including me, each in his or her own way, were sorting through their electronic records, correspondence, telephone logs, calendars, and notes and then copying anything that might be relevant under the broadly encompassing specifications of the Justice Department request.

On Monday, in response to follow-up questions, I confirmed at the briefing that I had spoken with Karl, Scooter, and Elliott and that each had denied any involvement in the leaking of Plame's identity. As I'd suspected they would, reporters wondered why I had questioned these three particular staff members, and why the president was not demanding that other staff members be asked the same question. I did some verbal dancing in response, knowing I was not authorized to get into the full backstory.

In hindsight, the president should have overruled his advisers and demanded that an internal investigation be conducted to determine whether there might have been any White House involvement. He also should have ordered the public release of as much information as possible as soon as it was known, so that the scandal would not take on a life of its own. But he chose not to do so, perhaps feeling that keeping clear of the story would insulate him and protect him from potential political damage. Instead it gave the story broader and longer life, only helping to reinforce the permanent state of suspicion and partisan warfare he had pledged to move Washington beyond.

Dan Bartlett later shared with me that David Addington, the vice president's counsel, had expressed concern after learning that I had publicly exonerated Scooter. Addington specifically warned Bartlett that I should not be out there talking about the investigation or discussing what anyone had done or not done. Bartlett responded, "It was your boss who told us to." I grimaced ever so briefly as Dan and I shook our heads. We were a bit incredulous.

Addington is publicly perceived as one of the most secretive officials in the White House. Over time, however, I would find that he was also one of the most helpful to me. He shared information or advice privately so that I would not misstep publicly as press secretary. Nothing was more important to me than getting the full picture when seeking information from a colleague. It was not always easy in a White House where some cared little for the press or viewed it as another "special interest." But David was considerate of my need to be fully briefed on things in order to be effective, and accurate. If he knew something he felt would help, he did not need prompting to share it or a game of twenty questions to guess it.

Unfortunately, Addington's advice was apparently neither heard nor heeded by those pushing me further into the abyss I had already unwittingly stepped into.

AT THE FRIDAY, OCTOBER 10, BRIEFING, I made my final comments about Rove's and Libby's assurances. Soon FBI agents and Justice Department prosecutors would begin interviewing White House officials.

I talked with Al and David about my personal situation after being contacted by the FBI. After reminding me that neither he nor Al was my personal attorney, David remarked, "This is not like being the White House spokesman. You want to answer questions completely and openly, as opposed to only the limited information you might share as a spokesman. You don't necessarily have to volunteer information beyond what they ask, but you need to be candid and responsive to what they do ask." The advice came as no surprise, but it was helpful to have it reinforced beforehand.

Al and David also offered to provide someone from their office to sit in on any conversations I might have with the FBI. I realized this would also be a convenient way for them to keep tabs on the investigation and any possible fallout for the president. Nevertheless, I was glad to take them up on their offer.

Within days, I had my first meeting with FBI agents in a second-floor conference room the counsel's office had set aside in the Eisenhower Executive Office Building on the White House grounds, just across the West Executive driveway from the West Wing staff entrance. The high-ceilinged room was lit by large windows on one side. Other than that, there was just a large wooden conference table surrounded by leather chairs.

John Eckenrode, the special agent in charge of the investigation for the FBI from day one, led the discussion. He was joined by two other agents who were seated on the side of the table facing the door; I was on the other side, facing the windows behind them.

They had been provided copies of all the documents from my work files that I had turned over to the counsel's office the second week in October. I remember one email I'd handed over from a friend of my personal assistant, Carmen Ingwell. Carmen's friend had attended a class or lecture event at a California university a few years earlier featuring Joe Wilson, during which, she said, Wilson had mentioned that his wife worked for the CIA. I had no idea whether the story was true or not.

It was early in the investigation, and the agents seemed to be focused on learning about how the White House, including the White House communications team, operated and interacted with the media.

Ted Ullyot, a smart, capable, thirty-something attorney in the White House counsel's office, listened in as I answered questions. I already knew Ted a little from working with him on other issues, and he had always come across as open and helpful. He and his colleague Raul Yanes had been tasked as the point people for the investigation in the counsel's office. I came to know Ted and Raul better during that time, and I thought that Al and David could not have chosen two finer individuals for such a controversial, high-profile task.

After that first meeting with FBI investigators, I remember saying to Ted, as we walked down the Executive Office Building hallway back to the West Wing, "I was surprised they didn't ask any substantive questions about what I might know, such as my conversations with Rove and Libby." The second meeting, I believe within a couple of weeks, was more targeted to what I might know. Neither meeting lasted much more than an hour.

On December 30, 2003, deputy attorney general Jim Comey held a news conference at the Department of Justice. He announced that attorney general John Ashcroft had recused himself from the investigation to avoid any appearance of conflict of interest. Comey then announced that he was naming a special prosecutor to oversee the leak investigation—Patrick J. Fitzgerald of Chicago. Fitzgerald was a highly regarded U.S. attorney who had a reputation for playing by the book and not being swayed by politics.

Comey would not publicly discuss what had led to the decision to appoint the special counsel except to say that "an accumulation of facts" over the previous several months had led to the decision. "We don't want people that we might be interested in to know that we're interested in them. We also don't want to smear somebody who might be innocent and might not be charged."

Ron Roos, the deputy to the head of the Justice Department's counterespionage unit run by John Dion, contacted me to arrange a time to meet with the team overseeing the investigation days before I was subpoenaed to appear before the grand jury. This time he asked if I would come alone without anyone from the counsel's office. They preferred to talk to me alone, he indicated. I agreed. It made little difference to me one way or the other, although I appreciated hearing any feedback Ted was able to offer. I suspected that the investigative team wanted to keep information as closely held as possible as they proceeded with grand jury testimony.

Early on, when I knew that I would be questioned in light of my public exonerations of Rove, Libby, and Abrams, I consulted my sister-in-law Stephanie McClellan, a former assistant district attorney in San Jose County, and my brother Dudley, a former clerk to a federal judge in Austin.

Stephanie thought I should hire an attorney, even though I told her I did not know anything about the actual leak and that my role was limited to defending the White House and a couple of staffers after the fact. She perceptively pointed out that one can never know with certainty how words spoken might be construed or, worse, twisted, particularly in the context of a high-profile political investigation taking place during an election campaign.

Dudley was noncommittal, just advising me as a brother and knowledgeable attorney on the pro's of hiring counsel. I would later ask him some basic, substantive questions. He, his twin, Bradley, and our eldest brother, Mark, may have picked on me growing up but we are as close as any brothers can be. It was reassuring to know I could call on him when push came to shove.

Colleagues thought I would be crazy not to hire an attorney. My deputy Claire Buchan, a good friend who always looked out for me, basically said, "You *have* to hire an attorney."

However, unlike many of my colleagues, I decided not to. I would tell investigators the truth—what I knew and what I remembered. With nothing to hide and with my only involvement coming in the aftermath of the leak, I felt comfortable with the decision. (I don't mean to imply that my colleagues had something to hide, I'm just expressing my own feeling about the decision.)

So there I was that cold afternoon at the counterespionage unit's office, several floors up in a Justice Department office building a few blocks from the White House.

The conference room where we met was rather dark. The table was long. I saw the FBI agents who had previously interviewed me. Ron Roos introduced himself and the others present. I sat at the center of the table across from the FBI agents, as I had in the previous meetings in the Executive Office Building. Prosecutorial team members sat across the table as well as to my right. Fitzgerald was not in the room.

While the previous meetings were straightforward and free of tension, this one started differently. Roos, who struck me as a serious and professional prosecutor, asked why I had exonerated Rove and Libby. Then he asked why I had not mentioned in the first meeting that Karl had spoken to Novak. Somewhat taken aback, I looked at one of the FBI agents and said, "I told you all when you asked me in the second meeting. You didn't ask about it in the first meeting." The agent said nothing. I thought, Okay, they're playing tough to make sure I have told them everything I know or can recall, and to make sure they have been thorough in seeking to learn the truth.

A few minutes later, Peter Zeidenberg, a prosecutor from the public integrity unit, entered the room. He introduced himself and seemed friendly. Professional and courteous, he quickly won my respect and trust.

He played good cop to Ross's bad cop, indicating they were just trying to verify facts. He said he had seen many times how a witness's memory can be hazy when they're asked to recollect something that happened weeks or months earlier, and they just wanted to make sure they talked to me before my grand jury appearance. From his comments, I assumed he had been watching the initial discussion through what appeared to be a one-way window to my right, like one would see on the television show *Law and Order*.

The meeting did not last much longer, and I was soon back at the White House to tend to my press secretary duties. Still, I wondered about their initial hard-edged approach. I felt a little unsettled, since I had always been fully co-operative and open with them. I imagined they used the tactic to try to rattle those being questioned to see if they were being truthful. But I was comforted by the way the meeting had ended, and felt they had reassured themselves I had nothing to hide.

My appearance before a federal grand jury loomed before me. As I sensed was true of my colleagues, it weighed on my mind because of the high-stakes nature of the investigation. White House staffers long ago had stopped talking to one another about anything specific related to the leak investigation, including whether they'd been questioned and whether or not they'd hired an attorney (as with any high-profile Washington investigation, almost every White House aide going before the grand jury hired a lawyer out of an abundance of caution, even if they knew they were not involved). About the only thing I heard from colleagues was when they were headed to the grand jury, since the press was camped out by the grand jury room on a daily basis and my colleagues did not want me to be blindsided by hearing it from a reporter first. Besides the silence we shared, we all sensed the same anxiety hanging over us.

Somewhat unnerved, I wondered: Was Stephanie's advice right? Should I be leaning on an attorney's advice? When you agree to work for the president of the United States, you don't picture being interrogated by the FBI or testifying before a grand jury under threat of perjury as part of the job description.

The grand jury reportedly began hearing testimony in late January 2004. I was called to appear before the jurors on Friday afternoon, February 6.

I met Roos and one of the agents outside in the hallway in the upstairs area of the Prettyman federal courthouse building, near the Capitol on Pennsylvania Avenue. The afternoon weather was overcast and cold, although not unusually so for Washington that time of year. There was a little drizzle of rain now and then.

They told me they would be ready for me soon, and just to hang tight. Both were very friendly that afternoon. I sat in a chair in the barren, ill-lit hallway.

I walked to the grand jury room through a narrow, short hall. Not quite sure what to expect, I entered the room and was directed to sit down in a

wooden chair near the door at the short end of an L-shaped table. The prosecutorial team was to my right facing the jurors, who were seated theater-style in
front and above us. At a guess, I'd say there were thirty-five or forty jurors present. Across the way a stenographer took down everything I was asked and said.

Zeidenberg, the public integrity unit prosecutor, asked the questions.
Given where my chair was positioned, it was hard to know who exactly was
present, and no introductions were made. Maybe Patrick Fitzgerald, the man I
felt I now knew from all the press attention he'd received but had not yet met,
was there, but I did not see him. I was focused on answering questions.

I turned slightly to the left, so I could partially face the jury while looking
at Zeidenberg. The first thing he asked was whether it was correct that I was
not represented by counsel. I indicated that I had not hired an attorney, but
had just talked a few times with my brother Dudley.

Then we went through a series of questions before the grand jury, most of
which I had answered on previous occasions, including accounts of my conversations with Karl and Scooter and the assurances they'd provided me that
they were not involved in the leaking of Plame's identity.

But there were a couple of questions they had not previously asked me.
Zeidenberg asked whether I'd told Condi Rice that she should say that Karl was
not involved before she went on the Sunday talk shows back on September 28,
2003. (Rice hadn't in fact addressed this specific matter on those shows.)

I thought hard. I knew I'd spoken to Condi that Saturday—the same Saturday I'd called Rove after first learning that he'd spoken to Novak and he'd
assured me he had not been involved in leaking classified information—as I
usually did with administration officials ahead of their Sunday show appearances. It was a way to prep them for responses to likely questions and make
sure everyone was on the same page; we knew the Sunday *Post* piece would
likely prompt questions about possible White House involvement in the leak.
Had I coached Condi on what to say about Karl Rove?

I said I might have but could not remember with certainty. I indicated it
was more likely I told her what I'd said publicly, and suggested she could refer
back to what I said without getting into it herself.

After hearing the second new question, I was momentarily taken aback.
Zeidenberg asked if it was true the president told me in the Oval Office that
Karl Rove told him he was not involved? It was the first time I'd been asked
about something the president knew or said. Since the president had not been

questioned yet, I knew that Andy must have discussed it with investigators at some earlier point. Knowing the president's preference that his private conversations remain private, I hesitated momentarily. But this was different. I knew forthrightness was the only option. A frog in my throat, I managed to confirm that the president had indeed made such a statement.

Zeidenberg wrapped up his questioning and asked jurors if they had any questions. Only a young African American woman seated at the far end of the room in the first row had a question. She asked me to define what "background," "deep background," and "off the record" meant to me.

I responded by saying that the terms meant slightly different things to different reporters. "My understanding," I said, "is that 'background' means a reporter can quote you but not reference you by name. The reporter and the source will usually agree as to what the attribution should be: 'a senior White House official,' 'a senior administration official,' or if the source wants to have more distance, maybe 'a Republican official' or 'a U.S. government official.' As for 'deep background,' most reporters view it as information they can use in their reporting but can't attribute in any way or directly quote the source. And 'off the record' means to me that the reporter can't use the information in any way in his reporting."

The session was over within an hour. Roos and one of the agents thanked me as they walked me back out to the hallway. They also said that, while I was legally free to talk about it, they would prefer that I keep my grand jury testimony private.

As I headed toward the stairs, a journalist standing in the hallway recognized me and followed me down the stairs. She introduced herself as a CBS producer and asked where my attorney was. I looked behind me and playfully said, "I don't know, you didn't see him back there?" After she looked around for a few seconds, I said I didn't have one. She expressed surprise since everyone else she had seen come in, did.

A few other reporters were gathered just outside the courthouse, trying to get some cover from the day's light drizzle. I put on a nonchalant smile as I stopped to answer a few questions. "Just glad to do my part to fully cooperate with the investigation, as the president directed us to do," I said before getting into my car.

The investigation continued for months without causing any real distraction during the successful reelection campaign. Still, White House staff would not speak with one another about it. The counsel's office had long ago put the kibosh on anyone talking publicly about it, including myself. And privately people had spent enough money on attorneys and enough time responding to investigators that no one wanted to do anything that might cause more of our government paychecks and already stretched schedules to be eaten up.

I imagine some people slipped at times and found themselves complaining about their hours before the grand jury or gossiping about "who dunnit." On a few occasions, even the president couldn't help himself. I remember hearing him in the Oval or on Air Force One grousing about having to hire an attorney and about the atmospherics of being questioned.

The president was interviewed by Patrick Fitzgerald and some of his team for about seventy minutes in the Oval in late June 2004. "Shooter," as the president nicknamed his private lawyer, Jim Sharp, was also present.

Al Gonzales had testified to the grand jury several days earlier, and the vice president had been interviewed at the beginning of June. I have no knowledge of what any of them told prosecutors.

Karl Rove's first appearance before the grand jury was on October 15, 2004. Coming just weeks before election day, it was used by Democrats as an opportunity to take shots at the president. The Kerry campaign, seeking any political mileage they could get at that late stage in the game, called for Rove and the White House "to come clean about their role in this insidious act." It would be Rove's only grand jury appearance before the election, but it would not be his last.

From the outset of the investigation, the president had made a decision not to pursue the matter internally. He said he wanted to get to the bottom of questionable activity surrounding the leak episode, but he did not order any White House staff members to mount an investigation, nor to take any other proactive steps to uncover the truth or inform the public. At least in part on the advice of White House lawyers and other key advisers, he chose to leave the leak and its consequences solely to the special counsel.

The approach stood in stark contrast to the way the White House had approached the sixteen words controversy that led to the scandal. In that case, once the decision had been made to determine how the words had made it into the presidential address, we got to the bottom of what happened fairly quickly and shared information as completely as possible. By approaching the controversy openly and forthrightly, we shortened its shelf life in the news and diminished any momentum for the outside investigation on the specific controversy at the time that congressional Democrats initially advocated it.

But when it came to the disclosure of Plame's identity, we left it to outside inquiries by reporters and prosecutors, allowing the matter to "harden into a permanent state of suspicion and warfare," as Bob Woodward, in *Shadow*, described the legacy of Watergate and its effect on Nixon's successors.

The risks of taking this approach should have been clear. But in the bubble of the White House, sometimes you learn the wrong lessons of history and fail to recognize this reality. You become so focused on protecting the president, you don't realize you're rolling the dice and losing control of the problem.

I didn't know anything about the leak or its causes. Uninformed about efforts to discredit Wilson, I simply assumed the best about them and key advisers to the president. I believed, based in no small part on the categorical assurances I'd received from Libby and Rove, that the White House had not been involved in leaking classified information or creating an environment that led to its disclosure. Sadly, I eventually learned otherwise.

Would I have pushed for addressing the matter openly and directly if I'd been more knowledgeable about the facts and circumstances, if I'd been on the job longer, or if I'd had previous experience with criminal investigations? I like to think so. I've always believed the term "no comment" is a terrible communications strategy. It inevitably comes across as suspicious and defensive. But in this case I went along with the decision that was in place. Now I wish I hadn't.

During the 2000 campaign, candidate George W. Bush had pledged to be different, but at the White House he chose to be the same. Just as the Clinton presidency had done when it came to questionable activity, we perpetuated the endless investigations and scandals we'd vowed to move beyond by engaging in spin, stonewalling, hedging, evasion, denial, noncommunication, and deceit by omission.

The decision to invade Iraq, more than anything else, took the Bush presidency off course, and our excessive embrace of the political tactics at the heart of Washington's culture of deception kept it there. When candor could have helped minimize the political fallout from the unraveling of the chief rationale for war, spin and evasion were instead what we employed.

While those tactics worked to our short-term advantage and did nothing to hurt the president's reelection cause—our primary objective at the beginning—the longer-term effect was to undermine his presidency and to keep Washington from moving beyond the partisan warfare that had engulfed it years before.

As for Patrick Fitzgerald, the special counsel, he was determined to do only one thing—his job. That meant not worrying about the partisan back-and-forth or any artificial timetables for getting to the truth in Washington's otherwise truth-deficient culture. Unknown to anyone outside his determined team of professionals, obstruction of justice charges were already being considered against at least one, and possibly two White House officials.

In the grand scheme of things, the leak episode didn't help our efforts to address the challenges and problems in Iraq or the volatile Middle East, or our own security interests there. It just served to perpetuate Washington's destructive culture of deception, rooted in the partisan warfare embraced by our elected leaders in Washington. All of this at a time when America's men and women in uniform were fighting abroad, hoping only to return home one day and reunite with loved ones.

But those of us at the White House during that time can only fault ourselves for all the attention the leak received. The lack of openness, forthrightness, and straightforward honesty to this day still fuels critics and raises questions about the president's truthfulness and honesty, traits at one time perceived to be among his greatest personal attributes.

And through it all, ironically, the White House successfully kept the potentially most embarrassing and damaging issue for the president from being closely scrutinized, the larger issue at the heart of the original sixteen-word controversy: how policymakers used the intelligence on Iraq to make the case that Iraq was a "grave and gathering" threat sufficient to justify a preemptive war.

Questions surrounding that larger issue are paramount to understanding the decision to invade Iraq and its lessons for history. Exploring those questions, and the decision by the president and his key advisers to avoid the potential consequences of openness and forthrightness about them, is also at the heart of understanding what took his presidency off course and prevented it from getting back on track.

Instead of embracing candor and honesty when they were most needed and using them to his advantage, the president decided to avoid them for fear of political damage. His advisers went along with his decision. The result would be a sustained loss of standing with the public, and a president left clinging to the belief that history and posterity will overlook the inherent deception in such an approach and burnish his legacy if his vision of success in Iraq can ultimately be achieved.

But I wouldn't come to realize any of this for many months. Back in late 2004, the president was on his way to making history another way: by winning a prized second term.

13

TRIUMPH
AND ILLUSION

I HEADED TO THE OVAL OFFICE late on the morning of November 3, 2004. I was expecting to witness the president receiving a concession call from his re-election opponent, Senator John Kerry. It had been a long night. Even the usually early-to-bed Bush had stayed up until 5:00 A.M.—about the time he typically would awake—and was operating on about two hours' sleep. I had left the White House around 5:30 A.M. and returned a few hours later.

The day before had reminded me a bit of Election Day 2000, only this time the drama centered on Ohio, not Florida. In the late afternoon, just before polls around the country started to close, the mood was grim. The president and Mrs. Bush had voted in Crawford and then stopped in Ohio before Air Force One transported them and their daughters—and those of us on the senior staff with him—back to Washington. Before we jumped into the staff vans to take us back to the White House, Dan Bartlett heard from Karl Rove, who had received word from the president's chief pollster, Matthew Dowd, that exit polls spelled trouble for the president. The grim diagnosis left all of us in the upper echelons of Bush World feeling anxious.

But by evening our mood had begun to change. When results in states like South Carolina and Virginia started coming in, it was clear the exit polls were off-base. Things were tight but seemed to be tilting our way. Cautious optimism permeated the atmosphere. I alternated between my West Wing office and the adjacent Roosevelt Room, which had been set up for the senior staff victory watch party. My wife, Jill, and I—we'd been married the previous November—enjoyed visiting with former president George H. W. Bush for several minutes when he popped in to say hello to the assembled advisers. Jill, who had never met him personally, was thrilled to talk with the warm, gracious elder statesman. The current president was following the news from the private residence in the White House with immediate and extended family— parents, siblings, and their spouses—as well as several longtime friends.

Later I headed over to the Old Family Dining Room, just below the private residence, which Karl Rove had arranged to use as the election night war room. It was conveniently located just a staircase away from the president if he decided to check in personally. He did just that several times during the evening, while maintaining continuous contact with Karl by phone. On one side of the room were tables with several computers where staffers, including Rove, could monitor state-by-state results. On the other were large flat-screen TVs tuned in to the network political coverage.

The original plan was to limit access to the room to a few key political aides—Rove, his top assistants Israel Hernandez and Susan Ralston, and a handful of others. But as the night progressed and the election race continued neck and neck, some other senior White House staff arrived to get the up-to-the-minute scoop about where things were headed. I was one.

Near midnight, the networks started calling Florida for Bush. The Old Family Dining Room was filled with cheers and excitement. Although the numbers-crunching Rove felt we had won Ohio too, none of the stations were close to calling it yet. Andy Card had already begun reaching out to the Kerry campaign, delicately taking its pulse and gently encouraging them to consider making the dreaded concession call. A victory party was under way in the atrium of the Ronald Reagan Building just down the street. At the White House, we were all hoping that we'd soon be able to celebrate and watch the president give a victory speech.

But still the night dragged on. The wee hours of the morning arrived and the national networks—perhaps overly cautious after having been badly burned in 2000—were still hesitating to call Ohio, with its crucial cargo of electoral votes.

As we headed into the 4:00 A.M. hour, we felt that our cushion of about 150,000 votes in Ohio would give us the state and the election. But the networks were still holding back, and Kerry and some in his campaign were still holding out hope that Ohio's provisional ballots would somehow turn it around. At the White House, a few advisers wanted Bush to declare victory without a concession by Kerry. They hoped this move would discourage Democrats from bringing in the lawyers and turning 2004 into a new version of 2000. But others urged Bush to wait, and that's how matters stood when the president called it a night and headed up to the residence at 5:00 A.M.

Word had filtered back to us confidentially via Mike McCurry of the Kerry campaign that, if we just gave Kerry some time to reflect, he would come around. Later that morning, he did.

When I arrived back at the White House that morning after a couple hours of rest, I immediately popped into the Oval to see the president. "Congratulations, sir," I said. "Nice win."

"Thanks, Scott," Bush replied. "You did a great job, a really great job."

A little later, Rove, Karen Hughes, Dan Bartlett, chief speechwriter Mike Gerson, and I were visiting with the president in the Oval. We were expecting Kerry's call at any moment. Don Rumsfeld, grinning ear to ear, popped his head in briefly to congratulate the president.

At 11:02 A.M., Bush's assistant Ashley Estes appeared. "Mr. President, Senator Kerry is on the line." The president walked back to his desk to sit down and pick up the phone. We could only hear Bush's side of the conversation: "I think you were an admirable, worthy opponent. You waged one tough campaign. I hope you are proud of the effort you put in. You should be."

When Bush hung up after three or four minutes, he said, slightly choking up, "That was very gracious." Then he started to tear up. It was a sentimental moment. Bush had secured a place in history by winning a coveted second term. He started hugging each of us, as our eyes also began to well up. The embraces were warm and heartfelt. Within minutes, Andy Card arrived to join the hug fest, along with Joe Hagin, Blake Gottesman, and Ashley. Bush then went down the hall to the vice president's office, and the two congratulated each other. Mrs. Bush called just after he left, and a short time later Bush went to the residence to see her and get in a workout before his afternoon victory speech.

I remember pulling up underneath the Reagan Building in the motorcade that afternoon for the celebration. The staff vans were packed full with joyful senior staff. This was a time for us to enjoy the moment of euphoria we'd been deprived of four years earlier. Inside, the building was packed with cheering supporters and staff.

Bush's remarks were brief. He thanked his supporters and staff—singling out a few like "the architect," Karl Rove—and reached out to those who supported his opponent. He talked about the record turnout and the historic victory. And then he turned to the agenda for his second term. "Because we have done the hard work, we are entering a season of hope," he said. He pledged to build on the recent economic progress, reform the tax code, strengthen Social Security, and continue improving public schools. He also reaffirmed a commitment to helping the "emerging democracies in Iraq and Afghanistan" and to continuing the war on terrorism. Befitting the occasion, it was an upbeat, hopeful speech, filled with expectation about the great accomplishments he looked forward to during his second term.

The next morning, Dan held a communications team celebration in the Roosevelt Room. The president made a brief surprise visit to thank everyone for their work. As he finished, he gave me a shout-out. "Where's Scott?" he asked. "Is he here?"

Some others pointed to me. "I especially want to thank Scott," Bush continued. "Scott did a great job. You didn't make any news," he added in his jocular mood. "I want to thank you for saying—nothing."

The line got the chuckle it deserved. But it also reflected Bush's sentiment about not wanting his press secretary stirring up controversy unnecessarily, particularly in the heat of a campaign. He'd used a similar line at Ari Fleischer's departure party, saying he'd done a great job of saying nothing at all.

Midmorning, Bush held a cabinet meeting. "I expect there to be lots of rumors and speculation about changes in the cabinet for our second term," he began. "Well, a few changes are very likely, but I haven't had time to think about them yet." Then he talked about the second-term agenda. He talked about the Medicare prescription drug benefit—soon to go into effect—and the need to make sure that the projected savings for seniors became "real and true." On the domestic front, education had helped Bush win the election, neutralizing a typically Democratic issue or even turning it into a Republican strength, he said, because we have "a vision and philosophy."

The second term would be a chance to solidify Bush's place in history. Retooling Democratic ideas of education, Medicare, and Social Security along conservative lines could take away Democratic dominance on these core issues for years to come, or so Bush and Karl Rove believed. With Republican majorities in the House and Senate, the two men—especially Rove—relished the prospect of launching a new era of Republican dominance as part of their legacy.

The president told the cabinet he would push for medical liability reform, insist on fiscal discipline, seek an energy bill, and then turn to the three biggest domestic initiatives: Social Security, tax reform, and budgetary reform.

Most important, Bush indicated that his approach to governing would be much the same as it had been during his first term. The permanent campaign would continue. "How we sell the big items is going to be very important as we move forward," Bush declared. "We already sold the American people on the agenda," he added, referring to the election victory. Now, he assured the cabinet, when it came to promoting his biggest agenda items, "we are going to go for it." The focus would be on swaying public opinion and thereby pressuring Congress to get on board.

It was a philosophy of governance he shared with the powerful Rove, to whom he now turned. Bush praised Rove as "a brilliant architect" who'd come up with a "perfect strategy" for the reelection and had run "a perfect campaign. It was incredibly well-managed. We had huge, magnificent crowds." It went without saying that the architect would now be turning his attention to running the campaign "to sell the big items" to the American people. It was as if Election Day merely represented a way station on a never-ending journey.

Then Dick Cheney made some brief comments. He recalled discussing plans with President Bush at the same time four years earlier. "I remember our conversation coming off the recount of 2000 about whether to trim the sails," the vice president said. "You said it was not an option, and it paid off. This time around, the mandate was clear." (The narrowness of the victory, one of the smallest margins for any reelection bid in presidential history, went unnoticed in this talk of a "mandate.") Cheney added that the next four years were "an opportunity to complete the task."

The conversation turned to Iraq. "Iraq is foremost in our mind," Secretary Powell said of the State Department. "We are working toward elections in '05. The insurgency must be put down, particularly in the Sunni triangle."

The president interjected, "It was a defining moment in Afghanistan when elections took place. You've got to have faith people want to be free, even in impoverished areas. Iraq will change the world." But, he acknowledged, achieving the results you want can sometimes be "ugly."

Defense Secretary Donald Rumsfeld referred to military families and parents. "I kept thinking about them," he said. "The election ending must be enormously reassuring [to them]." He talked about how the Iraqi people were "resisting intimidation" amid the "tough stuff" they faced—vaguely alluding, like Powell, to the chaotic and deadly situation in areas like Fallujah, where terrorists and insurgents were causing mayhem. And he also stressed the importance of the upcoming January Iraqi election to elect a transitional national assembly.

The president agreed. "Elections are important," he said. "It forces people to make a choice. Either they miss the train or get on the train" of democracy. Bush added that he had spoken with Iraqi leaders Yawer and Allawi about the U.S. election results, and said they were "relieved" about Bush's victory.

"They were toast if you lost," Rumsfeld said.

"French toast," replied Bush, to a burst of laughter in the room.

The victory speech and cabinet meeting made Bush's state of mind crystal clear to anyone who knew him. He was dead set on pushing ahead aggressively, selling his big ideas, and leaving his mark on history. The election, he believed, had validated his first-term policies, including the decision to invade Iraq, and it had given him a mandate for the second-term agenda he'd outlined. Now all he had to do was what he did best—campaign. He would travel the country, shaping the media narrative to his advantage, and winning the battle for public opinion one voter, one poll, one state at a time. Soon Congress would be forced to come to the table and negotiate on Bush's terms. Bipartisan give-and-take and compromise from the outset would be unnecessary. Those techniques, so vital to Bush's success in Texas, were irrelevant to the Washington game.

The same spirit was obvious in Bush's first postelection news conference. He expressed his intent to spend his "political capital" in pursuit of an ambitious agenda, beginning with overhauling Social Security. When pressed about working with Democrats, Bush said he was willing to do so. He even made passing reference to the theme of uniting the country on which he'd run four years earlier. "One of the disappointments of being here in Washington is how bitter this town can become and how divisive," said Bush. "I'm not blaming one party or the other. It's just the reality of Washington, D.C., sometimes exacerbated by you [the media], because it's great sport. It's really—it's enter-taining for some. It also makes it difficult to govern at times. But nevertheless, my commitment is there" to work with Democrats.

But Bush also made it clear that, if he had to push something through with little Democratic support, as he'd done with the Medicare prescription drug bill, he would do that. "Results really do matter," he said, and it was clear that, for Bush, "results" meant getting his agenda through the way he (and Rove) envisioned it—not a watered-down version tainted by Democratic in-put. In hindsight, the commitment to transcending partisanship was largely perfunctory.

Of course, Iraq was still a top priority. In his press conference, the presi-dent articulated the same view he and his national security team spoke about in private: it was just a matter of time before democracy took hold in Iraq. Then Iraqis would step forward and assume responsibility for their own secu-rity, and the drawdown of American troops could begin in earnest. The up-coming January elections were being viewed as a milestone moment in this process. "We will work with the Allawi government," Bush said, "to achieve our objective, which is elections, on the path to stability, and we'll continue to train the troops. Our commanders will have that which they need to complete their missions."

It was all part of Bush's idealistic vision of Iraq as a launching pad for transforming the Middle East. He defended that vision in his press confer-ence. "There is a certain attitude in the world, by some, that says that it's a waste of time to try to promote free societies in parts of the world," he said. "I've heard that criticism. . . . I just strongly disagree with those who do not see the wisdom of trying to promote free societies around the world. If we are interested in protecting our country for the long term, the best way to do so is to promote freedom and democracy."

The agenda for the second term was nothing if not ambitious: to reform some of America's biggest and most controversial domestic programs, to create the conditions for a lasting Republican majority, and to simultaneously bring a major foreign war to a successful conclusion, thereby beginning the transfor-mation of a volatile region into an oasis of peace and democracy. But Bush and those of us on his team were confident. We put faith in the president's hands-off leadership style, which left many of the crucial details to his trusted team of subordinates. Unlike Presidents Johnson and Carter, who'd gotten lost in the weeds thanks to their penchant for micromanaging, Bush would stick to the big picture and so achieve success on multiple fronts at once.

Bush's top policy and strategy advisers believed they understood the reality of how to win the Washington way. But was their self-confidence in our "mandate" illusory? Had they succumbed to one of the perennial dangers faced by successful campaigners—believing their own spin and ignoring just how shaky public support was for Bush?

The next couple of years would tell the tale. For now, an eager and determined Bush and a reenergized White House team were triumphantly charging forward.

BUSH LEFT FOR CAMP DAVID WITH Mrs. Bush that Thursday afternoon to clear his head and relax after a grueling campaign. But he would also begin serious discussions with Andy Card about the cabinet and White House staff. A number of cabinet members were planning on leaving, and Andy would encourage a few others to see the benefits of submitting resignation letters rather than waiting to be dismissed.

Periodic change is critical to any effective White House. A president needs a diversity of advice that is informed, honest, and clear-sighted. Fresh blood can help keep these sources vibrant and energetic. Furthermore, working as a member of the senior White House staff is all-consuming and exhausting, a well-worn path to burnout. And the longer you remain inside the White House bubble, the harder it becomes to see things clearly and objectively. So knowing when and how to implement change is critical for a president and his chief of staff.

Andy Card understood all this. He'd warned many of us future West Wingers from the outset that one of the most important things we needed to know was "when to leave." Now he set out to Camp David to encourage the president to start this process by bringing in a new chief of staff.

I stayed in close contact with Andy throughout the planning period. The Washington rumor mill was already beginning to speculate about the changes to come, and I didn't want to be blindsided at a press briefing by any sudden moves. At the same time, I understood that this would be a tightly compartmentalized process. The president believed in keeping plans confidential until they were finalized. Andy and the president would seek ideas from trusted advisers; the White House counsel's office would quietly vet any potential new faces. Specific names would usually circulate within the inner circle, which is when I would usually find out, if not from the president himself. The goal was to make most of the changes around the same time, and to have a complete second-term cabinet in place before the end of the year.

On Friday at Camp David, the president also participated in a national security meeting on Iraq. Via secure videoconference, General Abizaid, the head of Central Command, General Casey, the head of the Iraqi theater, and John Negroponte, the U.S. ambassador to Iraq, offered their perspectives.

A priority topic of discussion was the situation in the city of Fallujah, an area of concern ever since the end of the first battles there months earlier. Insurgents still controlled the city, and Bush and his team had decided that they must be defeated once and for all before the upcoming elections. That first week in November, Prime Minister Maliki had publicly warned the insurgents that their window for reaching a peaceful settlement with the government was closing fast; U.S. forces had already begun pounding the city with air strikes and artillery fire. Now American forces were about to be joined by Iraqi forces in bloody, intense urban warfare, under the name of Operation Phantom Fury. They would gain firm control of the city within several days and move to mop-up operations by the middle of the month.

But during that same time period, increased violence broke out in other parts of Iraq, such as the city of Mosul. It was the beginning of what some have called the "whack-a-mole" period of the battle against insurgents: knock them down in one place and they pop up somewhere else.

The following Monday morning, after the president returned from Camp David, he made a rare visit to the senior staff meeting in the Roosevelt Room. "I've made one decision," he said. "I have asked Andy to remain as chief of staff." The senior staff applauded, and Andy expressed how honored he was.

The message here was one of continuity, not change. I have great admiration for Andy Card, and I always considered him one of the most honorable public servants in the Bush administration. Andy himself had believed the White House would be better served by a change at the chief of staff position. As Andy later told me, he'd urged the president to make such a change, only to have the suggestion firmly rejected. In hindsight, it foreshadowed what was to come in the way of second-term change.

People used to ask me why Bush's staff was so loyal to him. I would reply, "We are loyal to him, but he is also loyal to us. It is a two-way street, and our mutual loyalties feed each other."

Bush likes familiarity and does not like change, especially in regard to key staff members he has come to trust and rely on. This has led to a close bond between Bush and a number of us senior staffers, particularly fellow Texans and people like Andy. His personal charm and approachable demeanor also make for an enjoyable working environment where people *want* to stick around—maybe longer than they should.

It's a great personal strength of George W. Bush that he is able to inspire such loyalty. But for President Bush it is also a potential source of weakness. Bush's discomfort with change makes it difficult for him to step back from the bonds he develops and make clear-eyed decisions about what is best.

In hindsight, it's apparent that an opportunity was missed at the start of the second term to bring people with new perspectives onto the White House staff and the national security team. Instead, we saw the consolidation of an even more like-minded team within the cabinet and White House, particularly among the national security principals. There were changes, but they only increased the homogeneity of opinion among those with the president's ear.

Secretary of State Colin Powell was out. Card later told me that Powell and Bush had previously agreed that he would serve only until the end of the first term. By the time the transition came, Powell had reconsidered and was at least open to staying longer under certain conditions. But after meeting to discuss it, both men agreed the time for parting had come.

Like much of the country, I was sorry to see Powell go. I always knew him to offer straight, unvarnished advice based on his years of experience as a military and foreign policy leader. What's more, he never hesitated to make his position clear.

President Bush, however, apparently felt no continued need for Powell's moderate voice to counter the more hawkish views of Cheney and Rumsfeld. He would be replaced by the fully trusted and sometimes too accommodating Condi Rice, who was more than ready for a change from her position as national security adviser. That job had been fraught with enormous challenge and pressure—and, more recently, growing controversy over Iraq. I could tell she was eager to start anew in another capacity, and secretary of state was the only job she was interested in, as far as I could see.

Some on the Bush team, including the president, felt that Rice would bring the State Department bureaucracy (including its cadre of Democratic loyalists) more in line with administration policy, whether they agreed with it or not. By contrast, Secretary Powell had deferred more to the career foreign service officers. This stance, along with his independent views, caused others in the foreign policy hierarchy to consider him something less than a complete team player. As for me, I think he exemplified what it means to be a team player. He looked out for the interests of the man he served, as well as the country to whom both had sworn allegiance, with great care and wisdom. It was a mistake not to find a way to keep him around.

Condi Rice is hard to get to know. She plays her cards close to the vest, usually saving her views for private discussions with Bush. Over time, however, I was struck by how deft she is at protecting her reputation. No matter what went wrong, she was somehow able to keep her hands clean, even when the problems related to matters under her direct purview, including the WMD rationale for war in Iraq, the decision to invade Iraq, the sixteen words in the State of the Union address, and postwar planning and implementation of the strategy in Iraq. Some say she should have pushed harder to heed the threat warnings and focus the White House on terrorism prior to 9/11. Although she has been the president's top foreign policy adviser and coordinator of his national security team, she has largely allowed responsibility for all these matters to fall on people like former CIA director George Tenet, Paul Bremer, and Don Rumsfeld. If, as President Bush likes to say, results really do matter, then history will likely judge her harshly as the person responsible for overseeing a number of the defining—and, at least in the short term, ill-fated—policies of the Bush administration.

But whatever her policy management shortcomings, Rice knew public relations well. She knew how to adapt to potential trouble, dismiss brooding problems, and come out looking like a star. Few performed better under the spotlight, glossing over mistakes with her effortless eloquence and understated flair.

And in private, she complemented and reinforced Bush's instincts rather than challenging or questioning them. As far as I could tell from internal meetings and discussions, Condi invariably fell in line with Bush's thinking. If she wasn't actually shaping his thinking, she knew how to read him and how to translate his ideas, feelings, and proclivities into concrete policies.

As the new secretary of state, Rice got off to a strong start. With its public diplomacy component and its strong public relations role, it was a position that seemed well suited for her dynamic personality, and she surrounded herself with a trusted and tested team that served her interests well.

Steve Hadley moved up from his deputy position to become national security adviser. Low-key, even-keeled, bright, and tireless in his attention to detail, Hadley played the role of facilitator for the president's thinking and his national security council. He worked long hours and understood that he ultimately served the wishes of one person, President Bush. But he also made sure that every principal was fully informed and able to offer his or her full input into matters of policy, so that no one was ever excluded or blindsided.

Some reports later said that Andy Card had advocated a complete overhaul of the national security team, including the departure of Don Rumsfeld. It sounds credible to me, though this is something Andy would never say in public. (His role as an honest broker of the policy process, he felt, demanded such discretion.) In any case, the president decided Rumsfeld would stay. Rumsfeld is a strong personality, relentless in pursuing his goals and utterly convinced that his years of government and corporate experience make him uniquely informed and the only qualified judge of his own decisions. Bush always seemed to show him great deference—sometimes too much. Keeping him in place at the start of the second term meant that Defense would continue to be managed the only way Rumsfeld knew—his way.

Changes were made in a few other key administration posts. Alberto Gonzalez, who had served as the White House Counsel during the first term, was tapped to head the Justice Department. Al was the consummate Bush loyalist, a friend and associate from the Texas days who had doggedly served Bush's personal interests all the way into the White House. He had treated the post of White House Counsel very much as that of the president's personal lawyer, working hard to find legal justifications and protections for some of the most controversial policy choices of the administration. These particularly included certain positions championed internally by Cheney and his counsel, David Addington—for example, the decision to broaden authority that would permit the use of once forbidden interrogation tactics on terror detainees, the administration position that "enemy combatants" from the war on terror were not entitled to the protections of the Geneva Convention, and the decision to use military tribunals rather than civilian courts to try terror suspects.

It's easy to see why Bush, always loyal to trusted, longtime friends and averse to change, would want Al in the attorney general's spot. (Harriet Miers, yet another friend from Texas, was named to take Gonzalez's place as White House Counsel.) But the transition would prove to be more problematic than either man anticipated. It's all right for a White House Counsel to be personally dedicated to the president; it's much more questionable when the same is true of an attorney general, whose job is to impartially administer the law of the land, even when the results may be damaging to the president and his party.

Because of Al's controversial past positions, his nomination to the job was only narrowly approved on a largely partisan vote: sixty senators (only six of them Democrats) voted in favor of the nomination, while thirty-six were opposed (all Democrats). The close call in the confirmation process foreshadowed what would be a troubled tenure in office. Unable to detach himself from his close association to the president and exert independence, and too closely aligned with the White House's political machinations, Al became caught up in a number of damaging controversies, including one that continues to raise suspicion, over whether or not the Justice Department dismissed several U.S. attorneys for partisan reasons. Whipsawed by charges and countercharges, Al ended up resigning in August 2007, and his time as attorney general has been widely viewed as ineffective.

Another cabinet department in need of new leadership as the second term began was Homeland Security, still in its infancy and still struggling to define its identity. A vast, unwieldy agglomeration of dozens of formerly independent agencies, now bundled together under one name and with a new focus (physical threats to the American "homeland") that sometimes contradicted the old mandates, Homeland Security was hampered by bureaucratic infighting, incredibly complex coordination challenges, and slumping employee morale.

The department needed a leader with great people skills, administrative ability, a powerful overarching vision, and unquestioned integrity. Unfortunately the first person President Bush selected for the job fell far short of these qualities—Bernard Kerik, a former New York City police commissioner who'd been warmly recommended for the job by Rudolph Giuliani, the former mayor.

Giuliani and Kerik had a close personal relationship not unlike that between Bush and some of his Texas loyalists. In retrospect, it was probably *too* close. Their friendship may have led Giuliani to overlook a series of ethical missteps that had deeply tainted Kerik's record of public service. Some of

Kerik's lapses led to legal problems for him. In 2006 he pleaded guilty to two ethics violations and was fined for them, and in 2007 he was indicted on sixteen counts of wire fraud, mail fraud, conspiracy, and lying to the IRS. (He pleaded not guilty and has not yet been tried on the latter counts.)

After Bush nominated Kerik for secretary of Homeland Security in December 2004, revelations about his behavior began flying. This was one episode in which the media illustrated the vital role the press can play in uncovering genuine malfeasance by public officials. Frankly, the media did a better job of vetting Bernard Kerik than the Bush administration did. Kerik was left with no choice but to resign.

In January, Bush nominated Michael Chertoff for Homeland Security. A former federal prosecutor, judge on the U.S. Court of Appeals, and Justice Department official, Chertoff was a known quantity to the Bush White House. He had even (along with Viet Dinh) served as coauthor of the Patriot Act, a highly-touted administration initiative that also became highly controversial. But his qualifications for managing a vast, complex government bureaucracy were questionable, and the liability would come to haunt him during Katrina, in ways no one could have anticipated.

One of the most meaningful changes made in the 2004 transition was the expansion of Karl Rove's official role within the White House. Rove was named to replace Harriet Miers (the new White House Counsel) as deputy chief of staff for policy. The new title broadened Rove's portfolio by giving him a role in coordinating domestic policy, economic policy, national security (in a limited way, not including war policy), and homeland security—a wide-ranging assignment for someone many people, even in Washington, thought of chiefly as a canny political operative. As Peter Baker waggishly put it in the *Washington Post,* "During President Bush's first term, outsiders often suspected that Karl Rove was really behind virtually everything. Now it's official."

The move was seen as, in part, a reward for Karl's role as "the architect," the man who guided a successful reelection campaign for a president struggling with an increasingly difficult war in Iraq. But it also reconfirmed and strengthened the sense that the Bush administration was deeply committed to maintaining the permanent campaign as normal operating procedure in Washington. Not only would governing continue to be an offshoot of campaigning, but the master campaigner would now be openly in charge of governing—thus discarding even the pretense of a separation between the two disciplines. Karl was genuinely a policy wonk at heart, but foremost a political mastermind. It was impossible to separate the two.

And lurking behind it all remained the magic man, Vice President Cheney. No one knew better how to orchestrate what was happening from behind the curtain while the grand production was playing out on stage. Quietly slipping in and out of internal deliberations, his influence and wand waving barely discernible to the outside world, Cheney rarely showed all his cards and never disclosed how he made things happen. Yet somehow, in every policy area he cared about, from the invasion of Iraq to expansion of presidential power to the treatment of detainees and the use of surveillance against terror suspects, Cheney always seemed to get his way. He viewed the world as an ominous place where evil has to be fought by any means necessary—including some that are decidedly unpleasant.

All in all, the shape and direction of the second term were clear. The administration did *not* infuse fresh blood and new thinking from outside sources but eliminated some voices that had represented independent perspectives (such as Secretary Powell's) and elevated people who were known Bush loyalists, practically guaranteed not to challenge the conventional White House thinking (such as Condi Rice and Al Gonzales). And it reinforced the dominance of the permanent campaign within the administration by giving Karl Rove an even more powerful seat at the table, ensuring that political considerations would never be far from the center of any policy conversation during the second term.

Caught up inside the White House bubble, I publicly defended all of Bush's decisions. It was my job. I didn't fully appreciate their implications for the future of the administration, nor did I recognize the serious problems they would help to create during the next four years.

REENERGIZED AND EMBOLDENED BY the reelection victory, the Bush administration was ready to begin making the case for yet another aggressive attempt at transformational change. This time, the topic was Social Security. And we wouldn't be satisfied with just any plan for reform. The president had drawn a line in the sand: personal or private retirement accounts had to be part of the solution. The idea was to create an option for people to invest a small portion—2 to 4 percent—of their Social Security dollars into "safe" stocks, mutual funds, and other appropriate retirement vehicles. It was a perfect Republican initiative. It fit the president's oft-touted theme of "the ownership society"; it encouraged people to take control of and responsibility for their own future; and it was fiscally responsible to solve a large, unfunded liability.

It was the kind of bold domestic initiative Bush had always hoped would define his presidency. He would get it passed through a massive campaign to bring public pressure to bear on Congress.

A Social Security principals meeting was held in the White House on December 16 to discuss strategy for getting the president's Social Security plan passed in the coming year. The discussion centered on two battles we would have to wage. The first would be to "educate" the public about the economic and fiscal problems facing Social Security and the need to fix them. The goal of this effort was to create a crisis mentality, which would give us a better shot at getting the necessary public support to bring about bipartisan backing for our reform plan in Congress. The second battle would be to shape the solution and make sure that personal retirement accounts were part of it.

Bush's legislative liaison, David Hobbs, understood Congress and what its members respond to: "Seventy percent of the battle is defining the problem and putting congressional leaders on the spot. We need public pressure." The plan to create this pressure included extensive travel by the president to the states and districts where targeted members of Congress lived. Bush would use the reelection hopes of these crucial swing voters in Congress as the lever with which to apply the pressure required.

We agreed that the principals would meet once a week, our deputies more often. The reelection campaign concluded, the campaign to reshape America's thinking would be back in action, requiring complex, ever changing choreography among the key players to ensure that a consistent, appealing, powerful message was reaching the people through every channel available to us.

But looking back on how we launched this massive campaign effort early in 2005, I wonder whether we were investing our resources wisely. We were spending excessive effort on selling our sketchily designed plan while skimping on other elements of the process that probably should have been at least as important. We weren't spending much time deliberating with members of Congress to work out details of our reform plan. We were doing minimal outreach to Democrats to build the kind of consensus that would make such a dramatic change in the law easier to pass. Instead, we were leapfrogging many of the vital steps and jumping straight to the stage in the process we found most congenial—the public relations effort.

It was all vaguely reminiscent of the way we'd short-circuited debate over the necessity for war in Iraq and chose instead to turn it into the subject of a massive marketing blitz. We used a similar approach as we planned the Social Security campaign. With Iraq it was a threat that needed confronting, with Social Security it was a crisis that needed solving.

And even as our plans were taking shape, we were being dogged by bad news relating to the subject of our last big campaign—the war in Iraq. Throughout the last two months of 2004, insurgents and terrorists in Iraq were continuing to wreak havoc. The ongoing violence was a concern, especially with the first scheduled elections just around the corner. By early December, the president decided to increase U.S. troop levels in Iraq to upwards of 150,000 to provide additional security for the elections in January and to keep pressure on the insurgency.

Around the same time, on December 7, 2004, the *New York Times* reported that a classified cable from the CIA Baghdad chief was warning of a deteriorating situation in Iraq that was unlikely to rebound anytime soon. According to the paper, another CIA official who had visited Iraq a short time earlier had offered a similar assessment. The article also noted that Bush had dismissed an earlier national intelligence estimate including a "dark forecast for Iraq's future through the end of 2005," calling it simply one possibility among many.

It was an early indication that the reelection victory was not going to alter the administration's attitude toward bad news. A president who has been handed an electoral mandate and faces no more future election contests might very well take advantage of those circumstances and to reach out, to seek a consensus approach for improving a policy whose results were less than satisfactory. But Bush and his team chose not to do so.

On Wednesday, December 8, with the high levels of violence in Iraq continuing and the security situation deteriorating, Secretary Rumsfeld met with soldiers about to be deployed to Iraq at their staging base in Kuwait. He was asked pointed questions about poor equipment and extended deployments. Tennessee National Guard Army Specialist Thomas Wilson asked about the lack of sufficient numbers of armored combat vehicles. "Why do we soldiers have to dig through local landfills for pieces of scrap metal and compromised ballistic glass to up-armor our vehicles?" asked Wilson.

Rumsfeld's response would prove to be a defining moment of his career—and not a positive one. "As you know, you go to war with the army you have," replied the defense secretary. "They're not the army you might want or wish to have at a later time. If you think about it, you can have all the armor in the world on a tank and a tank can be blown up," he later added.

Democratic leaders in Congress jumped on Rumsfeld's comments, calling them "stunning" and "callous." When asked about them at the next morning's gaggle, I defended Rumsfeld personally, but I knew better than to try to defend his comments. "Secretary Rumsfeld has a practice of speaking directly with our troops in harm's way," I said. "You saw that yesterday. The secretary is someone who cares deeply about our men and women in uniform, and he is committed to doing all he can to address their concerns." But his comments helped solidify an already accepted media narrative: the administration was sending troops that were ill equipped to fight the IED threat from terrorists and insurgents; worse still, administration officials were either unaware of the problems, unable to fix them, or totally unconcerned.

Even well-intentioned gestures designed to create positive impressions of the war effort seemed to backfire during this period. On December 14, the president awarded the Medal of Freedom, the nation's highest civil award, given to men and women of exceptional merit, integrity, and achievement, to three leaders he described as "men who have played pivotal roles in great events, and whose efforts have made our country more secure and advanced the cause of human liberty." The three were key players in his Iraq policy: former CIA director George Tenet, former head of Central Command retired General Tommy Franks, and former head of the Coalition Provisional Authority in Iraq, Paul Bremer.

Against a backdrop of discouraging news from Iraq, as well as a mounting chorus of criticism specifically aimed at all three men—particularly Tenet, who had reportedly described the flawed Iraq WMD intelligence as "a slam dunk," and Bremer, who had made several major miscalculations during the early months of the occupation—the ceremony drew plenty of criticism. Wasn't this supposed to be an administration that prided itself on results and believed in responsibility and accountability? If so, why the rush to hand out medals to people who had helped organize what was now looking like a badly botched, ill-conceived war?

The growing backlash against the war threatened to engulf the president himself. At Bush's end-of-year news conference on December 20, he was pressed to defend his secretary of defense. He did so in a personal way:

> I know Secretary Rumsfeld's heart. I know how much he cares for the troops. He and his wife go out to Walter Reed in Bethesda all the time to provide comfort and solace. I have seen the anguish in his—or heard the anguish in his voice and seen his eyes when we talk about the danger in Iraq, and the fact that youngsters are over there in harm's way. And he is—he's a good, decent man. He's a caring fellow. Sometimes perhaps his demeanor is rough and gruff, but beneath that rough and gruff, no-nonsense demeanor is a good human being who cares deeply about the military, and deeply about the grief that war causes.

It was a typical assessment by Bush, who often speaks about the people he likes in terms of their inner character—a good man, a decent man—rather than in terms of their concrete behaviors and actions. Bush didn't try to defend Rumsfeld's badly chosen words in Kuwait or his errors in judgment over the management of the war. Instead, he simply assessed the hidden qualities of the man, as if these outweighed his actions and erased their negative consequences. One might call this a redemptive, Christian perspective, in which forgiveness is seen as washing away every misdeed. But it didn't jibe with the self-image of an administration supposedly focused on accountability results, nor did it satisfy the growing unhappiness of Americans who were wondering whether their children and their treasure were being squandered to no good purpose.

In the same conference, following a strategy we'd discussed behind the scenes, the president also tried to give what would be referred to in the media as a "candid and sober assessment" of the situation in Iraq. He spoke about the suicide bombings and IEDs, and he acknowledged that difficulties remained. He also left the impression that our troops would need to remain in Iraq for a while, without saying specifically how long.

The next day's *Washington Post* poll showed that 56 percent of Americans now believed the war was a "mistake" and "not worth fighting." A majority also said Rumsfeld should resign. The administration had tried positive spin, denial, and now—belatedly—candor and realism, but to no avail. The stark news on the ground was conveying its own message, and it was one the American people found increasingly troubling.

But those of us inside the White House, as we headed into the new year, missed the multiplying warning signs. The president's approval rating was shaky, hovering just above the majority mark, the lowest it had been prior to any previous State of the Union address. Clearly the president received no postelection bounce. The goodwill evident four years earlier as he began his presidency was nowhere to be found, and Bush was doing little to build any. He seemed determined to play the game Washington's way, not appreciating how much his policies and actions had contributed to poisoning the atmosphere.

The narrow election victory supplied no real mandate. There was only division and polarization, and none of us in the president's inner circle seemed to realize how problematic it was at the time. Instead, we clung to the notion of a mandate, refusing to accept it for what it was—an illusion.

And all the while, the situation in Iraq continued to worsen. As far as the president and his foreign policy team were concerned, the strategy was in place and the resources were in position to confront the approaching storm. Our troops would continue to aggressively pursue the insurgents and terrorists. Our diplomats would continue to push the political process forward. The January elections were a foremost priority, a potential turning point that might give hope to Iraqis and dampen the will and spirit of the insurgency. After a provisional government had been elected, the focus could shift to smaller reconstruction projects that could provide concrete help and hope to citizens across the country. Meanwhile, we would push ahead on training Iraqi forces so they could assume increasing responsibility for the country's security. In the formula we often used, as they stood up, American forces could stand down.

It was a logical-sounding program for long-term success in Iraq. The problem was that it didn't match up with reality. There were serious problems still not being identified and addressed.

U.S. force levels inside Iraq were insufficient and were being stretched to the limit through repeated redeployments. The troops would continue carrying an immense burden and doing it well, but ending the violence and securing the expansive country was a major challenge and problem given the force level. Reconstruction was increasingly hampered by the deteriorating security situation. Projects were slowed by the frequent attacks, thereby denying Iraqis essential services. The length of time it was taking to equip and train Iraqi forces to assume security responsibilities independent of American help was too long. And underlying it all was growing sectarian division rooted in history and fomented by insurgents, unsanctioned militias, and terrorists. American troops were doing their job well, but they could only do so much. They needed more from Washington, but it was growing more polarized as the conflict dragged on.

Bush's way of managing the problems in Iraq was proving inadequate to the task. He received regular updates and held frequent meetings as he sought to improve the situation through personal persuasion and pressure on Iraqi leaders. But he was insulated from the reality of events on the ground and consequently began falling into the trap of believing his own spin. He failed to spend enough time seeking independent input from a broad range of outside experts, those beyond the White House bubble who had firsthand experience on the ground in Iraq, and—perhaps most important—those with differing points of view, including those who disagreed with his policies.

The failure to open up the Bush White House to fresh perspectives in the second term was already beginning to exact a price.

14

REVELATION
AND HUMILIATION

By MID-2004, SPECIAL PROSECUTOR Patrick Fitzgerald had been pushing ahead to wrap up the leak investigation. Speculation was swirling that Fitzgerald was either seeking an indictment or two or was just trying to wrap up a complicated, messy investigation. But he needed the help of two reporters to complete his investigation and had sought their grand jury testimony for the better part of a year.

One was Matthew Cooper, a quick-witted, soft-spoken *Time* magazine White House correspondent. The other was *New York Times* Washington reporter Judith Miller, who had written extensively about Saddam's weapons of mass destruction, based on intelligence from the U.S. government and foreign governments, during the lead-up to the invasion.

Cooper and Miller refused to tell Fitzgerald what they knew about the leak case. They were holding steadfast to the journalistic credo not to divulge confidential, anonymous sources to anyone, and especially not in a way that might cause them to become known publicly. For Cooper and Miller, this was a fundamental freedom of the press issue. Reporters often depend on anonymous sources to get information that helps hold government officials accountable. If contempt of court rulings were used to force disclosure of such sources, it could inhibit people from talking to reporters at all, making investigative journalism far more difficult in the future.

Of course, there was a curious twist to the defense used by Cooper and Miller in this case. By refusing to divulge the names of their sources in the leak case, the two reporters were not protecting courageous whistle-blowers revealing government wrongdoing in the public interest. Rather, they were shielding government officials who administration critics believed had used leaks as weapons of partisan warfare. It was hard for some in the public, and especially those critical of the administration, to see this as an act of journalistic courage. In the days of Watergate, crusading newspaper reporters battling for the truth were depicted on movie screens by actors like Robert Redford and Dustin Hoffman. This episode, however, seemed to confirm for at least some administration critics that reporters were no longer heroic figures but were now participating in the same partisan warfare they covered.

Fitzgerald, who had subpoenaed both reporters early in the investigation, dismissed the freedom of the press defense and said their testimony was crucial to his ability to wrap up his investigation and make a determination whether or not a crime had been committed. He had obtained signed waivers from administration officials that absolved reporters of any previous confidentiality agreements, and he sought a court order compelling their testimony. If Cooper and Miller refused, he said the court should hold them in contempt and send them to jail until they were willing to talk.

For Cooper and Miller, the waivers changed nothing, since their sources could have felt forced to sign them in the face of a criminal investigation. This was not, in their view, a voluntary, uncoerced assurance. For Fitzgerald, it was a matter of finding out the truth about possible criminal wrongdoing, and what the appeals court would uphold as the government's "critical need" for their testimony.

The issue generated intense media attention as Cooper and Miller dug in their heels. A feeding frenzy ensued outside the federal courthouse building whenever the two reporters appeared.

In August 2004, Judge Thomas F. Hogan of the U.S. District Court for the District of Columbia found both Cooper and *Time* magazine in contempt of court. Miller suffered a similar blow the following October. Both were fined and ordered to serve jail time. The judge, with Fitzgerald's agreement, stayed the orders until their appeals were exhausted.

Miller would ultimately be sentenced to prison for contempt of court. Starting on July 6, 2005, she would spend eighty-five days of a four-month sentence in jail before finally receiving uncoerced personal assurance from the source she was protecting. It was Scooter Libby, who had told her, according to Miller's later testimony, that Wilson's wife worked at the CIA, though she had never reported the fact. Cooper, after a last-minute voluntary release from confidentially from his source—Karl Rove—avoided jail time.

By July 2005, reports had begun circulating that Rove had spoken with Matt Cooper for the story he'd written about Joe Wilson's mission to Niger. On July 4, 2005, Michael Isikoff, a respected investigative journalist for *Newsweek*, broke the story that Karl was one of Cooper's sources. He received confirmation from Robert Luskin, Karl's personal attorney. However, Luskin told Isikoff that Karl had neither "knowingly disclosed classified information" nor told "any reporter that Valerie Plame worked for the CIA." Isikoff noted that exactly what passed between Cooper and Rove was "unclear."

And on Sunday, July 10, 2005—halfway into the first year of the president's second term and nearly two years after Robert Novak's column revealing the identity of Valerie Plame—another critical piece of information that Cooper had previously refused to divulge became public for the first time.

I'd heard through the grapevine that Isikoff had another scoop for *Newsweek* with specifics about what Karl told Cooper. I remember speculating that, more than likely, Cooper had asked him about Wilson's wife, but as Karl had indicated to Claire and me about his call with Novak, he could not confirm anything because he did not know. And the president had told me that he too had been personally assured that Karl did not leak the information. Maybe I did not want to believe that Karl had not been completely forthcoming, or that what he had told me—and the president—was not true.

Later that morning, Harriet Miers, a longtime Bush loyalist from Texas who had taken over as White House counsel when Al Gonzalez was confirmed as attorney general, called me through the White House operator. Like me, Harriet had served in the Bush White House since day one. The West Wing was quiet that day. I had come in to catch up on work, watch some of the Sunday political shows that were taped, and prepare for the week ahead free from interruptions.

Harriet was calling from her office and said she needed to come and talk to me about something important. She walked in, closed the door behind her, and said, "There's some news that's likely to come out tomorrow about Karl in the leak investigation that may appear to contradict what you said nearly two years ago."

"I heard," I said, thinking about Isikoff's report but not taking time to let what she had just said fully sink in. Harriet reiterated to me that we still could not comment on the investigation publicly. In effect, she was forbidding me from talking and setting the record straight about my previous comments.

Then, just before she headed out of my office, Harriet said, "You know, Scott, I always feel bad because I feel like I only make your job tougher."

"That's okay, it's my job," I said, almost reflexively, so as to lessen any angst for a person I really liked. After she left, I wondered about what the article would say and how it would contradict what I had said. Later that day, I learned the truth. Isikoff's article revealed that Karl had spoken with Cooper specifically about Wilson's wife working at the CIA.

According to Isikoff, Cooper had written in an email to his boss, *Time* Washington bureau chief Michael Duffy, that Karl had warned him not to "get too far out on Wilson." Cooper's email went on to note that Karl said Wilson's trip was not authorized by CIA director George Tenet. "It was, KR said, Wilson's wife, who apparently works at the agency on WMD issues who authorized the trip." Cooper continued, "Not only the genesis of the trip is flawed an[d] suspect but so is the report. he [Rove] implied strongly there's still plenty to implicate iraqi interest in acquiring uranium fro[m] Niger."

Cooper stated up front in the email that it was confidential, and that Rove had only spoken to him "on double super secret background for about two minutes before he went on vacation," according to Isikoff.

The date of the email was Friday morning, July 11, 2003—three days before Novak's column revealing Plame's identity was published. It related to the story *Time* was working on about Wilson, his trip to Niger, and the White House efforts to discredit him: "A War on Wilson?" published on July 17, 2003.

In his *Newsweek* article, Isikoff placed this latest bombshell in context:

Rove's words on the Plame case have always been carefully chosen. "I didn't know her name. I didn't leak her name," Rove told CNN last year when asked if he had anything to do with the Plame leak. Rove has never publicly acknowledged talking to any reporter about former ambassador Joseph Wilson and his wife. But last week, his lawyer, Robert Luskin, confirmed to *Newsweek* that Rove did—and that Rove was the secret source who, at the request of both Cooper's lawyer and the prosecutor, gave Cooper permission to testify.

"Nothing in the Cooper e-mail suggests that Rove used Plame's name or knew she was a covert operative," Isikoff wrote. "Nonetheless, it is significant that Rove was speaking to Cooper before Novak's column appeared; in other words, before Plame's identity had been published. Fitzgerald has been looking for evidence that Rove spoke to other reporters as well."

According to Isikoff, "a source close to Rove" said that "a fair reading of the e-mail makes clear that the information conveyed was not part of an organized effort to disclose Plame's identity, but was an effort to discourage *Time* from publishing things that turned out to be false."

The most likely source was Luskin, Karl's attorney, since he was quoted in other parts of the article. Reportedly the source was concerned about being quoted on the record discussing publicly what Karl had testified to privately before the grand jury as part of an investigation that was still under way. Clearly I had allowed myself to be deceived. In the coming weeks and months, I would discover that the deceit went well beyond Rove.

These revelations would soon have a painful, chilling effect on my relationships with reporters. On CNN's *Late Edition* for Sunday, July 17, 2005, John King, the guest host who had been CNN's chief White House correspondent for years, summed up the attitude of his colleagues in the briefing room. They were willing to vouch for me to a point because they had come to know me and my reputation, but they could not go too far without a public explanation of events from me.

The reporters' attitude would prove hurtful but understandable. It wasn't so much an indictment of me as of the administration I worked for. The implication was clear: if some of the highest-ranking officials of the Bush White House hadn't been forthright with the president's chief spokesman, how could anyone assume they were honest with the public? The White House had a serious credibility problem, and I was now going to take the heat for it.

THE IMPACT OF THAT SUNDAY CONVERSATION and the imminent *Newsweek* scoop was the equivalent of getting whacked upside the head with a two-by-four.

I never saw it coming, given Karl's personal assurances to me and the president, at least not until the final few days before it became public. And even then I convinced myself not to believe the growing buzz in Washington because of the personal assurances I had received.

The Monday briefing following Isikoff's jolting revelation was brutal. After the initial period of the leak episode nearly two years earlier, I had used the line, "I am not going to comment on an ongoing investigation." It would end the questioning quickly, but not this day, given what I had so confidently asserted at the outset in the fall of 2003. John Roberts of CBS made sure to point out that I had in fact commented while the investigation had been under way for nearly two weeks, and he wondered why the change. Roberts was right, and I knew it. Although I had cleared Rove initially before notice of any investigation, I had not cleared Libby at the vice president's request and the president's direction until after we were informed about it.

NBC's David Gregory mockingly said it was "ridiculous" that I would not answer whether I stood by my previous assertions of no involvement by Rove, Libby, and Abrams, chiding me for unresponsively "not saying anything" about the Newsweek revelations. Then Terry Moran of ABC swung the piñata stick, saying I was in "a tough spot" before derisively asking, "All of a sudden you have respect for the sanctity of the criminal investigation?" Eventually, long after leaving the White House, I came to see that standing in front of the speeding press bus in those days had much more to do with protecting the president and White House from further political embarrassment than respecting the sanctity of the investigation.

We would get to other topics that day, but reporters kept coming back to issue number one. The newscasts that evening were about as negative and biting as they could be.

I could feel something fall out of me into the abyss as each reporter took a turn whacking me. It was my reputation crumbling away, bit by bit. And my affection for the job eventually followed it. I kept going through the motions, much as I had when my older brothers occasionally pounded me when we fought as kids (at least before I caught up with them in size and strength). I was unable to do a thing about it other than put on a brave face and refuse to let them know they had gotten the best of me. The briefing could not end soon enough.

The ridicule I received that day and the following ones, though dispiriting and humiliating, was justified, given what I had previously said. Since my hands were tied, about all I could do was go into a defensive crouch and stonewall.

The postbriefing critique with my deputies was somber. They knew I had been put in an impossible spot. "It is what it is," said one deputy, Trent Duffy, a constant source of candid advice. "Nothing you can do about it. You're in a tough spot." The other two, Dana Perino and NSC spokesman Fred Jones, expressed their sincere empathy for me personally.

Back in my office later that afternoon, I received a phone call from Karl Rove. "I just want to say, I'm sorry for what you're going through." Given the continuing investigation, I knew that was as full an apology as he would offer. It's clear to me, Karl was only concerned about protecting himself from possible legal action and preventing his many critics from bringing him down.

The network news coverage by White House correspondents that night was understandably unforgiving—harsh on the White House and on my credibility, which didn't help the president's either. Each played clips of my statements in the fall of 2003, and reported how they were now being contradicted. John Roberts summed it up: "It was a bad day at the White House, unable to defend its own on-the-record statements, unable to explain why what it repeatedly said with such certainty twenty-one months ago now would appear so demonstrably false."

Roberts's colleague, Bill Plante, concluded his report the following morning by saying, "There are other people involved in this controversy over the outing of the CIA officer, but if Rove is truly not a target of this investigation, the White House, at worst, still looks stupid."

That same morning, Karl ran the senior staff meeting in Andy's absence. Usually I was the second one to speak, following a quick rundown of the president's public schedule for the day. Before Karl turned it over to me, he said for all our senior staff colleagues to hear that he was "really sorry" for what I was going through.

Karl paused momentarily, looking at me intently, almost waiting for me to say, "Don't worry about it. No big deal." But all I could do was grimace expressionlessly, nod my head slightly, and acknowledge his remorse by softly uttering, "Thank you, appreciate it." The next day, I found a handwritten apology from Karl waiting on the chair in my office.

Later that week, it would become known (confirmed anonymously by Karl's attorney, Robert Luskin) that Karl had been the second source for

Novak's original column disclosing Plame's identity. Dick Stevenson, a White House correspondent, and his *New York Times* colleague David Johnston got the scoop for that Friday's story. It was part of Karl's and Luskin's strategy.

Karl's attorney insisted to reporters that he had not leaked or disclosed Plame's identity. Novak, according to Luskin, had said he'd heard Wilson's wife worked at the CIA, and Karl had responded, "I heard that too." And the *Times* article said the anonymous source (Luskin) "discussed the matter in the belief that Mr. Rove was truthful in saying that he had not disclosed Ms. Wilson's identity."

The *Times* story said that Novak had described the "two senior administration officials" in a follow-on column published October 1, 2003. His primary source, who was yet to be revealed, was "no partisan gunslinger" according to Novak, and the second official (Rove) had only confirmed that "Oh, you know about it."

At a press conference the following Monday held with visiting Prime Minister Singh of India, the AP's Terry Hunt asked the president about Karl and the leak investigation. "Mr. President," Hunt said, "you said you don't want to talk about an ongoing investigation, so I'd like to ask you, regardless of whether a crime was committed, do you still intend to fire anyone found to be involved in the CIA leak case? And are you displeased that Karl Rove told a reporter that Ambassador Joe Wilson's wife worked for the Agency on WMD issues?"

"We have a serious ongoing investigation here," the president said. He then continued:

> And it's being played out in the press. And I think it's best that people wait until the investigation is complete before you jump to conclusions. And I will do so, as well. I don't know all the facts. I want to know all the facts. The best place for the facts to be done is by somebody who's spending time investigating it. I would like this to end as quickly as possible so we know the facts, and if someone committed a crime, they will no longer work in my administration.

The last line was part of a strategy for the president to "clarify" the terms of firing. Dan Bartlett thought the president needed to have something to say to that very question we knew would come up, and that it was best to go ahead and redefine the terms of firing someone who might have been involved in the leak, specifically Karl. Feeling psychologically battered, I quietly went along with Dan's construct, barely objecting that it did not square with what the president had previously committed to do.

The media played it up as a changed position, as we knew they would, but it was best to go ahead and do it sooner than later. I was disappointed to see the president backpedal, but I understood his motivation. The whole situation surrounding Karl, who still maintained he had never knowingly or intentionally leaked Plame's classified identity, was murky, at least as the president would have seen it, and Karl was a very important part of the president's team.

One day around that time, I don't even remember how it came up, I recall Andy saying to me in private something about how some staffers felt bad for me because I'd been left hanging out to dry unable to defend myself, whereas other staffers felt the White House should vigorously defend Karl. I think Andy felt bad for the spot I had been put in, partly as a result of his call to me that first Saturday morning in October 2003. But the Rove revelations were not the last time my words and credibility would be undermined.

Three months later, the vice president's chief of staff, Scooter Libby, whom I'd been specifically directed to exonerate, would be indicted by Special Counsel Patrick Fitzgerald for one count of obstruction of justice, two counts of making false statements to FBI agents and two counts of perjury before the grand jury. It would be revealed at the time that, in addition to Miller, he had spoken to Cooper, though not Novak, about Plame—contrary to my public assertions that he had assured me otherwise. It was also revealed that he had shared the classified information with my predecessor, Ari Fleischer, in an apparently successful effort to use him to leak the information to reporters. (Fleischer later testified that he did not know the information was classified.)

Over the coming weeks and months, Karl was vigorously defended by the Republican National Committee, whose hand-picked chairman, Ken Mehlman, had previously been Karl's top White House aide and my former colleague. Conservative pundits and opinion leaders joined in the defense, orchestrated, in part, through Karl's attorney, Mehlman, and Mark Corallo, the veteran spokesman Karl had personally hired to deal with the investigation.

In the end, after several lengthy grand jury appearances, Karl escaped indictment. Reports indicated he had not revealed his discussion with Matt Cooper about Plame initially to the grand jury. Then after his attorney, Robert Luskin, learned about it in casual conversation from another *Time* reporter, Rove reportedly threw himself on the mercy of the jury.

Ken Mehlman strongly defended my honor and integrity in talk show appearances, as Dan Bartlett did on CNN. But my most credible defenders were the same well-known White House correspondents who had pounded me that week of the Rove revelation and later the week of the Libby indictment. And they were credible because they were not spinning or obfuscating for partisan purposes, but simply expressing what they knew to be true.

For example, during an appearance on *Hardball* with Chris Matthews on October 31, 2005, David Gregory, the chief White House correspondent for NBC News and my toughest, least courteous nemesis in the briefing room, was asked about my position. It was the Monday following Fitzgerald's single indictment in the investigation, with Fitzgerald continuing to investigate Karl's role as I continued my defensive "no comment" posture at the podium about the whole affair.

"It gets kind of hot in that briefing room, doesn't it, these days?" Matthews asked Gregory.

"It can and it does, certainly when it has to do with Scott McClellan's statements about these individuals not being involved in any way, shape, or form," Gregory said. Then he added:

> I mean, Scott is in a tough position, we understand that, because he's being told as are all White House employees, by the White House counsel, Harriet Miers, by the way, not to talk about any of this.
>
> But the reality is that he made a public statement about getting assurances directly from Karl Rove and Scooter Libby that they were not involved with any of this, and that was not the case. Because even if it is not a crime, and we know that Scooter Libby has been accused of committing a crime of obstruction of justice and perjury, Karl Rove has not been accused of any crime, they were, indeed, involved in conversations about a covert officer of the CIA. And you don't have to believe me, that's what Special Prosecutor Fitzgerald said of [Plame's] . . . classification.
>
> So that's the spot that he's in. And it's a question of credibility. And Scott said to us, look, you the members of the press corps know me, I'm a credible guy. That's true. He has a sterling reputation. But it's a question for the

American people, you know. It's a real question if you say something that turns out not to be true.

The previous day on CNN's *Reliable Sources* with *Washington Post* media reporter Howard Kurtz, CBS's John Roberts had come to my defense. "John Roberts, do you believe that Scott McClellan owes the press and the public an apology for his—what turned out to be misleading denial in the CIA leak case?" Kurtz asked.

"Well, you know, Howie, I may be one of the people in the minority, but I think that he's getting a really rough deal on this," Roberts said.

> You know, he doesn't go out and free-lance this stuff . . . he goes out there, and he tries to faithfully articulate whatever it is that the White House tells him. Obviously in October of 2003, he got some pretty bad information. Is it his fault that he conveyed that information? I don't think so. I think the people who are at fault are—the ones at fault are the ones who gave him what now appears to be bad information.
>
> So I think that Scott—you know, I have known him for a number of years now. I have got a pretty good working relationship with him. I think that he is a truth-teller. I think he is a stand-up guy. And I just think that he was just told to carry somebody else's water, and it just turned out that that water was foul.

On the same day, in a roundtable appearance on *This Week with George Stephanopoulos*, Terry Moran, ABC's chief White House correspondent, also defended my reputation with his candor. "What does the White House do now about their press secretary Scott McClellan and the fact on occasion after occasion after occasion he had absolute blanket denials—there was no involvement by Rove, no involvement by Libby?" Stephanopoulos asked.

"It's an incredibly difficult position to put the press secretary in," Moran responded. "I was in the room. He was telling falsehoods right at us over and over unwittingly."

"But do you think he knew?" panelist Cokie Roberts inquired.

"No," said Moran. "And he signaled that he wants to tell us the story," he added, referring to my sincere comments at the podium that I would like nothing more than to be able to talk about events surrounding my public exoneration of Rove and Libby.

"I got to press this, then," Stephanopoulos said. "Okay, you say he didn't know it so that means that Karl Rove lied to him?"

"Yes," Moran said. "Yes."

"What does the president do about that?" Stephanopoulos asked.

"He's got to do something," Moran said, before correctly predicting the continued awful communications strategy of stonewalling. "My sense is right now they'll kick this down the road. They'll say it's a continuing criminal case and we're going to kick it down the road."

"We had a presidency just recently where the president lied to his press secretary and everybody else in the White House," Roberts added in reference to Bill Clinton.

"But what does the president do?" Stephanopoulos pressed.

George Will jumped in. "At this point, change the subject," he said. "It's an old axiom in politics if you don't like the news go out and make some of your own," as he correctly suggested the president would do by naming a new Supreme Court nominee following Harriet Miers's withdrawal just days earlier.

The president nominated Sam Alito to the bench the very next morning. But that did nothing to alleviate my painful humiliation or ward off the continued blows to the credibility of the Bush administration.

IN AN INTERVIEW WITH REPUBLICAN party chairman Mehlman, John King of CNN said:

> You call Scott McClellan a good man. I agree with you. A little dangerous for me. I'm supposed to be objective here. He is a good guy. He has one of the toughest jobs in Washington. I've been in that briefing room during questions like this in this administration, questions like this in the Clinton administration. He has, if you watch, fairly or unfairly, suffered some damage in that room. His credibility is at question with the people who cover the president every day because of this.

King then asked Mehlman, "So you're essentially saying that it is a fair price, Scott McClellan, a man who has been loyal to this president back to his days as governor of Texas, his credibility is a fair price to defend Karl Rove?"

"What I'm saying is that Scott McClellan and Karl Rove and George W. Bush are less worried about personal credibility than they are about a process," Mehlman said.

> They want to get to the bottom of this. They want to make sure that justice gets done. And the way justice gets done is not to have the White House and president making comments from the podium about an investigation of the White House. And so I think what he is doing is, frankly, very admirable, and I think the fact that he's willing to put himself second and put the process first is exactly what we talk about when we say somebody who's coming to Washington to serve rather than worry about themselves.

Clinging to the candid words from my briefing room inquisitors, I deceived myself further by thinking my reputation and credibility with the press could survive in the absence of an honest personal explanation, which I was prevented from making because I went along with directions not to comment.

In hindsight, the strong relationship of trust that I had established with the White House press corps could do little except permit a badly wounded spokesman and his damaged credibility to survive the next several months—and just barely.

There is only one moment during the leak episode that I am reluctant to discuss. However, since I am committed to telling the truth as I know it, and since the moment seems to be of some relevance given its timing and nature, I feel that full disclosure is the only option.

It was in 2005 during a time when attention was focusing on Rove and Libby, and it sticks vividly in my mind. I don't recollect the exact day, but it was following a staff meeting in Andy Card's office. He shared a two-office suite. Three staff assistants worked in a common area that connected the two offices and served as waiting area and entrance to both. The second office was for the deputy chief of staff for policy, who at the time was Karl Rove.

The meeting in Andy's office included some principals, or assistants to the president, and some deputies, or deputy assistants to the president. I believe some special assistants were also in attendance.

Following the meeting some of us, maybe a handful, were still working our way out the door of the suite's common area and mingling at its entryway, near the door to Karl's office and in front of his able assistant Taylor Hughes's desk. Scooter Libby was walking to the entryway as he prepared to depart when Karl turned to get his attention.

"You have time to visit?" Karl asked.

"Yeah," replied Libby.

They were just a few feet from me before they disappeared behind the closing door to Karl's office.

I have no idea what they discussed, but it seemed suspicious for these two, whom I had never noticed spending any one-on-one time together, to go behind closed doors and visit privately. Karl's office door was always open unless there was a real need for privacy. It was not unusual for me to stick my head in his door and briefly interrupt. Karl always tended to be busy working on countless issues, events, or plans. If I needed to get information from him to prepare for the press briefing, information I always had to obtain under time constraints, the easiest way was to just go to him.

Why would I remember this moment so vividly?

Because these are the two colleagues, one a fellow Texan, I put my credibility on the line to defend. The two who assured me unequivocally they were not involved in leaking the identity of Valerie Plame. At least one of them, Rove, it was publicly known by that time, had at best misled me by not sharing relevant information, and credible rumors were spreading that the other, Libby, had done at least as much.

The confidential meeting also occurred at a moment when I was being battered by the press for publicly vouching for the two by claiming they were not involved in leaking Plame's identity when recently revealed information was now indicating otherwise. In the four years we had all worked together at the White House, I had never seen the two meet one-on-one. Now, here they were, meeting privately behind closed doors late in the game when both were under investigation and intensifying public scrutiny.

I do not know what was discussed, but what would any knowledgeable person reasonably and logically conclude was the topic? Like the whole truth of people's involvement, we will likely never know with any degree of confidence.

A GROWING SENSE OF BURNOUT LED me to briefly consider resigning. But I never felt the president himself had knowingly misled me or withheld relevant information from me. And despite some uncertainties from within about the course we were on, I remained determined to honor my commitment to him, without appreciating how difficult it would be.

I imagine some believe my resignation at that moment could have helped the president. Maybe so. But it was Bush's unconscious acquiescence and, at times, enabling of deception that put us in such a precarious position. It would continue plaguing his presidency and his standing with the public. Instead of embracing openness and forthrightness to prevent the scandal from taking hold, he allowed suspicion to grow and partisan warfare to flourish.

More than thirty years later, Nixon's legacy of the permanent scandal culture was bedeviling yet another president who'd failed to learn the lessons of Watergate. I certainly paid a price as a result. But a far greater price was paid by the Bush administration—and by the nation it was pledged to serve.

15

OUT OF TOUCH

THE CONFERENCE CALL BEGAN AT AROUND 5:00 A.M. on Tuesday, August 30, 2005. I'd been up a while, unable to sleep. We'd arrived in California the day before from Texas, where the president, as usual, was spending much of August working out of his home in Crawford. Along with many others on the staff, he was still operating on Central Standard Time. The president had come to San Diego to make some remarks commemorating the sixtieth anniversary of V-J Day in a speech to veterans, Marines, special operations forces, Navy officers, sailors, and aviators at Naval Air Station North Island. Secretary Rumsfeld, traveling separately, was there as well. After that, Bush was scheduled to visit some wounded Navy SEALs and Marines at the nearby medical facility before returning to Crawford for the last few days of the summer.

One of the fringe benefits of being on the president's traveling staff, or "road crew," as we often referred to ourselves, was staying with him in luxury hotels. On this trip, my room in the historic Hotel Del Coronado—a five-star resort on San Diego's Del Mar beach, locally known as the Del—was just a few rooms down the hall from the president's.

The trip west had been planned long in advance. No one could have anticipated that this would be the weekend when a catastrophic hurricane would hit the United States. The sheer size of Hurricane Katrina's reach and destructive power, covering more than 90,000 square miles, was difficult to imagine. The purpose of this morning's conference call was to update some of the president's key team members on the current situation in the aftermath of the storm and, most important, make a determination about Bush's immediate plans.

We'd known for a while that the hurricane would be a bad one. President Bush had taken the unusual step of declaring both Louisiana and Mississippi disaster areas on the previous Saturday and Sunday, respectively, *before* the hurricane hit. (He'd made these declarations at the request of governors Kathleen Blanco and Haley Barbour, with whom the administration had been in contact, in part so that the cost of the emergency preparations being made by the states could be reimbursed after the fact by the federal government.) A series of increasingly drastic preparatory steps had been taken, including, on Sunday morning, the first mandatory evacuation order in the history of New Orleans, issued by Mayor Ray Nagin (the president had urged him to do so in a call).

Yet as the hours ticked by, the news kept getting worse. Hence the need for this morning's conference call.

Back in Washington, Dan Bartlett had initiated the call through the White House signal, a military-run operator service for national security matters and senior staff that's part of the White House Communications Agency (WHCA). WHCA provides full communications support to the president, the vice president, the National Security Council, the Secret Service, and the White House senior staff, including secure and nonsecure communications. Among those on the call were chief of staff Andy Card, who was vacationing in Maine, deputy chief of staff for policy and senior adviser Karl Rove, Bartlett, deputy chief of staff for operations Joe Hagin, and myself. Hagin and I were traveling with President Bush. Among his other White House duties, he served as the internal point person for coordinating with administration officials in charge of natural disaster response.

In retrospect, I wasn't at my best during that time period. Just a few weeks earlier I'd been exposed as having passed along the false assertion that Karl Rove had not been involved in leaking the identity of Valerie Plame. As a result, my credibility as presidential spokesperson had suffered quite a blow, something I was reminded about frequently during my increasingly stressful hours at the podium in the White House press room in the immediate aftermath of the revelation. Those events had taken an enormous psychic toll on me, and I needed a break from Washington—away from colleagues, away from the spotlight, a time to clear my head and recover. So my wife Jill and I had taken a few days off and traveled to a remote hideaway in North Carolina with our two dogs. Nonetheless, I was still feeling sapped and a little depressed as that fateful week began.

Unshowered and unshaven, clad only in a T-shirt and shorts, I had just started to scan some of the morning news programs. The newspapers delivered to my door said that New Orleans had apparently been spared a catastrophic hit, but the morning programs with journalists on the spot were showing just the opposite. I had yet to receive my daily morning summary, which would include an internal Katrina situation report from the White House Situation Room.

The phone rang. Dan Bartlett and I were the first connected to the call. In the moments before the others logged on, Dan gave me a brief update on what he knew about the situation. "It's bad," Dan said. "A worst-case scenario in New Orleans. A lot of the Gulf Coast along southeast Louisiana and Mississippi was wiped out, too."

But the most shocking news concerned the devastation of New Orleans. Much of the city rests below sea level in a bowl-shaped depression encircled by levees and floodwalls. Katrina was a massive Category 3 hurricane with storm surges of up to twenty-five feet as its eye passed some forty miles to the city's southeast. Its width had expanded as it reached shore, and hurricane force winds extended 103 miles from its center. The levees were now definitively confirmed to have been breached, which meant that the floodwaters would not be going away anytime soon.

One by one, the president's team members were connected to the call. We did not share a detailed situation report; we'd all heard how bad the situation had become, either through the pictures and words on our TV screens or through internal White House reports. We understood that Katrina had wreaked enormous havoc and came to quick agreement that the president needed to return to Washington sooner rather than later.

The plan we formulated was to have the president return home to Crawford immediately following his morning visit to the naval base and the hospital. That would give everyone in the president's entourage the evening to pack their belongings in Texas and return to Washington the following morning. In retrospect, we should have gone straight back to D.C., but no one seemed to feel that the circuitous route back would hurt as long as the president was staying on top of things and the public knew he was cutting short his Texas stay.

"Yeah, and can we have the president do a flyover in Air Force One?" Karl Rove suggested. "We should have him looking out and surveying the damage in New Orleans and along the coast of Mississippi and Alabama as he returns to D.C." As usual, Rove was thinking about the political perceptions. That was Rove's job, and no one did it better. His thinking in this case was obvious: a flyover would at least reflect the president's concern.

Rove's political instincts in such situations were usually on target, but this suggestion made me uneasy. I didn't like the idea, and I spoke up quickly. "I think that's a bad idea," I asserted. "He'll be 10,000 feet up in the air, looking down at people being rescued off rooftops. He'll look out of touch and detached. If he goes, he needs to be on the ground visiting with those affected and seeing the damage up close."

I added, "Or at least an aerial tour in a helicopter if he can't go on the ground. If he can't do that, then he should just go straight back to D.C., without a flyover."

"I agree," Bartlett added instantly, and no one else objected. I felt the matter had been put to rest: there would be no Katrina flyover.

I was pretty confident my instincts and judgment on this issue were sound. I remembered as a kid tagging along with my mother when she was mayor of Austin as she personally visited a neighborhood ravaged by a killer flood. And I remembered how, only a year before, Joe Hagin and I had accompanied the president as he visited Florida four times in a few weeks, each after a major hurricane damaged homes and neighborhoods.

The president understood his role as comforter in chief in such situations, and he performed it remarkably well, showing genuine care and concern for victims. He would take walking tours of damaged neighborhoods, observing the wreckage to homes and offering comfort and support to devastated families. His Florida trips had included helicopter tours with the governor (his brother Jeb) and other officials so he could see the scope of the damage firsthand. Hagin understood this dynamic well, and always worked to make sure events were planned accordingly.

By contrast, a Katrina flyover in the luxury of the world's most recognizable 747 would create in the minds of the press and the people an image of a callous, unconcerned president. If we weren't going to hit the ground immediately, I felt it was better to get back to D.C. and assume greater control over the emergency response.

So I was glad to get that sense of reassurance from the conference call that there would be no flyover in Air Force One. Unfortunately, I'd accepted that reassurance a little too quickly.

The conversation wrapped up a short time later as final plans were discussed. "At the first event this morning," I said, "I will tell the press pool about the change in plans. I'll let them know a trip to the Gulf Coast region is expected by the end of the week. I'll also let reporters know about the updates the president is receiving and that he'll likely participate in a videoconference tomorrow morning from his ranch."

Everybody was good with the game plan.

But President Bush was one step ahead of us. When the call ended and Hagin went to tell him what we thought, Bush spoke first. He told Hagin he had already decided he needed to return to Washington. The entire team swung into action, beginning a new, improvised scene in the elaborately choreographed dance that is a presidential trip.

As press secretary, I focused on the story we delivered to the news media about President Bush's response to Katrina. I knew how important this was. Natural disasters are widely viewed as tests of presidential leadership. The press and the people want to see their president behaving assertively and authoritatively in the immediate aftermath of a disaster. They also expect to see him visiting the affected area as quickly as possible, with the press in particular using this as a measuring stick of his concern.

The current situation was complicated by the fact that, according to the press, the president was currently "vacationing in Crawford," which our critics regularly used to imply he was not tending to important business. Frankly, as someone who lived it from within, such an assertion is off the mark and too easily embraced to fit a convenient political narrative—particularly when a problem is erupting somewhere in the world as it was this week. A president is never really on vacation. Occasionally he may go somewhere to decompress, clear his head, and escape the bubble of Washington, but he never has a full day off, particularly in our age of advanced telecommunications technology. Everything and everybody he needs is either with him or within reach twenty-four hours a day, seven days a week, from security briefings and classified news updates to instant connections with leaders around the nation and the world.

And this week, our stay in Crawford had been used as a jumping-off point for a western trip aimed in part at educating seniors about the new Medicare prescription drug benefit that was about to go into effect, as well as the V-J Day commemoration and the planned visit with Navy wounded. The average person with a schedule like this—a corporate CEO making a string of speeches, for example—would consider it fairly grueling. But that did not stop our critics from jumping on the president "vacationing in Crawford" to fuel a growing perception. I remember having to set the record straight months later when a *New York Times* article stated as fact that the president felt relieved the day after New Orleans had been spared a catastrophic hit while he was "on vacation in Texas." He was actually in San Diego and we were not relieved. But the vacation line fit a convenient story line—that we had made misjudgments, which was true.

I understood it was all part of Washington politics. But I wanted to make sure that Bush's so-called vacation didn't get interpreted as "president relaxes while New Orleans drowns." Hence the importance of carefully orchestrating the travel plans and communicating them clearly and fully to the media. Unfortunately, it would still be overshadowed by the larger policy and management problems that would come to light in the coming week.

The question of when we would travel to New Orleans offered its own set of complications. The standard practice of the Bush White House was not to have the president rush to the scene of a natural disaster. First and foremost, we wanted to make sure that nothing interfered with emergency response and recovery efforts in the immediate aftermath. Even a scaled-down presidential trip, with staff, the press corps, secret service agents, and support elements, involves quite an entourage, not to mention the advance staff that must go ahead of the president to coordinate everything with those on the ground. When disaster strikes and lives are in the balance, it doesn't make a lot of sense to divert scores of workers and officials from rescue efforts to focus on making arrangements for a presidential visit.

Second, President Bush never wanted to give the appearance of capitalizing on a tragedy for political purposes. For these two reasons, leaving a little breathing space between a disaster and his visit always seemed to President Bush the most appropriate thing to do. For example, he didn't visit Ground

Zero in New York until September 14, three full days after the attacks in 2001, and then only after great care was taken to avoid disrupting the rescue and recovery efforts by the first responders.

Our New Orleans schedule was developed with these considerations in mind, and I intended to explain this to the media before the president spoke at our first event that morning on August 30 in San Diego. But as sometimes happens, my plans went slightly awry. With time short because of the president's penchant to start an event as soon as he arrives, I hurried across the roped off area in front of the stage to the area reserved for the press pool. I managed to announce to the pool that the president would be returning to D.C. the following morning. But before I could give further details, the always punctual president appeared on stage, ready to start his remarks. I stopped and told the reporters I would fill them in after the speech, not wanting to distract the president or have him glare down at me, wondering why I was talking while he was giving a speech.

President Bush began his speech by addressing the storm damage:

This morning our hearts and prayers are with our fellow citizens along the Gulf Coast who have suffered so much from Hurricane Katrina. These are trying times for the people of these communities. We know that many are anxious to return to their homes. It's not possible at this moment. Right now our priority is on saving lives, and we are still in the midst of search and rescue operations. I urge everyone in the affected areas to continue to follow instructions from state and local authorities.

President Bush then proceeded with the rest of his speech, which dealt with commemorating the anniversary of V-J Day. When he finished, I immediately began detailing the change of plans with the press pool, informing reporters of the schedule we'd discussed in our senior staff conference call and letting them know that the president had received an update on the latest damage assessment and the ongoing response.

One reporter asked whether the trip back to Washington was essentially symbolic, since the president could carry out his duties from Crawford. "No," I said. "This is one of the most devastating storms in our nation's history, and the president, after receiving a further update this morning, made the decision that he wanted to get back to D.C. and oversee the response efforts from there. This is going to—there are many agencies involved in this—in this response effort, and it's going to require a long and sustained effort on behalf of all the federal agencies working closely with state and local officials to help people recover from the destruction and devastation."

A few yards away, the president was finishing shaking hands with local well-wishers along the rope line. As he proceeded backstage, assistant press secretary Josh Deckard indicated we needed to wrap things up. He wanted the press pool to get into the motorcade to be ready to leave as soon as the president was set to depart. As he escorted the pool, I headed backstage, where the president and Secretary Rumsfeld were shaking hands with VIPs and dignitaries.

Standing off to the side, I turned and noticed Martha Raddatz, then the Pentagon correspondent for ABC News, in the company of a small group of army officers traveling with Rumsfeld. I wondered what she was doing back-stage, since that area is normally not open to the press. It's a place where the president can relax a little and not worry about being "on his game," since no one is recording his every word and movement.

I spotted Eric Ruff, a veteran Republican communications operative and Rumsfeld spokesman I had known for several years, and pulled him aside. "What is she doing back here?" I asked, referring to Raddatz. Ruff looked sur-prised. "She's traveling with the secretary," he said, "but I have no idea why she's backstage." Ruff immediately set out to have Raddatz escorted out of the area. But it was too late.

As Ruff headed toward Raddatz, I noticed that she was carrying a small camera. Later that day I learned one of her shots captured a private moment. Mark Wills, a country music singer who had performed at the V-J commem-oration prior to the president's arrival, handed Bush a small present—a gui-tar bearing the presidential seal. Bush accepted the guitar with a smile and playfully strummed a couple of chords. It was a nice little interlude in a hec-tic day, and I'm sure Wills was tickled by Bush's gesture. But to Raddatz, the image of Bush strumming the guitar was newsworthy, I would learn later in the day.

Raddatz was escorted from the backstage area. But her snapshot soon hit the AP wire, juxtaposed with one showing a stranded family in coastal Missis-sippi being rescued from the rooftop of their SUV, and others showing New Orleanians clinging to the rooftops of their submerged homes.

This was exactly what I'd feared: the image of a seemingly carefree Presi-dent Bush pursuing his original schedule and disregarding the plight of Katrina's victims—the dead, the homeless, the lost. Was it fair? You decide. There were other moments from the president's morning that could have been highlighted: his remarks about the seriousness of the Katrina disaster and his decision to alter his plans to focus on it; his visit with wounded Navy SEALs and Marines in the military hospital. But the media and our critics chose to pounce on the guitar photo. It was a handy symbol of what many in the press had already chosen to believe about President Bush and his priorities.

UNFORTUNATELY, THE PROBLEM WAS MUCH larger than one photo. It would be a day or two before we would begin to fully grasp it, but we had already blown our initial response to Katrina. In the process, we'd made ourselves vulnerable to exactly the kind of criticism that Raddatz and her photo unleashed.

With 20/20 hindsight, it's clear that President Bush should have canceled his two-day western trip and headed back to Washington on Saturday or Sunday, *before* Katrina unleashed its fury. Even if we'd left Texas for D.C. on Monday morning, it would have helped greatly. A clear message would have been sent: the president understands this emergency, he takes it seriously, he is personally involved, and he wants the federal response to be the highest priority for everyone in the administration. Instead, we delayed and temporized and partially continued with business as usual, and thereby sent exactly the opposite impression: the Bush White House is focused on everything *but* Katrina.

How did we screw up so badly? The problem wasn't lack of information. The potential seriousness of the storm had been clearly conveyed to us in advance by Max Mayfield, the director of the National Hurricane Center. And while the information we received after Katrina's landfall, on Monday and Tuesday, was fragmentary, chaotic, and sometimes inaccurate, we were getting enough data to know that this was a very bad storm—possibly "the big one" residents of New Orleans and emergency management professionals had long worried about.

The problem lay in our mind-set. Our White House team had already weathered many disasters, from the hurricanes of the previous year all the way back to the unprecedented calamity of 9/11. As a result, we were probably a little numb ("What, another tragedy?") and perhaps a little complacent ("We've been through this before"). We assumed that local and federal officials would do their usual yeoman's work at minimizing the devastation, much as the more seasoned Florida officials had done the year before, and we recalled how President Bush had excelled at reassuring and comforting the nation in the wake of past calamities. Instead of planning and acting for the potential worst-case scenario, we took a chance that Katrina would not be as unmanageable, overwhelming, or catastrophic as it turned out. So we allowed our institutional response to go on autopilot. Rather than seizing the initiative and getting in front of what was happening on the ground in New Orleans, we let events control us. It was a costly blunder.

And things soon got a lot worse. One horrific media story line—a tale of indifference—would soon be joined by another—a tale of incompetence. Over the next three days, as the government's response to Katrina proved to be slow and inadequate, the press and the public would link the image of a seemingly carefree president with the news of his administration's clumsy management of the disaster, creating a narrative of government failure that would be irresistible and, once established, practically indelible.

As of that Tuesday morning, however, we had no idea what was about to hit us. We blithely headed to Texas to get our belongings and a good night's rest before departing for D.C. the following day.

Meanwhile, thousands of people were stranded in attics and on rooftops or elsewhere in New Orleans, waiting for help with little more than the clothes on their bodies. Hospitals filled with gravely ill patients were losing power. Makeshift shelters, including the New Orleans Superdome and the Convention Center, were filling up with tens of thousands of displaced people, hungry, sick, and scared. Conflicting, confusing accounts filtering out of the city added to the sense of chaos: people were talking about widespread looting, rioting, armed bands of thugs terrorizing the city. (Some of these stories eventually proved overblown, but at the time it was impossible to sort fact from fiction.)

The substantive problems the Bush White House had to address were huge and pressing. It didn't help that a parallel public relations disaster was unfolding. Sometime Wednesday morning, I learned that Karl Rove, still pushing his ill-conceived suggestion from Tuesday's conference call, had actually persuaded the president to do a flyover of the Katrina disaster area.

Dan Bartlett and I talked about it by phone. I still stressed that it was a bad idea. Dan did not disagree, but indicated Karl was convinced we needed to do it—and the president agreed.

There was little fight left in me. My will to push back had been severely diminished in the aftermath of the recent media flare-up over my earlier assertions in the Plame affair. I shrugged it all off and went along. I did not bring it up with the president. I knew it was a mistake, but I had no idea how devastating the image would turn out to be.

Before we took off from Crawford, I briefed reporters on the tarmac. I explained how the president had held a videoconference on hurricane relief efforts from his ranch. I emphasized that the president was focused first and foremost on saving lives, and second on developing a long-term strategy for addressing the needs of hundreds of thousands of displaced citizens. Then we boarded Air Force One for the flight to Washington, including the flyover Karl Rove had insisted on.

From a technical standpoint, the flyover proceeded beautifully. As Air Force One neared New Orleans, it descended to a lower altitude, and the president moved from his private cabin to the left side of the plane where the head of his Secret Service detail normally sits. This location provided him the best view of Katrina's devastation. He was joined by Karl Rove, deputy national security adviser J. D. Crouch, one of the pilots, and me. The still photographers in the pool were brought forward to snap shots for a couple of minutes while Bush looked out over the inundated Crescent City.

In all, we spent about thirty-five minutes flying at about 2,500 feet over New Orleans and the Mississippi coastal cities of Slidell, Waveland, Pass Christian, Gulfport, Biloxi, and Pascagoula. In Waveland and Pass Christian, slabs of concrete were left where wooden houses had once stood, the debris "looking from the air like nothing more than piles of matchsticks as far as the eye could see," as described in the pool report by *Washington Post* reporter Peter Baker. The mood in the cabin was somber. All of us, including the president, were struck by just how devastating the storm had been.

Newscasts that night included pictures of Bush gazing out the window, and the following morning newspapers across the country followed suit. The image I most feared was captured in each picture. Authors Wayne Slater and James Moore summed it up succinctly in their book *The Architect: Karl Rove and the Master Plan for Absolute Power*:

> The photo of Bush gazing out the window in the gentle half-light, amid the security and considerable comfort of Air Force One, peering down on a city

lost and ruined and rapidly descending into chaos, dominated the front pages the next morning. It was among the most damaging photos of his presidency. The president appeared detached and powerless, unable even to comprehend how he might use the government to help his own people. Worse, the picture conveyed no sense that the president cared or was worried about the catastrophe unfolding beneath the aircraft's big wings.

My earlier briefing with the press pool mattered little after the photos hit the news wires. The picture I had drawn was of a president deeply concerned and fully engaged. Photos of him peering down from Air Force One at people stranded by the floodwaters below painted a very different image. It was quite an object lesson in the supreme power of images in today's visually oriented world.

The president was certainly moved by the devastation he witnessed during the flyover, but it's impossible to truly feel the agony of those below from the luxury and comfort of Air Force One. Real empathy can only happen when meeting victims face-to-face. Bush fully grasped Katrina's destructiveness during our first visit to the region a couple of days later, although even then he didn't meet those in New Orleans who'd suffered the most.

The way we define "leadership" in America today is a funny thing. It demands strength, steadfastness, and resolve, as well as an unwavering focus on the duties at hand. But it also involves visible displays of emotion, empathy, compassion, and sorrow—softer qualities that may conflict with the toughness we expect from our leaders. Bush understood both of these roles, and in addressing the demands of his office, he had come to rely on his uncanny ability to compartmentalize—to wall off within himself the varying emotional and psychological responses triggered by the multitude of challenging issues facing him every day.

This strategy enabled him to exhibit calm, steady leadership during times of crisis. Bush regarded such calm as one sign of a disciplined leader who focuses on making hard decisions and wisely delegating responsibilities, in the manner of an effective corporate CEO. And by this point in his presidency, having lived through a number of trying crises, he knew how easy it could be to let emotion overpower him and paralyze his thinking. It had happened to another Texan president, Lyndon Johnson, during the height of Vietnam.

Bush was determined not to let it happen to him, either from war abroad or catastrophe at home.

For Bush, being a strong leader in a time of crisis means not allowing himself to be overwhelmed with anguish or anxiety. It means working to solve problems coolly, deliberately, and strategically. But as a result, he sometimes seems disconnected from the realities of people's lives. And that's what happened in Katrina's wake. People across the country were witnessing horrific images on their television sets: dead bodies floating in the floodwaters or lying face down on the pavement; families stranded on rooftops, calling out for food and water; people huddled under cardboard boxes for shelter. Bush needed to show that he was in control. But he also needed to show that he cared—that he understood the situation and shared Americans' sense of horror and anger, that he was determined to do whatever it took to make the bureaucracy respond. The flyover images showed none of this. And while privately Bush was quickly becoming more engaged, it was too little, too late.

Over the next couple of days, Dan Bartlett and I struggled with the PR side of the problem. We talked a lot with President Bush about the need to show he was fully engaged in public. But the public policy side of the problem was far more serious, and it was still lacking.

Many within the White House were in denial about the administration's responsibility for Katrina. Throughout that first week, we focused on how poorly prepared and overwhelmed state and local officials had been in responding to the storm. This was true. But we largely ignored the fact that the federal government was the vital backup, the fail-safe mechanism supposed to compensate for breakdowns at the lower levels. When you're president, the buck stops with you—a lesson George W. Bush still hadn't fully absorbed.

Back at the White House on Wednesday afternoon, the president chaired the first meeting of a newly formed cabinet-level White House task force on Katrina. "We will be dealing with this for a long time," he said at the start of the meeting. He continued:

> Coordinating responsibility closely with state and local officials is important. There are issues on the ground we must deal with. We need to make sure we know who is in charge, who is running the show on the ground. I just spoke

with [Louisiana] Governor [Kathleen] Blanco and told her if she wants it to be us, then we will [run the show].

It is a terrible disaster. Parts of Mississippi are just wiped out. It's beyond description. In New Orleans, neighborhoods are gone. We are talking about rebuilding a city. It is indescribable how terrible it is.

Bush concluded his opening by saying simply, "We got a problem to solve." Homeland Security secretary Chertoff had already begun daily media briefings along with FEMA officials, including Mike Brown. He then gave a situation update and reviewed the short-, mid-, and long-term priorities. The immediate needs were daunting: to save lives, stabilize the flooding, completely evacuate New Orleans, deliver food and water to the stranded, address the security problems, and get medical care to those who needed it. And complicating all these matters was a scarcity of reliable information. "Situational awareness has been a problem," Chertoff admitted. Even now, when the president asked about the emergency communications capabilities of state and local responders, he was told that they only had a limited number of satellite phones. Secretary Rumsfeld followed with an update about the military assets being deployed in the area, particularly to New Orleans. This led the president to speak about the possible need to federalize the response in New Orleans. Alluding to the deteriorating security situation in the city, he declared, "This is a war zone, I am telling you. I worry about riots breaking out. We will need to make up our minds [about putting the federal government in charge] in the next couple of days."

Several other cabinet members addressed priorities that fell under their purview, such as transportation, health, energy, and environmental matters. "We will have meetings quite frequently until we are on top of the problem," the president concluded. It had been a grim session.

As FEMA and the cabinet officers focused on concrete steps to help the devastated region, we tried to get the communications challenge under control. It did not go well. The disconnect between the reassuring, upbeat messages we wanted to convey and the bitter realities on the ground was simply too wide and too obvious.

Following the task force meeting, President Bush spoke to the nation from the Rose Garden. He outlined the steps being taken to save lives as well as the comprehensive planning under way for the long-term recovery. He tried to leave the impression that essential supplies of food, water, and medicine were getting to those most in need. It was true that the Coast Guard and other search-and-rescue teams were exerting heroic efforts. But the TV images of tens of thousands of people stranded or trapped in New Orleans short of supplies were also real, and left the president looking like a purveyor of illusory positive spin that the response was going fine. Later that same day, New Orleans Mayor Ray Nagin suggested the death toll in the city would likely be in the thousands. (Thankfully, his estimate turned out to be way too high, but no one had any way of knowing that at the time.)

Dan Bartlett was working to make sure the communications effort at the federal level was aggressive. In addition to the daily briefings by his agency, FEMA director Mike Brown was encouraged to do a continual round of interviews, particularly with the television networks. Secretary Chertoff, the cabinet member with ultimate responsibility for the response, also gave more interviews. But both Brown and Chertoff came across as out of touch. In an interview with Ted Koppel on *Nightline*, Brown said the Convention Center held some 5,000 people and that food and water had been supplied there by FEMA. The true number was closer to 25,000, and the center actually had no supplies at all. Similarly, Chertoff dismissed stories about the terrible conditions at the Convention Center as mere rumors.

With optimistic administration appraisals being vividly contradicted by media accounts and images, the rose-colored statements by Brown, Chertoff, and other officials were pounced on by reporters—understandably so.

While Bartlett was leading the broader communications strategy, I focused on day-to-day details, seeking to coordinate closely with some of my counterparts at relevant agencies—for example, by instituting a daily conference call to share the most crucial new information. Of course, explaining operational matters was best left to those closest to the situation. My role was to talk about what the president was doing, the meetings he was holding, and the bigger picture as we understood it in the White House.

But here too, the disjunction between message and reality was continuing to undercut us. On Thursday, President Bush's live interview with Diane Sawyer for ABC's *Good Morning America* created another defining reference point in the spiraling fiasco that was Katrina. This time, the problem was not the visual image but the words Bush uttered. Asked why he and his team had remained "on vacation" as Katrina bore down on the Gulf Coast, the president defensively snapped, "I started organizing on Tuesday when we realized the extent of the storm. And I said, look, when I get back to Washington on Wednesday afternoon I want to have a report on my desk and a cabinet meeting for you to tell me exactly what your departments are going to do to alleviate the situation."

Millions of Americans found the president's response less than reassuring. Was it true that no one in the administration had "realized the extent of the storm" until Tuesday, when Bush himself had declared a state of emergency three days earlier? And Americans who'd long heard, and agreed with, the president's own jaundiced, critical comments contrasting the bureaucratic mind-set with the can-do spirit of real leadership were dismayed to hear that Bush had demanded little more than "a report on my desk" by Wednesday afternoon—over fifty hours after Katrina's landfall. It sounded as though, in a moment of crisis, the president had practiced the worst sort of out-of-touch bureaucratic management—just the opposite of what he'd promised the voters.

Of course, this communications failure is much easier for me to see in retrospect than it was at the time. Like the rest of the president's team, I was immersed in trying to meet the enormous immediate challenges we faced, including both the practical steps to alleviate the tragedy and the communications efforts to reassure and inform the public. Only in looking back from today's perspective—outside the bubble—are the mistakes we all made obvious.

On Friday morning at 7:00 A.M., just before his first visit to the Gulf Coast region, the president chaired a joint Katrina briefing with leaders from the Department of Defense and the Department of Homeland Security. It was held in a secure conference room in the White House Situation Room. For three full days, Americans had been witnessing terrible images of human suffering on their television screens. It was gut-wrenching. Many wondered how the federal government, with its vast resources, could allow this to happen. They were demanding answers.

Urged on by his key advisers, Bush started this meeting by sending a stern message. He was blunt and to the point. "We are not winning," he said. "On the ground, it is chaotic. We've got to get New Orleans under control. We've got to establish order as soon as possible." He expressed continuing concern about the command-and-control issues that were hampering cooperation between the state and federal governments. Then, after noting that a lot of hard work and good effort were being exerted, he said flatly, "I am not pleased at all with the results." The message was clear. Further failures in the Katrina response would not be acceptable. The president concluded his opening remarks by asking General Myers, chairman of the Joint Chiefs of Staff, to bring home any Guard troops deployed abroad whose families had been uprooted by Katrina.

Secretary Rumsfeld called on Admiral Keating, who appeared on video screen from Northern Command in Colorado, which is responsible for homeland defense. Keating outlined the military's priorities—saving and sustaining lives in support of federal, state, and local response efforts. He outlined the command-and-control system that was in place and the assets being deployed, including several naval ships, nearly two hundred helicopters, and a growing number of National Guard troops. All were under the command of Joint Task Force Katrina based at Camp Shelby, Mississippi, and headed by General Russel Honoré, who was on another video screen from the Gulf Coast.

Named to head the task force only two days earlier, Honoré and his no-nonsense, take-charge approach had left a strong impression on Bush. Now Honoré stated that Louisiana was still "a big problem," while noting that Mississippi was fairly stable. The New Orleans Superdome was "under control and stable," he reported. In just the past twenty-four hours, 15,000 people had been evacuated from the stadium. Now the Convention Center was the focus of attention. Some 25,000 to 30,000 people were still there four days after the storm had struck, and getting food, water, and medicine to them was the priority. Honoré mentioned reports of "shootings and lawlessness," describing the situation at the civic center as "a crisis" that they needed "to get under control in the next twelve hours." National Guard troops, he said, were being moved in to secure the area. General Honoré came across as fully in command, well informed about what needed to get done, and hard at work making it happen.

Additional discussion ensued about the security situation. In response to a question from Secretary Chertoff, Honoré said that there had been isolated shootings, but reports of rapes around the Superdome and Convention Center appeared to be unsubstantiated. He said that people at the Convention Center just wanted to get out. As for looting, Honoré acknowledged, people "are scavenging for food because they don't have any." There were adequate supplies of food and water as well as military strength on the way, but it would take time to secure the area and begin distributing goods.

General Carl Strock, commander of the U.S. Army Corps of Engineers, updated the efforts to fix the levees and alleviate the flooding in New Orleans. He noted that the floodwaters had stabilized and would continue to recede.

The discussion then turned to the possibility of federalizing the response and asserting U.S. military control over New Orleans, an option that had been under serious discussion since earlier in the week. Bush believed that the military was the only organization disciplined and organized enough to come in and stabilize the situation quickly. Agreeing that there was an "issue of confidence" when it came to current response and relief efforts, Admiral Keating said the troops were ready if the orders came. But no final decision was made.

That led to a discussion of the images of human suffering being played in the media. Someone noted that some of the images were three days old, yet they were being replayed without explanation on the news networks. Under the circumstances, it was no wonder that Americans' sense of confidence in the government response was so low. Bush concluded the meeting by saying, "We have a duty and responsibility to think clearly." He was right, of course. But this was Friday, September 2. The message was a solid week too late.

Bush's visit to the flood zone that afternoon did little to improve public perceptions of the administration's handling of Katrina. In fact, as far as most Americans are concerned, it produced only two noteworthy moments, both of them embarrassments for the president. The first was his off-key focus on the heavily damaged vacation home of Republican Senator Trent Lott. "Out of the rubble of Trent Lott's house—he's lost his entire house—there's going to be a fantastic house," Bush raved, and he went on to declare that he was looking forward to sitting on Lott's new porch with him. Surrounded as he was by the devastated homes of thousands of Mississippians—many of them poor people who could scarcely afford to repair one house, let alone build a posh vacation home—the remarks seemed ill timed at best, callous at worst.

The second clinker from this trip has become even more famous. In an informal gathering before TV cameras, ringed by federal and local officials, President Bush singled out the beleaguered Michael Brown for praise, using a line that has become infamous: "Brownie, you're doing a heck of a job!" Even Brown looked embarrassed, and no wonder; most Americans had already concluded that the FEMA director was in over his head. They were simply beginning to wonder how and when he would get the ax and who would replace him. (Brown ultimately resigned ten days later, on September 12.) For Bush to commend him publicly suggested either that the president's well-known belief in personal loyalty was overwhelming his judgment or that he still didn't realize how bad things were on the Gulf Coast. Either way, the incident said something bad about the Bush administration.

The president later told us he had little choice but to praise "Brownie" at that moment. "He was standing right there, and I was trying to pump up everybody's morale," he explained. "What was I supposed to do?" he asked rhetorically. He had a little bit of a point. We should not have put him in such a position. The motivation was understandable, even laudable. But the execution was just another blow to the administration's already tottering credibility.

And once a particular story line, good or bad, has been established in the media, it's very difficult to slow its momentum. By now, the story line "Bush administration ignores hurricane devastation" had fully taken hold, and details that were basically irrelevant were being swept up into the narrative. Secretary of State Condi Rice had taken a couple of days off to visit New York this week, and while in the Big Apple she'd been spotted shopping for shoes in an upscale boutique. There was nothing terribly newsworthy about this, particularly since the secretary of state doesn't have any direct involvement in domestic disaster relief efforts. That didn't stop critics or the media from pouncing on the incident as further "proof" of the indifference of the Bush administration to human suffering. New York's most popular newspaper, the *Daily News*, ran a gleeful headline, AS SOUTH DROWNS, RICE SOAKS IN N.Y., and the story got widely circulated for weeks afterward.

Such incidents show that, even when there is plenty of real substance to criticize and there are noteworthy facts to uncover, the inclination for critics to exploit trivia for political advantage and the media to give play to something it considers conveniently and symbolically important is too difficult to resist and often leads to silly political sniping that adds little value to the search for the truth. In the case of Katrina, however, the substance of our problems was so great and so unmistakable that it overwhelmed the petty stories like the one about Condi's shoe shopping.

I'VE COVERED ONLY A SMALL PART OF the story of the national response to Hurricane Katrina, focusing especially on the early events I observed during that first devastating week. As New Orleans and the rest of the Gulf region continue to work toward full recovery from the horrific damage done by the storm, historians and reporters have begun to publish detailed accounts of what went wrong before, during, and after the hurricane. It's an important episode filled with lessons for the future.

For the purposes of this book, however, I want to stress that Katrina was a defining turning point for Bush and his administration. It left an indelible stain on his presidency. The tardy efforts to help the people of the Gulf Coast did not convince Americans to forgive the initial ill-prepared response and the inadequate preparations and plans.

The Bush administration was caught flat-footed partly because it believed it had mastered the art of emergency management. But Katrina was different, and New Orleans was different. Unfortunately the White House and the Federal Emergency Management Agency tackled Katrina in the same way it had dealt with the four major hurricanes that had hit Florida the year before. Extraordinary measures were not taken from the beginning. The cavalry was needed, but only a limited number of foot soldiers were deployed initially, despite the fact that we knew Katrina could be the "Big One" New Orleanians had feared for so long. For example, even though an unprecedented amount of supplies—MREs, water, ice, and medicine—had been pre-positioned in preparation for Katrina's landfall, the quantities were still too small given the massive scale of the tragedy, and they weren't moved to those who needed them quickly and effectively in the first few days of the disaster.

It was a failure of imagination and initiative. And when the storm hit and the damage proved worse than anyone expected, our inability to adjust bespoke a failure of responsibility.

We spent most of the first week in a state of denial. The tendency to shift responsibility and minimize unpleasant realities is a part of human nature that has to be kept in check. It was not. And we on the communications team bore our share of the blame. As we sought to protect the president and his reputation, instead of just accepting fault outright and moving aggressively to remedy the problem, we tried to deflect responsibility away from the White House and the federal government.

One of the worst disasters in our nation's history became one of the biggest disasters in Bush's presidency. Katrina and the botched federal response to it would largely come to define Bush's second term. And the perception of this catastrophe was made worse by previous decisions President Bush had made, including, first and foremost, the failure to be open and forthright on Iraq and rushing to war with inadequate planning and preparation for its aftermath.

The continuing violence in Iraq—suicide bombings, improvised explosive devices, sniper fire, and daily loss of life among American soldiers—was already causing many at home to lose hope and develop deep reservations about the postinvasion effort. The incompetence and blindness exhibited in the response to Katrina would soon become the lens through which many Americans, particularly independents and other centrist supporters of the war, would come to view Bush and his administration's management of post-Saddam Iraq.

16

AFTER THE TRIAL

Iᴛ ᴡᴀs ᴀ sɪᴍᴘʟᴇ sᴛᴀᴛᴇᴍᴇɴᴛ, ᴊᴜsᴛ three words from the mouth of the president, uttered in a blunt, matter-of-fact tone: "Yeah, I did." But the words left me in stunned disbelief. And their aftermath proved to be my breaking point—the final painful blow that made me realize I couldn't go on working for the Bush administration indefinitely.

I was boarding Air Force One in Charlotte, North Carolina, in the early afternoon of April 6, 2006. The president was sitting in his onboard office, and when he spotted me he caught my attention and that of Dan Bartlett. We had both just boarded the plane behind him. "What was he shouting out?" Bush asked us.

He was referring to a question that Geoff Morrell, an ABC News correspondent who covered the White House, had yelled out to Bush on the tarmac just a few moments earlier. That morning, the president had made some remarks on our Iraq strategy and participated in a question and answer session with members of Charlotte's World Affairs Council. Meanwhile, back in Washington, the Senate had been making some notable progress on comprehensive immigration reform, and we decided to have the president issue a statement at the airport to applaud the bipartisan efforts.

Bush wasn't taking questions that afternoon, but Morrell was eager to get the president's response to the day's major breaking news story, about a court filing related to the trial of Scooter Libby by Special Counsel Patrick J. Fitzgerald.

Dan had heard Morrell's question, and now he explained it to Bush. Dan stated that he was asking about Libby's grand jury testimony and the leak of the NIE that Fitzgerald just disclosed in legal proceedings.

"He asserted you authorized the leak of part of the NIE," I added.

"Yeah, I did," Bush simply replied. The look on his face said he didn't want to discuss the matter any further. Nor did I expect him to, since he had already been advised by his personal attorney Jim Sharp, not to discuss any details related to the Libby trial.

I wasn't sure what to say. I was only just learning about Fitzgerald's court filing from the media reports myself. But it was a bombshell that, if true, would add significantly to the damage that the Valerie Plame affair had done to the Bush administration—and to me as its chief spokesman. I was shocked to hear the president casually acknowledge its accuracy, as if discussing something no more important than a baseball score or the latest tidbit of inside-the-Beltway gossip.

The story had its roots back in July 2003, as I was preparing to take over as White House press secretary. At the time, the intertwined controversies over the sixteen dubious words in the State of the Union address, including the un-reliable claim about uranium from Niger, and the leaking of Valerie Plame's name and identity as a CIA agent were all raging. In the midst of those debates, then-National Security Adviser Condoleezza Rice had publicly suggested that the October 2002 national intelligence estimate (NIE) had offered evidence supporting the notion that Iraq had tried to acquire uranium from Africa, and specifically from Niger. But when she'd been asked whether the NIE could be declassified so that the American people could judge the evidence for them-selves, Rice had replied—in keeping with administration policy—that the White House did not "want to try to get into [a] kind of selective declassifica-tion," though she added that we were looking into whether parts of it could be shared publicly by declassifying it through formal channels.

According to Libby's grand jury testimony at the very time Rice asserted that the White House opposed "selective declassification," President Bush had actually engaged in just such selective declassification himself. He'd authorized the use of parts of the October NIE in the effort to discredit Joe Wilson's attacks on the credibility of the administration—the campaign that had ultimately in-cluded the leak of Plame's identity and led to the indictment of Scooter Libby.

Now, with those three simple words, "Yeah, I did," the president was telling me that Libby's testimony on the NIE—which I would soon learn about in greater detail—was accurate, and his and my public statements about the sanctity of classified intelligence rang hollow.

Democrats didn't hesitate to pounce on this latest evidence of hiding the truth, at the least, by the Bush administration. Senator Charles Schumer of New York said that if the president had authorized the leaking, then the American people "ought to know what distinguishes his leaking information from all the others who leaked information and were condemned by the president."

President Bush had often decried the selective leaking of classified information. The previous December, he had publicly condemned the leaking to the *New York Times* of information about the highly classified warrantless surveillance program that had been authorized in the aftermath of 9/11 to allow the National Security Agency to listen in on international communications involving known or suspected al Qaeda terrorists.

Now the fact that he himself had authorized the selective leaking of national security information to reporters made him look hypocritical. The president has inherent legal authority to declassify anything he chooses. But Democrats were quick to point out that the secret way he'd done it, as well as the underlying objective—to anonymously discredit a White House critic—smacked of politics.

In time, we would learn that the president's penchant for compartmentalization had played an important role in the declassification story. The only person the president had shared the declassification with personally was Vice President Cheney. Two days after the Fitzgerald disclosure, Cheney's lawyer told reporters that the president had "declassified the information and authorized and directed the vice president to get it out" but "didn't get into how it would be done." Then the vice president had directed his top aide, Scooter Libby, to supply the information anonymously to reporters.

No one else was told about the secret declassification—not Chief of Staff Andy Card, not National Security Adviser Condi Rice. When Rice was publicly rejecting the notion of selective declassification on July 11, 2003, Scooter Libby had already leaked it to Judith Miller on July 8—at the vice president's direction with authority from the president.

A week later, on July 18, Condi Rice requested formal declassification of part of the October NIE, including the "key judgments" section and the paragraphs relating to Iraqi attempts to secure uranium in Africa. This was done through the normal CIA channels the same day, and Tenet personally spoke with Cheney and Rumsfeld that day to let them know it had happened. (Even the CIA director did not know the president had already declassified parts of it earlier.) And in response to a reporter's question, I announced publicly that it had been officially declassified that day as well.

Now, in April 2006, with breaking news of the secret declassification authorized by the president, reporters began to press me on the distinction between this secret action and the formal declassification of July 18, 2003. Of course, what I'd announced on that date almost three years earlier had been correct: the official declassification had occurred then. As for the president's earlier action, I wasn't permitted to get into any details about that, since we were not commenting on the legal proceedings in the Libby trial. All I could do was point out that there are two ways to declassify information—the president can do it on his own, or it can go through the official declassification process, as had happened on July 18. It was a clear distinction, though a slightly arcane one.

The larger issue of hypocrisy was thornier. About all I could say was that the president would never declassify information if he thought it would compromise national security. It was in the nation's interest to declassify the NIE because of the accusations we'd been fielding of having manipulated or misused intelligence. In the context of the sixteen words controversy, I said, the president's declassification of information was in the interest of public debate, while the leaks he criticized were ones that could harm national security. This struck many as a distinction without a difference, and the argument fell flat with a skeptical public.

The president received plenty of criticism in the press as a result of this revelation—legitimately so. TV news programs played the news that he'd authorized the declassification against videos from 2003 of Bush saying, "There are too many leaks of classified information" and declaring, "If there is a leak out of my administration, I want to know who it is."

Questions were also raised about whether the president's action had set in motion the unauthorized disclosure of Valerie Plame's identity. Although we could not comment publicly, we did our best to distance him from this suggestion by pointing to the comments of Libby's lawyer that Bush had only authorized Cheney to "get the information out." He hadn't told him how to do it or what kinds of tactics to use. In other words, Bush hadn't explicitly talked about leaking. It was a narrow and ultimately tenuous thread.

In the days following the revelation of the NIE declassification I reached my personal breaking point. The secret declassification undermined what the president had repeatedly said and what I had echoed just as often. I don't believe President Bush intended to mislead me or senior advisers like Condi. But his secret actions meant that we had been deceived, intentionally or not. It was a painful revelation for me. And there were more to come.

WHEN THE NIE DECLASSIFICATION WAS revealed, the Bush administration was already going through a rocky time. The optimism and energy we'd felt after the successful reelection campaign had swiftly dissipated. The administration had been rebuffed in our attempt to win over public opinion and pressure Congress to reform Social Security. Despite a massive administration campaign aimed at generating support for reform, polls showed majorities of Americans rejecting our favored concept of personal accounts and resisting the idea that major changes needed to be made in the popular program. In late May 2005, when House majority whip Roy Blunt listed "priority legislation" to be acted on after Memorial Day, Social Security was not included, effectively signaling the death of entitlement reform as a short-term goal of the Republican party. When Katrina hit, any hope of regaining momentum for it was washed away for good.

By the spring of 2006, we in the Bush White House had been struggling for months, trying to overcome the perception of incompetence created by the botched initial response to Hurricane Katrina, the worsening situation in Iraq (including the February 2006 bombing of the Golden Mosque in Samara, which had intensified the raging sectarian conflict), and the accompanying drop in the president's approval ratings.

On March 28, Andy Card had announced his resignation as chief of staff. He had virtually forced it on the president, not the way he or anyone would want to leave the White House. But it was past time for change, and Andy, a longtime, selfless public servant, knew it. He was willing to take the hit if it could help improve the public perception of Bush and his leadership team.

"Think about it," Andy had said to me when we talked it over in his office. "There are really only four, maybe five people in the administration whose departure could make a real difference with the public. There's me. There's the vice president, and that is not going to happen. There's Condi, and that won't happen. And there's Rumsfeld, and that's not likely but that's between him and the president." The only choice Andy really saw was to resign himself and let a new chief of staff come in to run the show.

This conversation with Andy had helped solidify my thinking about a change in my own status at the White House. I'd begun thinking about it back in July 2005 when it had been revealed that what I had said in defense of Rove and then later Libby over the Plame leak controversy was false. I was feeling burned out. We had gone through the warrantless wiretapping disclosure, a former top policy aide being indicted for stealing from Target, and the vice president's infamous hunting accident. With the secret declassification of the NIE revealed, I had been burned internally one too many times. But I didn't want to leave the president in the midst of a raging controversy. That would be unfair to him and bad for the administration, I felt. I'd begun to think that the three-year mark of my starting date as press secretary—July 15, 2006— would be a good time to take the next step in my career. I'd announce it when the time was right, maybe in May, I decided.

With Andy Card on the way out, Josh Bolten would soon be taking over as chief of staff. He had previously been the director of the Office of Management and Budget and, before that, the deputy chief of staff for policy. He was a trusted loyalist who had worked for Bush since serving as policy director during the first presidential campaign.

I talked to Josh the day he was announced as Andy's replacement (so I could brief the press fully), which occurred simultaneously with Andy's resignation announcement. He also indicated that he wanted to visit with me soon, but didn't suggest there was anything pressing on his mind or that he had any particular concerns to discuss—just that he wanted to get my thoughts about White House communications.

But the following week, after the president departed for a long Easter weekend at Camp David on Thursday, Josh requested that I come visit with him in his OMB office. There were already reports suggesting that he had decided a change was needed in the press secretary position, and I was prepared to tell Josh that I was ready to go at a mutually agreed date, no later than July 15. I assumed he would be okay with my planned July departure. I preferred to get past the media feeding frenzy about possible personnel changes that usually follows the installation of a new chief of staff. My assumption was wrong.

Josh welcomed me in and I sat down on his couch. Before I could say a word, in a soft and measured tone, he got straight to his point. "This is not something pleasant for me," he began. "You are really liked around here. I really like you. But I believe this is a White House that is severely crippled and in need of change. One area that I have decided needs to change is your position. When the president asked me to serve as chief of staff, he assured me that I would have full authority to make changes I deemed necessary to turn things around. This is not something he decided. It is not something Dan Bartlett decided. This is a decision I made."

I sat there taking it all in, not necessarily happy about Josh starting off before he had a chance to hear what I wanted to say. Then I spoke up. "I understand," I said. "You should know that I was already thinking about leaving. I have been in this position a long time. I was already thinking this July, my three-year mark, would be a good time to leave."

"Oh," Josh said. "Well, in that case, that makes this easier. I was going to tell senior staff on Monday that anyone who is thinking about leaving within the next several months should go ahead and do so. I want the team that will be here through the end of the year to be in place within the next couple of weeks. You can tell the press that is why you are leaving now. I thought tomorrow might be a good day for you to make the announcement."

Gone within two weeks? Make an announcement tomorrow? That isn't what I'd had in mind.

My emotional response was strong and immediate. I thought to myself, *He's ready to throw me to the wolves.* I thought about how long I had worked for the president, about how loyal I had been to him, about how I threw myself in front of the bus during the controversy over the Valerie Plame leak—how I sacrificed my own credibility for the sake of the administration. *And now he doesn't even care to let the current storm blow over. Thanks for everything, Scott— and don't let the door hit you on the way out.*

Yet at the same time, my rational side understood all too well what was happening. I knew this was nothing personal. Josh was doing what he felt needed to be done, and he wanted it done quickly. I had been on the defensive too often since the Rove revelations in July. A press secretary cannot survive for long under such circumstances.

Still, I wasn't going to just capitulate. I told Josh I wanted a few days to sort things through. "Early next week might be better than tomorrow," I said.

Josh ended the meeting by saying that I should talk with Dan and work out when to make an announcement.

It was an interesting time on the Bush administration personnel front. Some former top military commanders were calling on Defense Secretary Rumsfeld to resign or be replaced. I had been asked about this at the briefing just before Josh and I met. I strongly defended Rumsfeld, saying the president thought he was "doing a very fine job during a challenging period in our nation's history." General Pete Pace, chairman of the Joint Chiefs of Staff, had also spoken out strongly in support of the secretary earlier in the day.

The next morning, after reading the front-page coverage in the *New York Times* and other papers, Josh spoke with Dan and me. He felt we needed to mount an even more vigorous defense of Rumsfeld by having the president make a statement. I thought it would be overkill to have the press pool go out to Camp David. We settled on having the president call the secretary and then issue a statement of support for him. (Rumsfeld ultimately left the administration in November 2006, in the wake of major Republican losses in the midterm elections. The first time I heard the president mention the possibility of Rumsfeld leaving was in casual conversation days after I announced my own resignation.)

I left early that Good Friday for an Easter weekend getaway—my wife, Jill, and I spent the holiday at a place in southern Virginia along the Chesapeake Bay. We talked it all over, as married couples do. Jill wasn't happy about the way she felt Josh was shoving me out the door. I understood her feelings, but, having stepped back from the situation since the initial discussion, I tried to get her to take a more philosophical attitude. After all, I said, I was ready to go anyway, and while I would have preferred to do it on my own terms, a few months one way or another wouldn't make a big difference in the long run.

Jill pushed back. She couldn't understand, she said, how the president could let Josh handle the situation this way after all I'd done for him. Again, I understood her feelings. Jill and I had enjoyed spending a couple of weekends at Camp David with the president and Mrs. Bush and a select few others. Like me, she'd developed tremendous affection for both of them. It was hard for me to explain that this was nothing personal.

"I'm sure the president and I will talk about it next week," I finally said. "Let's enjoy the weekend and not worry about it." And we did enjoy the weekend, although I won't claim that thoughts about the White House and my changing situation didn't creep into my head once or twice.

I connected with Dan over the weekend by phone. Jill and I were just settling into our room on the Chesapeake Bay. Dan and I agreed on the following Tuesday or Wednesday as the time for me to make my announcement.

"I'm sorry about how this is turning out," Dan remarked.

"It's okay," I assured him. "I'm ready to move on. We've been through an awful lot the past few years. I could use a change. Jill's a little upset about things. She's having trouble understanding. But I'm fine."

That Monday morning in the nine o'clock hour, the president summoned me over to the Oval.

"I hear you spoke with Josh last week," he began as I sat in the chair right next to his desk. "I told him I didn't think there was anyone better we could find than you."

Bush went on speaking for a moment or two about how much he appreciated my service and how much he would miss me. His charm was on full display, but it was hard to know if it was sincere or just an attempt to make me feel better. But as he continued, something I had never seen before happened: tears were streaming down both cheeks.

I found myself in the funny position of consoling the president. "It's okay, sir," I said. "I am ready to go. It's been a long ride."

We visited a little while longer and had a warm embrace. As we were about to leave the office together, Bush turned to me. "I hear Jill is pretty upset," he said.

"Yes sir, she is. It's hard for her to understand. And it's not easy for me to explain to her, since politics isn't her background."

"She loves you very much," Bush said, "and her only concern is you. Should I call her?"

I paused for a second. "I think she would appreciate that. And it might help a little. She has a lot of affection for you and Mrs. Bush."

"I will call her," he said.

I spoke to Jill later that afternoon. "Did the president call you?" I asked.

"Yes," she said. "He and Josh both called me separately."

"How was it?" I asked.

"The president didn't have to do that," she said. "He was very nice and tried to help me understand. And Josh was fine."

I could tell Jill was touched by the president taking the time to call. She didn't have a lot more to say about those two conversations. She was still pretty emotional about what was happening to me, and Josh Bolten, understandably, wasn't on her list of favorite people at the moment.

That Wednesday, before a trip to Tuskegee, Alabama, the president and I walked out to Marine One together. But we had a stop to make first—a place on the south lawn outside the Oval where the press had been alerted to wait for a statement. It was much the same as when the president had made the announcement nearly three years earlier that I would be replacing Ari Fleischer as press secretary. As we walked from the office to the waiting microphone, the president told me he would try to keep from choking up.

The press knew as soon as they saw us move in their direction that I was a dead man walking. I spoke first:

> Good morning, everybody. I am here to announce that I will be resigning as White House Press Secretary. Mr. President [here I had to clear my throat ever so briefly as I momentarily choked up], it has been an extraordinary honor and privilege to have served you for more than seven years now, the last two years and nine months as your Press Secretary. The White House is going through a period of transition; change can be helpful, and this is a good time and good position to help bring about change. I am ready to move on. I've been in this position a long time, and my wife and I are excited about beginning the next chapter in our life together. You have accomplished a lot over the last several years with this team, and I have been honored and grateful to be a small part of a terrific and talented team of really good people. Our relationship began back in Texas, and I look forward to continuing it, particularly when we are both back in Texas. ["That's right," the president said, provoking laughter.] Although I hope to get there before you. [Laughter.] I have given it my all, sir, and I've given you my all. And I will continue to do so as we transition to a new Press Secretary over the next two to three weeks. Thank you for the opportunity.

Then it was the president's turn:

> First of all, I thank Scott for his service to our country. I don't know whether or not the press corps realizes this, but his is a challenging assignment dealing with you all on a regular basis. And I thought he handled his assignment

with class, integrity. He really represents the best of his family, our state and our country. It's going to be hard to replace Scott. But, nevertheless, he's made the decision and I accept it. One of these days he and I are going to be rocking on chairs in Texas, talking about the good old days and his time as the Press Secretary. And I can assure you I will feel the same way then that I feel now, that I can say to Scott, job well done.

The announcement went fine. But when the president talked about us sitting in rocking chairs, I glanced at him and thought to myself, *I'm not that old, sir!* I remember looking at some of the reporters' faces, the ones I had come to know so well. They were there doing their jobs, covering yet another story in the endless round of White House news. But I also saw expressions of sympathy on a number of faces. We had developed a good relationship despite all the contentiousness and sparring during a controversial period. But they were human beings too, and it felt nice to see the look of human concern and fellow feeling on their faces.

So this is what the end of the road feels like. The good-byes, the going-away parties, the kind letters and words had come and gone. Three weeks earlier I had announced my resignation. Now it was just me, carrying one last box of belongings, walking down the stairs to the ground floor toward West Executive Avenue, which I would drive down one last time that pleasant spring afternoon.

There was only one other person present—Woody, the veteran officer of the Secret Service's uniformed division, looking as professional as ever in his white uniform, sitting at his station guarding the area just inside the staff entrance to the West Wing, where cabinet members are often filmed by news crews as they get out of their cars for a meeting. Woody was more to me than someone who protected the president and those of us on his team. I'd come to know him as a friend.

As he turned and noticed me walking toward him, Woody rose to stand behind the arched desk.

At that moment, my duties now finished, I could feel my emotions starting to get the better of me for the first time that day. It had been quite a roller-coaster ride, with more twists, turns, ups, and downs than any of us could have imagined back on January 20, 2001. We had just returned earlier that day from my final trip with the president—an overnight one to Florida.

"Good-bye, Woody," I said as I shook his hand and looked him in the eye. "Thank you for everything. It has been an honor."

"The pleasure has been mine," Woody said. "You're a good man, Scott. Best of luck to you."

"Thanks, Woody," I replied. "Take care."

"You too, Scott."

I would have preferred to chat a little longer, but my voice was starting to crack and my eyes were tearing up. So I turned my head and continued out the door. I didn't want to lose it in front of Woody, a good man who represented the many career men and women who keep the White House running and secure. We staff members come and go, but they remain, providing a sense of continuity and familiarity reminding us that the White House belongs not to any president or party but to all the people.

As I got in my car, I took a deep breath. With my sunglasses in place and the tears now contained, I drove through the checkpoints, waving one final time to Woody's colleagues in the uniformed division. I don't know if it was just the way they are or if the brownies Jill used to bake them made a difference, but the officers were always courteous, professional, and kind to me. It had been more than five years since I'd first driven into the White House complex past those smiling, ever-vigilant faces. It had been nearly three years since the officer at the checkpoint to West Executive Avenue had leaned toward me and said, "You're Matrix now, you know that."

Matrix was the code name the Secret Service used for the White House press secretary. "I know," I'd said with a smile. Now I was Matrix for the very last time.

The moment was emotional for me, since I had invested so much in my time at the White House. But the moment was also calmly surreal. I had an acute awareness of everything around me as I took a final look around, slowly driving through the grounds. As I exited the first checkpoint, the officer waved good-bye. At the next, I saw the officer extend a wave back to me, as if to say, "Take care of yourself," much as I'd just waved to him.

Then it was past the final checkpoint, where I waved to the officer with the bomb-sniffing dog and the one manning the guard post before turning to exit the White House grounds one final time. I was headed home to be with my wife, Jill, and to plan for our future together.

But after more than five years of living inside the bubble of a presidency once filled with so much promise and now woefully off course, little seemed completely clear to me. I was still wondering what happened.

NOT QUITE A YEAR LATER, IN EARLY 2007, I would follow the Scooter Libby trial in Washington, D.C., curious to learn more about the truth. While we are never likely to know all the facts of the Valerie Plame leak episode, much had been revealed by the time Libby's trial ended.

No one was able to learn more about the truth of the Valerie Plame episode than Special Counsel Patrick J. Fitzgerald and his team. They had access to all the documents and records that were available. They interviewed many people. They questioned many under oath before a grand jury. They had all the pieces of the puzzle that could be uncovered. Some of those that are still unknown are locked away by law, unlikely to be made public. Other pieces will likely never be made public by individuals like Cheney, Libby, and Rove who have no reason to reveal them.

But Fitzgerald is a highly respected, straight-shooting prosecutor. He presented the facts at the Libby trial in a straightforward manner. The case he set forth was compelling to the jury and outside observers. As a result, Libby was convicted on four felony counts for perjury and obstruction. The judge fined Libby $250,000 and sentenced him to thirty months in federal prison.

Unfortunately, there is no way the trial could answer all the questions that Americans have been wondering about. In the next few pages, I'll give my tentative conclusions, for what they're worth.

Did the White House deliberately seek to blow Valerie Plame's covert status to punish her husband, Joe Wilson, for his accusations about the administration's misuse of intelligence? I don't believe it was to punish him. Rather, I believe she simply became a talking point for some in a larger campaign led by the vice president to discredit Wilson publicly and thereby diminish the effectiveness of his criticisms. The president was only generally aware of this larger campaign and authorized Cheney to use parts of the NIE to support it. When the vice president sought to find out how Wilson was selected by the CIA to go on the trip to Niger, his wife's identity and role at the Agency became known. As documents disclosed by Fitzgerald with the vice president's handwriting on them show, Cheney wondered whether the trip was a junket based on nepotism that his wife helped arrange. As Cheney and Scooter Libby, his chief of staff and national security adviser, began to dig into the story, Plame's identity started to circulate among administration officials at the CIA, State Department, and Vice President's Office.

Some have defended Libby and Rove, saying they weren't the ones who leaked Plame's identity to Novak. In fact, Deputy Secretary of State Richard Armitage was the first to do so. But before Novak publicly disclosed Plame's identity, Libby and Rove did tell other reporters about her—and Rove became Novak's second confirming source for his article.

Libby became a key player in the effort to discredit Wilson, while, as Fitzgerald stated in his closing arguments, Plame's identity became just another weapon for him in the Washington political wars. As far as Libby was concerned, Fitzgerald said, "she wasn't Valerie Wilson, she wasn't a person. She was an argument, a fact to use against Joe Wilson." I think Fitzgerald was right.

Did the vice president specifically direct Libby to disclose Plame's identity? I don't know. Libby's lawyers claimed that Fitzgerald was seeking to suggest a "cloud" over the vice presidency at the trial without any evidence. But the special counsel strongly disagreed. "We didn't put that cloud there. That cloud remains because the defendant obstructed justice and lied about what happened," Fitzgerald stated.

Was Bush aware of the disclosure of Plame's identity? I know of nothing to suggest he was, nor do I believe he was, based on my conversations with him at the time. In fact, his words to me indicate that he was misled by Rove, too. Fitzgerald also stated in court filings that "the President was unaware" of the role that Libby "had in fact played in disclosing Ms. Wilson's CIA employment." Did his secret authorization for Cheney to get out parts of the NIE set in motion the disclosure of Plame's identity? Possibly. It certainly encouraged the anonymous efforts to counter Wilson's accusations. Sadly that's the way the game in Washington gets played.

Was an underlying crime committed by anyone in the administration by disclosing Plame's identity? I don't know. Armitage was Robert Novak's initial source concerning Plame's identity, and prosecutors seemed to believe that it was unintentional on Armitage's part. But it's false to assert that he was the only one who disclosed Plame's identity. We now know that Libby, Rove, and Ari Fleischer also disclosed her identity to reporters *before* Novak reported it. Fleischer apparently did so unaware of her classified status. Rove continues to maintain that he did not leak her name and that he disclosed her identity to Cooper only to prevent him from reporting something inaccurate.

Whether they committed a crime by revealing Plame's identity is something I don't know. It is in part a technical, legal issue that I'm not qualified to judge. None of these men were charged with a crime for revealing her identity. But I do know that what they did was wrong and harmful to national security, regardless of whether her disclosure was detrimental to any sources or methods. Plame was a covert CIA officer at the time, and they shouldn't have been discussing this with reporters, whether it was an indictable offense or not.

The vice president's office sought to find out why Wilson was sent to Niger. When his wife's name was mentioned, it started to circulate within the State Department and White House creating a permissive environment for her identity to be disclosed. As revealed in court filings, Libby sought to enlist Ari Fleischer's help in making it known to reporters. After Novak contacted Rove, Rove went to Libby and let him know that Novak was writing about her role. Rove also disclosed her identity to Matt Cooper of *Time* magazine.

As for what Rove and Libby told me when I was asked to publicly exonerate them, I can only conclude that they knowingly misled me. The facts have been recounted in this book. But set aside what I have written and consider another important fact. All objective observers, based on the facts that have become public, agree that what I said on their behalf was false; they were in fact involved in anonymously disclosing her identity—or leaking it—to some reporters. And I stated publicly at the time that my comments were based on personal assurances given to me by Karl and Scooter. I said they had "assured me they were not involved" in the leaking of classified information. I would never have made that statement had I known the facts above.

Neither man ever sought to correct the record when he could have. Instead he let my words stand for two years. Rove was being too cute by half when he told CNN and later ABC News back in 2004, "I did not know her name. I did not leak her name." He did not have to know Plame's name to leak her identity, as he did to *Time* magazine White House correspondent Matt Cooper and as he confirmed for Bob Novak. So both Rove and Libby deliberately allowed me to tell the public falsehoods on their behalf—a clear abuse of the White House press secretary's role. But I hold myself responsible for allowing that to happen. I should not have put myself in such a position—period.

It's also clear to me that Scooter Libby was guilty of the perjury and obstruction crimes for which he was convicted.

When the president commuted Libby's prison sentence and thereby protected him from serving even one day behind bars, I was disappointed. This kind of special treatment undermines our system of justice. It's not that I wanted to see someone I once worked alongside serve time. Prison is no joke, and I wouldn't wish it on anybody I knew or cared about. And it certainly has nothing to do with personal resentment on my part. Life is too short to waste time or energy on grudges. But I believe in the rule of law, and I think a president and those who serve a president have a special obligation to live up to both the letter and the spirit of the law. President Bush certainly has the right and the power to commute Libby's sentence. But in choosing to do so, he sent an unfortunate message to America and the world—that in the United States criminal behavior on behalf of a political cause may go unpunished if those who support that cause have the power to make it happen. Those in power have access to a different system of justice.

As I've explained in this book, I think it's unfortunate that the partisan, winner-take-all mentality of the permanent campaign has come to exert so much influence over the way our nation is governed. Intervening to circumvent a legally sound and morally just verdict because the defendant happens to be politically connected may be a symptom of just such a deplorable trend.

And what about the sixteen words controversy behind it all? Was the Bush administration guilty of a deliberate attempt to mislead the American people with the sixteen words? I don't think so. I think that the researchers at the Annenberg Political Fact Check, which describes itself as a nonpartisan advocate for voters that aims to reduce the level of deception and confusion in U.S. politics, gets it about right on its acclaimed website, factcheck.org:

> None of the new information suggests Iraq ever nailed down a deal to buy uranium, and the Senate report makes clear that US intelligence analysts have come to doubt whether Iraq was even trying to buy the stuff. In fact, both the White House and the CIA long ago conceded that the 16 words shouldn't have been part of Bush's speech.

But what he said—that Iraq sought uranium—is just what both British and US intelligence were telling him at the time. So Bush may indeed have been misinformed, but that's not the same as lying.

The "16 words" in Bush's State of the Union Address on Jan. 28, 2003 have been offered as evidence that the President led the US into war using false information intentionally. The new reports show Bush accurately stated what British intelligence was saying, and that CIA analysts believed the same thing.

This doesn't mean that the Bush administration was blameless in the way it handled intelligence during the run-up to war. As I've detailed in this book, the campaign mentality at times led the president and his chief advisers to spin, hide, shade, and exaggerate the truth, obscuring nuances and ignoring the caveats that should have accompanied their arguments. Rather than choosing to be forthright and candid, they chose to sell the war, and in so doing they did a disservice to the American people and to our democracy. However, this is not the same as saying they deliberately misled and lied—words that are emotionally charged and tend to obscure important truths and lessons in the fog of political sniping over difficult-to-prove accusations. As far as I can see, the evidence clearly supports one charge but not the other. However, embracing the permanent campaign tactics that increasingly fuel a culture of deception in Washington is just as problematic in its own way.

I don't believe the path to better democracy is served by exaggerated claims, distorted partisan attacks, or unsupported accusations of bad faith. Neither of our leading political parties is a repository of evil, and the vast majority of leaders on both sides of the aisle and at all levels of government are decent, well-meaning, and hard-working citizens who love our country and want to do the right thing. In diagnosing the problems we suffer from and the kinds of changes we need to make, I think it's crucial to cling to the truth, even when it is more nuanced, complex, and ambiguous than extreme partisans on either side may choose to believe.

17

CHANGING THE
CULTURE OF DECEPTION

W HEN GEORGE W. BUSH ARRIVED AT the White House, I believed he offered a real opportunity to move beyond the hyperpartisanship and excessive politicking that have come to characterize Washington. But it was not to be. The permanent campaign approach we publicly denounced and distanced ourselves from in the 2000 campaign was vigorously embraced after Election Day. The massive Bush campaign machine was integrally woven into his White House governance, without adequate controls or corresponding checks and balances. Ultimately, that machine worked not only to spin the media and defeat our opponents but to spin and defeat ourselves.

Imitation, they say, is the sincerest form of flattery. If so, members of the Clinton administration should feel deeply flattered when they look at the Bush administration. In our own way, we built on the art form the Clinton White House established and took it to a higher level. It worked well in a number of ways for Bush, as it had for Clinton. Bush was able to pass historic education reform, reduce taxes, implement important new measures to strengthen homeland security (including some that were controversial), give all seniors prescription drug coverage under Medicare, expand trade, and mount unprecedented efforts to combat debilitating disease in Africa—all in addition to notable successes in the war on terror abroad.

You may agree with some of these policies and disagree with others. But there's no denying that Bush's presidency has been enormously consequential. Its influence on the course of history is still unfolding and will continue to do so for years to come. In this sense, Bush is a president who achieved a tremendous political impact, for good or ill. It's another demonstration of the short-term power of the permanent campaign.

But if President Bush and his team had recognized and understood the many pitfalls of the permanent campaign approach to governance, the administration as well as the nation would have been better served. Our excessive embrace of the permanent campaign philosophy had the greatest consequences for the presidency of George W. Bush when it came to Iraq. No single decision caused the wheels to come off the Bush White House. But the way we went about executing the decision to go to war—from making the case to the public to inadequately planning and preparing for its aftermath as we rushed into it—sent us badly off track.

Selling war through a political marketing campaign rather than openly and forthrightly discussing the possible need for war with the American people is fraught with danger. Today we are seeing its destructive results play out. Washington is as polarized as ever, and Congress and the White House remain unable to come together for the good of the nation and our troops to forge a consensus way forward and bring the Iraq war to an acceptable, successful conclusion. The president has seen his once seemingly untouchable credibility—his honesty and trustworthiness—plummet, leaving questions of deliberate deception lingering in the public discourse.

I still like and admire George W. Bush. I consider him a fundamentally decent person, and I do not believe he or his White House deliberately or consciously sought to deceive the American people. But he and his advisers confused the propaganda campaign with the high level of candor and honesty so fundamentally needed to build and then sustain public support during a time of war. Had a high level of openness and forthrightness been embraced from the outset of his administration, I believe President Bush's public standing would be stronger today. His approval ratings have remained at historic lows for so long because both qualities have been lacking to this day. In this regard, he was terribly ill-served by his top advisers, especially those involved directly in national security.

All the president can do today is hope that his vision of Iraq will ultimately come true, putting the Middle East on a new path and vindicating his decision to go to war. I would welcome such a development as good for America, good for Iraq, and good for the world. Bush knows that posterity has a way of rewarding success over candor and honesty. But as history moves to render its judgment in the coming years and decades, we can't gloss over the hard truths this book has sought to address and the lessons we can learn from understanding them better. Allowing the permanent campaign culture to remain in control may not take us into another unnecessary war, but it will continue to limit the opportunity for careful deliberation, bipartisan compromise, and meaningful solutions to the major problems all Americans want to see solved.

I've tried to avoid becoming embroiled in the question of who started the partisan warfare and who is most responsible for the current culture of deception in Washington. It would take an entire book even to attempt to answer the question. My guess is that an objective, nonpartisan look at the facts would conclude that there is plenty of blame and responsibility to share— from presidents of both parties to Democratic and Republican leaders of Congress, from partisan pundits and interest group leaders to the complicit enablers in the Washington and national media.

Let the one who is without sin cast the first stone. It would be difficult if not impossible to find anyone who has lived in this destructive world of Washington—a world that has grown detached from the problems and priorities the American people care most about—who is truly "without sin." This is the reason so many Americans, especially those in the broad majority at the center, feel disenchanted and even disgusted with politics. And this is why we urgently need to get beyond blame and recrimination and focus instead on cleaning up the system. The good news is that a desire to see that happen is real and growing across the country.

Is it possible to divorce campaigning from governing? Should it be a crime to try to manipulate the sources of public approval for governing as the permanent campaign requires? I don't think so. That would be a dangerous road to travel. Our political leaders must be aware of popular opinion, and to govern effectively they need to appeal for the citizens' support. In this sense, campaigning and governing do go hand in hand, and pretending otherwise would be folly.

Fraud and deliberate deception, of course, are another matter. So is the misuse of government offices and funds for purely partisan purposes. These are crimes, and they should be. If there is hard evidence of anyone in government crossing the line of legality, then he or she must be held to account. But to try to define the modus operandi of establishment Washington as inherently scandalous misses the mark and allows the root problems to continue unabated. Unfortunately, elected leaders of both parties are having it both ways. They condemn the permanent campaign rhetorically even as they embrace its most destructive and inherently deceptive tactics.

The excesses of the permanent campaign need to be addressed and ended. They are deeply destructive to our national political discourse, and the consequences are all too real in terms of both policy and politics.

To criticize the system is not to excuse or absolve elected leaders of either party for the decisions, tactics, and means they have embraced that contribute to the destructive excesses of the permanent campaign. The vast majority are good people, but they were elected to lead, unite, compromise, and put our nation's best interest above that of their party. Too few have stepped forward to lead us beyond the partisan excesses. President Bush is paying a heavy price for his failure to do so. His public standing has been severely diminished as a result. But simply pointing the finger at one person obscures the bigger problems that need addressing and correcting.

Our elected leaders must begin the process of change by ending their inside-the-box mind-set of doing what everyone else does. They are in the best position to alter the status quo, and no one can do more than the president. No one has as loud a microphone or as prominent a stage as the president, and the primary responsibility for initiating change rests with him (or her).*

The president could exercise an immediate positive impact on the culture in Washington by taking some key steps that do not require an act of Congress. Not that these steps would be easy to accomplish and sustain. They require constant awareness of the excesses of the permanent campaign, of the long-term dangers of engaging in politics as war, and of the need to deprive the scandal culture of its life blood, including internal inaction, secretiveness, stonewalling, obfuscation, and dissembling.

Presidential candidates could start by informing themselves about the perils of the permanent campaign, not just in terms of current political tac-

---

*For the rest of this chapter, I'll refer to the hypothetical leaders of tomorrow simply as "he," to avoid the awkwardness of saying "he or she" repeatedly. No disrespect is intended to any current or future national leaders of the female gender.

tics but in the broader context of American history and its evolution over generations. Reading *The Permanent Campaign and Its Future*, the book edited by Norman J. Ornstein and Thomas E. Mann that I referenced in an earlier chapter, would enlighten many. Seeking wise counsel on how to deal with the problems of the permanent campaign from scholars who have studied it should be an early step as well.

As I witnessed with President Bush, it is not enough to preach unity and pledge to change the tone. Most Americans are ready for both. But rhetoric is meaningless without concrete steps. What institutional changes would a potential president make to counter and minimize the damaging aspects of the permanent campaign? In what ways would the potential president make bipartisan deliberation and compromise central to governing, something that is constantly and integrally embraced? It will not be an easy task to overcome the excesses of the permanent campaign. A president must have a specific plan that can reassure the public his commitment to reform amounts to more than empty words.

A president-elect should insist that those overseeing his transition into office learn about the permanent campaign—what it is, how it works, and the consequences of embracing it. A president-elect should also insist that his senior staff heed the same lessons. This could enable new administrations to avoid some of the pitfalls the Bush administration fell into, such as taking a massive campaign apparatus into the governing structure of the White House—a particularly dangerous mistake when there is no strong, counterbalancing force in place.

Once in office, the president must demonstrate an unyielding commitment to three important principles: (1) a high level of openness, forthrightness, and honesty when communicating with the American people; (2) a spirit of inclusiveness and unity, which reaches across partisan divisions and ideological differences to encourage cooperation among all groups and individuals; and (3) a readiness to consistently govern toward the center, seeking common ground from which to solve problems rather than appealing to a narrow base of opinion.

Most people, I think, would applaud these principles in the abstract. But how can they be practiced in concrete terms? There are a number of good ideas in the public domain already. Here are some to consider as well that do not require a lengthy implementation period or an act of Congress.

I'd recommend a significant change in the White House senior staff structure. I have thought about this based on my own experience, as well as through examining the structure of the White Houses that preceded the one I served. First, the president should appoint a deputy chief of staff for governing. This position would be responsible for making sure the president is continually and consistently committed to a high level of openness and forthrightness, and transcending partisanship to achieve unity.

Organizationally, this deputy would report directly to the president and the chief of staff. The policy directors, personnel director, senior political adviser, communications adviser, and White House counsel would be under his and the chief of staff's authority and direction. With such authority and responsibility, this person would also need some top talent working in his immediate office. He would likely need three dedicated assistants, each with important, specific responsibilities:

- An assistant to focus on unity, integrally involved in the legislative, policy, and political apparatuses. He would work to make sure that legislative, policy, and political priorities are set with an eye toward substantive engagement with leaders from the opposing party and the search for common ground. For example, when the details of a new health care program are being developed, he would ensure not only that legislators of both parties are consulted early and continually, but also that representatives of interest groups on all sides of the issue would have a chance to contribute to the conversation—doctors' and nurses' organizations, insurance companies, for-profit and not-for-profit health care companies, patients' rights associations, labor unions, employer groups, and many others.
- An assistant to focus on transparency, integrally involved in the presidential papers, and document processes, as well as responding to requests from citizens' groups and interest groups for information about the policy-making process within the White House. The transparency assistant might also oversee a potential reform of the process for classifying intelligence information and other government data, making sure that the secrecy needed to protect vital security interests isn't abused as a way of protecting an administration from revelations that are merely embarrassing or politically inconvenient.
- An assistant to focus on tone, integrally involved in the White House communications structure, including dealing with all high-profile

controversies that invariably arise in the executive branch. His job would include making sure that the messages the administration chooses to deliver reflect respect for the leaders of the other party and for the legitimate concerns and needs of all Americans. This assistant would have the responsibility for identifying and halting unsavory political tactics that foster needless division in Washington and among social, ethnic, religious, or geographic communities.

The deputy chief of staff for governing will need to be an experienced statesman who is knowledgeable, skillful, and respected enough to work across party lines. He should have a deep understanding and appreciation for the permanent campaign and its potential consequences, as well as a deep appreciation for alternative ways of governing—via deliberation, consensus, compromise, and cooperation. A strong presence or force of personality is also important. He must be someone who, when necessary, can look the president or his highest-ranking advisors in the eye and say, "With respect, you're wrong." The deputy chief of staff for governing would be critical to keeping the permanent campaign in check and making sure the senior political adviser or team of advisers does not exercise inordinate influence over events inside the White House.

This is an important concession to realism. I think it's unrealistic to hope that a president's top political advisers will *not* have significant influence in the White House. The goal should to be balance political considerations with nonpolitical ones. Creating a new position that focuses on governing is one way of achieving such balance.

The deputy chief of staff for governing would need to have full knowledge of what is going on inside the administration in order to fulfill his important role. He would need to be included in every senior-level policy, legislative, personnel, communications, and decision-making meeting, regarding both foreign and domestic issues. He would need to be provided with all relevant documents and information, and he would need to have full access to the president. Whereas the chief of staff might act as an honest broker, above and outside of the intramural battles that inevitably arise in any administration— a role that Andy Card filled—the deputy chief of staff for governing would be a strong advocate for his designated priorities. If he did his job well, he would probably butt heads with the president's political advisers from time to time.

In fact, if he rarely or never engaged in such conflict, it's almost certain that he would *not* be doing his job as I've envisioned it.

A deputy chief of staff for governance could do a lot to help the president move our country toward a style of leadership that is transparent, inclusive, and candid—qualities that I believe Americans are longing for and will readily embrace when they see them. Let me address each of these a bit more fully.

First, transparency. In our age of 24/7 news coverage and instantaneous communication, it defies logic to think that an administration can be success-ful without embracing transparency. The information age increasingly de-mands openness and forthrightness. No person or entity can control public opinion in a world with such a wide array of sources of public approval, from blogs to citizen journalists to growing advocacy journalism on the right and left and the diverse sources of news and opinion and ways to get them, espe-cially on the Internet. All of these trends are healthy for democracy, for ensur-ing accountability and getting to the truth.

Embracing secrecy beyond the necessary classified national security infor-mation is a recipe for disaster in such an environment, where what a White House tries to keep secret invariably comes to light. It is far better to be open and forthright about it than to let suspicion grow or allow others to determine the story line.

Just as important, embracing openness and forthrightness leads to posi-tive change and internal accountability. In an open environment, problems cannot be brushed under the rug. Transparency encourages corrective action, including holding people to account when needed.

As a leadership characteristic, inclusiveness means making sure that delib-eration and compromise with Congress is as much a focus as campaigning to manipulate sources of public approval. A president must constantly reach out to members of Congress and engage in good-faith deliberation and compro-mise to enact legislation and solve pressing priority problems, and the deputy chief of staff for governance would be charged with promoting and facilitat-ing these efforts.

Promoting inclusive leadership also means continually exposing the pres-ident to outside experts, scholars, and elder statesman of all points of view for advice and counsel—particularly on the most consequential or controversial matters. And it means making sure that the president's governing team is sig-nificantly more transpartisan than it has been in recent history, including a healthy number of members from the other party and possibly an independent leader or two. Such transpartisanship would be particularly important in today's hyperpartisan, ideologically driven Washington environment.

The president's cabinet should be the place to start. It's not enough for a president to name one or two members of the opposing party to minor cabinet posts (as President Bush named Democrat Norman Y. Mineta to the relatively obscure post of transportation secretary). Why not a secretary of state, defense, or treasury from the opposition party? It's easy to think of distinguished, capable, centrist figures from both the Democratic and Republican parties who are admirably suited to fill these roles. What a powerful gesture of national unity this would be coming from our next president!

It is also wise to have a cabinet that reflects the ethnic, racial, religious, geographic, and gender diversity of America. (This is a goal that President Bush did an admirable job of pursuing.) This can easily be achieved while reaching out across party lines to assemble the presidential team, and without sacrificing the paramount qualities of intellect, experience, training, judgment, and integrity.

The need for inclusiveness also means actively reaching out to leaders of various constituencies, both those who are naturally supportive of the administration and those who are not. The president serves all the people, and the White House should reflect that. The next Democratic president should make a point of spending time with such traditionally conservative groups as evangelical Christians, gun owners, pro-life activists, and tax-cut advocates, while the next Republican should reach out to gay rights groups, teachers unions, animal rights lobbyists, and environmentalists, to name a few. Even if no one's opinions are changed, some common ground may be discovered on which positive change can be built. And in any case, to show mutual respect and a simple willingness to listen would do much to reduce the toxicity that pervades the Washington atmosphere.

Inclusiveness also means constantly monitoring presidential and White House communications to ensure a tone that rises above partisan politics and minimizes or eliminates the use of scorched-earth politics—both internally and externally among key support organizations, including the national party apparatus.

There is nothing wrong with message discipline. It is useful and necessary in today's media environment. But it needs to be kept within the context of a high level of candor, honesty, and respect for the opposition. By the same token, campaigning to engage the public behind policy initiatives is also vital, but *not* at the expense of deliberation and compromise. Citizen groups, industry organizations, nonprofits, and activist associations shouldn't be regarded primarily as weapons to be deployed in partisan warfare but rather as partners who can help solve problems through mutual exploration of opportunities and options.

Emphasizing candor can help to ensure that the inevitable controversies that arise with every administration do not harden into a permanent state of suspicion and warfare. If the deputy chief of staff does his job, the president will not allow a controversy to turn into an outside investigation or legal proceeding without at least making an honest effort at resolving the problem internally. When scandals arise—as they will—the president must demand thorough investigations and necessary remedial action, including disclosure of the facts and holding people accountable, even if this costs the administration the services of talented subordinates.

In today's partisan climate, we sometimes hear "loyalty" described as a paramount political virtue. Presidents demand loyalty from their advisers and staff; they demonstrate their own loyalty in return by shielding them from accountability. This kind of loyalty often does a disservice to the American people. Public servants must remember that they take an oath to the Constitution of the United States. Our first loyalty is to the nation and its people. When conflicts arise, loyalty to the nation must take precedence over party loyalty or personal loyalty. If this means blowing the whistle on misdeeds or insisting that wrongdoing in office be fully and firmly punished, so be it. A readiness to adhere to this rule is essential for any presidency that seeks to transcend the corrupting atmosphere of today's politics.

A president committed to the core principles I've outlined and a White House structured to make sure he is following through on them could do a lot to set the right tone and discourage the practice of scorched-earth politics in Washington. But other players of the political game also have important roles.

Congress could help us move beyond partisan warfare and the culture of deception. Today, members are too consumed with raising money, appeasing special interests, and outmaneuvering the opposition to win the next election— all elements of the permanent campaign. A lot of good ideas have been proposed for changing the system in Congress. They are worth pursuing, but leadership can make a change in tone and attitudes happen now. Unfortunately, leaders of both parties are trending away from statesmanship and toward partisanship. It is these leaders—the speaker and the majority and minority leaders in the Senate and House—who must take the initiative.

The national media can help change our political culture as well. There is much they do right, but it is often overshadowed by what they do wrong.

Network news has been losing viewers in recent times. There are many reasons, including the proliferation of news sources, many now tailored toward specific audience interests. But one important reason, I believe, is that the networks are stuck in the past. Their national news desks remain focused on covering the horse race of the permanent campaign, not only during election years but continually, emphasizing controversy, and talking about who's winning and losing in Washington rather than really digging into the big issues Americans care about—the economy, health care, education, crime, war, and peace.

To break out of their slow ratings decline and their creative rut, the news media need to learn to think in new ways. The American public hungers for truth—not just as it relates to petty partisan squabbles and the controversy of the day, but larger truth, including the hard truths we too rarely hear emphasized on television or see written prominently about in our major newspapers and magazines. The network that can find a way to shift from excessively emphasizing controversy, the conventional horse race and image-driven coverage to give a greater emphasis to who is right and who is wrong, who is telling the truth and who is not, and the larger truths about our society and our world might achieve some amazing results in our fast-changing media environment. I'll bet I'm not the only viewer who would be energized by programming like this. The political drama is entertaining for me, as it is for most politicos, but Americans would be better served and more responsive to news that focuses more on the larger truth.

There are more mundane changes in media practices that could also make a big difference in our political culture. During electoral campaigns, reporters should work harder to pin the candidates down on policy specifics rather than accepting generalities and rhetorical flair. Newspapers and TV news programs should monitor the number of column-inches and the amount of airtime they dedicate to horse race stories about polls, campaign tactics, and strategies as compared to policy substance. They should set specific targets for each kind of coverage, so that sports-style coverage of the political game doesn't overwhelm what citizens need to know to make informed choices.

Media outlets should devote more resources to fact-checking ideas and information provided by political campaigns, politicians in office, or special interest organizations. When a candidate bends the truth, reporters shouldn't hesitate to point that out. When a television commercial uses emotional appeals, distorted imagery, or misleadingly selective facts to promote a particular point of view, news organizations should expose those tactics, even if it means braving the fury of an offended advertiser.

There are a number of organizations showing the way toward such improved media coverage. I've earlier cited the Annenberg Political Fact Check as an example of a nonpartisan group that is trying to improve the level of honesty in our political discourse. We need more organizations like this one. We also need to encourage the media to fulfill their vital role as advocates of honesty, transparency, and mutual respect among our political leaders, and there are encouraging signs that this is happening. "Truth tests" of campaign ads have become a normal part of political coverage in many newspapers, and CNN's "Keeping Them Honest" reports bring a similar fact-check approach to cable news. Now the media need to institutionalize this kind of coverage and make it a central focus of their political reporting.

The media too sometimes need help in staying honest. I'm happy to see that an increasing number of news organizations are employing ombudsmen to act as advocates for fairness and ethical standards. These ombudsmen investigate charges of bias, monitor newsroom practices, and criticize unfair or shoddy reporting whenever they find it. In a way, they play a role vis-à-vis the media not unlike the role I advocate for a deputy chief of staff for governing, serving as a kind of institutional conscience. This is a beneficial trend, and I hope it continues and spreads.

I hope that my friends in the media—including the solid professionals in the White House press corps I greatly enjoyed working with—will respond positively to the critique I've offered in this book. I know most reporters enter journalism with high ideals. I believe many of them agree with me that it's time for a rededication to those ideals, for the good of our nation.

Finally, there is a role for every citizen to play in changing the tone of our political system. We need all Americans to be involved in shaping the national conversation and in advocating—even demanding—that our political leaders respond to the real needs of the people. As I write these pages, it's exciting to see the enormous new outpouring of interest in the 2008 presidential campaign among millions of Americans, including many centrists in both parties, independents and individuals from groups that once showed relatively low rates of political involvement—young people and racial and religious minorities. I hope this trend continues and spreads in the years to come. With the right leadership from the president to Congress to the media, I believe it can.

New technologies already play a part in encouraging greater activism among ordinary citizens. The Internet provides a platform for millions of people to share their thoughts, opinions, observations, and reporting about local, national, and world affairs, giving voices to many who once had none. Social networking sites make it easy for citizens to form groups based around specific interests, from support of a particular candidate to concerns ranging from foreign policy to the environment. At times, the messages disseminated via blogs may be shrill and uncivil, and the videos popularized by YouTube may be vulgar or silly. But the fact that more people than ever feel able to express themselves and their opinions is a very good thing, and in time it should force political leaders to be more responsive to the will of an aroused and informed citizenry.

Most important, we as citizens can help change the tone of the national conversation by making an effort to reach across lines of party, ideology, and background within our own communities. Find ways to be involved. Join your local library board, PTA, or civic association, and learn to communicate with people whose worldview and environment may differ from yours. Listen to the concerns of neighbors who may vote for a different candidate than the one you favor, worship at a different church, synagogue, or temple than the one you attend (or none at all), and earn their living in a way you may never have considered. You may find you have more in common than you assume. And if we can find ways to work together constructively at the grass roots, maybe a little of the same spirit can filter its way up to the halls of Congress and the White House as well.

The Bush administration will soon recede into history. Future historians will debate the long-term consequences of the fateful decisions made by President Bush and his chief advisers for years to come. But I hope all Americans will participate in the conversation about what we can learn in regard to the right and wrong ways to govern from the last eight years of our shared history. It can be difficult, even painful, to look back on our own mistakes. It's tempting to focus on the obvious triumphs or ignore history altogether in our constant quest for a better tomorrow. But I'm convinced there's much to be gained from thoughtful, candid, and probing self-examination . . . and that requires an honest look at what happened.

ACKNOWLEDGMENTS

I OWE SPECIAL THANKS TO THE TEAM AT PublicAffairs, especially founder and editor-at-large Peter Osnos, and marketing director and senior editor Lisa Kaufman. Their commitment, support, and insights were invaluable. Lisa's editorial suggestions and questions were of tremendous benefit. Robert Kimzey and his production staff did excellent work, as did Chrisona Schmidt on the copy editing. Publisher Susan Weinberg and publicity director Whitney Peeling helped address the publishing and publicity challenges.

Karl Weber has my deepest appreciation. His editorial ideas, suggestions, and exceptional work kept this project moving forward and helped make sure it was completed in a timely manner. He delivered more than could have been expected, and I am grateful for his help.

Mimi Bardagjy provided some helpful research. I thank her for her great work and quick turnaround.

Craig Wiley, my literary agent and founder of the Craig Wiley Agency, helped me navigate the book publishing world. If not for Craig, I would never have been matched with such an outstanding group of people at PublicAffairs. He has my deep appreciation.

I had the honor of serving alongside many good people at the White House, none more so than those who worked in the office of the press secretary during my tenure. For all of my shortcomings and missteps, they did so much right. The credit for all the good we did belongs to them. I am forever grateful to Claire Buchan, Sean McCormack, Trent Duffy, Dana Perino, and Fred Jones. I also thank Kate Starr and Mike Anton. Carmen Ingwell and Tina Hervey did a wonderful job serving as my special assistants. Nathan Carleton, Joe Kildea, David Sherzer, and Brian Bravo stayed on top of the breaking news and did outstanding research work. Assistant press secretaries Pam Stevens,

Erin Healy, Ashley Snee, Adam Levine, Reed Dickens, and Josh Deckard did a terrific job. I appreciate Lois Cassano's great work and assistance. Special thanks go to all the staff assistants: Amanda DeVuono, Georgia Godfrey, Peter Watkins, John Roberts, Rachael Sunbarger, Will Holley, Theresa Pagliocca, Harry Wolff, Carlton Carroll, Greg Williams, and Liz Donnan.

I have also been blessed with a wonderful family. As always, they were there to support me from beginning to end during the writing of this book. I especially thank my mother, Carole Keeton Strayhorn.

Most importantly, I thank my wife, Jill, for her love, advice, comfort, and guidance throughout the course of my time as press secretary and during the writing of this book. I cannot imagine getting through it all without her.

INDEX

PublicAffairs is a publishing house founded in 1997. It is a tribute to the standards, values, and flair of three persons who have served as mentors to countless reporters, writers, editors, and book people of all kinds, including me.

I. F. STONE, proprietor of *I. F. Stone's Weekly*, combined a commitment to the First Amendment with entrepreneurial zeal and reporting skill and became one of the great independent journalists in American history. At the age of eighty, Izzy published *The Trial of Socrates*, which was a national bestseller. He wrote the book after he taught himself ancient Greek.

BENJAMIN C. BRADLEE was for nearly thirty years the charismatic editorial leader of *The Washington Post*. It was Ben who gave the *Post* the range and courage to pursue such historic issues as Watergate. He supported his reporters with a tenacity that made them fearless and it is no accident that so many became authors of influential, best-selling books.

ROBERT L. BERNSTEIN, the chief executive of Random House for more than a quarter century, guided one of the nation's premier publishing houses. Bob was personally responsible for many books of political dissent and argument that challenged tyranny around the globe. He is also the founder and longtime chair of Human Rights Watch, one of the most respected human rights organizations in the world.

. . .

For fifty years, the banner of Public Affairs Press was carried by its owner Morris B. Schnapper, who published Gandhi, Nasser, Toynbee, Truman, and about 1,500 other authors. In 1983, Schnapper was described by *The Washington Post* as "a redoubtable gadfly." His legacy will endure in the books to come.

Peter Osnos, *Founder and Editor-at-Large*